MW01167445

Not A Year Off

The Story Behind Language Stories

All content created and distributed by Lindsay Williams on behalf of Lindsay Does Languages. © 2019 Lindsay Williams, Lindsay Does Languages. All rights reserved.

First Edition, 2019.

This publication may be printed or photocopied for personal use. However no part of this publication may be reproduced, stored, distributed or transmitted in any form or by any means, including photocopying, scanning, recording or other electronic or mechanical methods for other purposes, without the prior written permission of the publisher, except in the case of brief quotations embodied in critical reviews and certain other noncommercial uses permitted by copyright law. Requests to the author and publisher for permission should be addressed to the following email: lindsay@doeslanguages.com.

Limitation of liability/disclaimer of warranty: While the publisher and author have used their best efforts in preparing this guide and workbook, they make no representations or warranties with respect to the accuracy or completeness of the contents of this document and specifically disclaim any implied warranties of merchantability or fitness for particular purpose. No warranty may be created or extended by sales representatives, promoters, or written sales materials.

The advice and strategies contained herein may not be suitable for your situation. You should consult with a professional where appropriate. Neither the publisher nor author shall be liable for any loss of profit or any other commercial damages, including but not limited to special, incidental, consequential, or other damages.

Due to the dynamic nature of the Internet, certain links and website information contained in this publication may have changed. The author and publisher make no representations to the current accuracy of the web information shared.

Contents

Guatemala

Season 1, Mini Episode 2: Star Wars: A Language Story

Season 1, Episode 5: Keeping K'iche'

Honduras

El Salvador

Nicaragua

Season 1, Episode 6: Nicaraguan Sign Language

Costa Rica

Panama

Season 1, Mini Episode 5: The Panama Canal

Ecuador

Peru

Paraguay

Season 1, Episode 7: Guarani in the Heart of South America

The 89 Hour Journey

Myanmar

Vietnam

Season 2, Episode 1: Learning Vietnamese

Season 2, Episode 4: Discovering Hmong

Season 2, Episode 6: Hands For Vietnam

Laos

Season 2, Episode 3: Teaching English in Laos

Cambodia

Japan

Malaysia

Season 2, Episode 5: Make Hokkien Cool Again

Season 2, Episode 7: Kristang: A Tale of Two Cities

Singapore

Season 2, Episode 2: Singapore Takes The Floor

Season 2, Episode 7: Kristang: A Tale of Two Cities

For Ashley,
So we can remember our own story too.

Introduction

We were never really quite sure what to call it.

Friends would ask if we were ready for our "break" and older relatives would ask us if we were looking forward to our "holiday".

Whatever it was, it was not that. It was not a year off.

I think it's important to start this book with that.

It's so easy in our filtered, Instagramable world to see someone we know (or perhaps don't *really* know) sharing photos from the beach, the mountains or the jungle and assume that they're simply taking an extended holiday. An escape from life. An overdue gap year. It looks so easy, right?

If that's what you're after - an overly glossy take on a year of life in various countries and climates across the planet - then you're probably not going to enjoy this book. This is not that. This is our story. Warts and all.

While we knew we wanted to spend a year or so travelling, and had some savings to do so, we also knew that to make it possible we'd still need some income in some way to pay for it.

I started working online in 2014, and although Ashley, my husband, would have to quit his job for "it"/"the trip", I'd be able to keep working on the road with him working with me too. We were lucky.

My job revolves around languages - learning them, teaching them, sharing about them. There was no way we could just travel aimlessly on a "holiday" or a "break" in these far-off places and not do something also revolving around languages.

We settled on Language Stories, a podcast and video language documentary series.

I knew some people in our first stop New York that we could interview, and in Montreal, our second stop, but after that we were well and truly flying solo. Would it work? We'd soon find out.

After years of dreaming and planning and more dreaming and more planning, in August 2017, we left our home and headed off into the unknown. Well, not quite the unknown. We had tickets to New York. We were starting in New York.

USA

Season 1, Episode 1: New York & The 7 Line

I can't think of the first time I knew of New York. Was it Kevin getting left there in Home Alone? Mara Wilson's innocent face starting up at Santa Claus in Miracle on 34th Street? The last dance at a wedding as drunken bodies, arms thrown carelessly around each other, focus all their efforts on lifting one foot in front of the other to Frank Sinatra crooning New York, New York?

It certainly wasn't reading Poeta en Nueva York by Federico Garcia Lorca for my A level coursework, nor was it my flatmate watching and rewatching the trailer for the first Sex and the City Movie. Those, arguably more personal, connections to the city that never sleeps came later.

And, I'm sure, if you were to write a chapter yourself on New York, your own reaching for that first reference would be equally as hazy and personal.

New York is so integrated into our geographical vocabulary, no matter where we grow up.

It could be claimed that London and Paris both clamber alongside NYC elegantly for the top spot of the most spoken of, referenced, and known of city in the world. However, do either Paris or London come close when we're talking language?

When I knew we'd be starting our trip in New York City, I instantly began scurrying around the internet for what had to be multiple organisations, clubs, societies, communities that spoke and stood for the various languages spoken in this city to potentially rival no other linguistically.

That 'potentially' was quickly wiped from the sentence upon discovering estimates from the Endangered Language Alliance, based in New York City, that 800 languages could well be spoken across the five boroughs.

Well, clearly that was one organisation we had to speak with. I emailed Ross Perlin at the Endangered Language Alliance asking for an interview for Language Stories and eagerly awaited a response.

Ross wasn't the first person I'd contacted regarding the New York episode whilst my feet remained firmly on British soil.

I already knew personally of Daniel Bogre-Udell and Freddie Andrade, who co-founded the non-profit organisation Wikitongues where I'd volunteered loosely for a few years on the blog team, and Benny Lewis of Fluent in 3 Months, who I'd met a few times at various language events.

Daniel, Freddie, and Benny all agreed to speak with us for Language Stories. It wasn't a pipedream any more. Language Stories was happening. Our trip had purpose.

That meant I could get planning to make the most of our 7 days there, including playing tourist on my birthday that would fall while we were there.

I started by looking up events and stumbled upon the Chinese Dragon Boat Festival happening the day after we arrived, no doubt weary eyed and jetlagged. It was way out east at Flushing in Queens. It was going to be a journey to get there, but it could be a great example of finding people who speak different languages in the city.

And so it was, that less than twenty-four hours after arriving in New York City, before we'd even come within twenty feet of the Empire State Building, the Statue of Liberty, or the Brooklyn Bridge, we were leaving the glamour of Manhattan for Flushing. The name alone tells you why it's not top of TripAdvisor.

The Dragon Boat Festival itself was interesting, a pleasant example of how multicultural and diverse New York City is. But it wasn't the only reason we'd come this far out.

For a few months before we left home, I'd been learning Guarani, a language we'll get to later in the book so I won't dwell on it too much here.

It was always due to be the final episode in season one of Language Stories, and I thought it would make for a cool little loopback if we could find something Guarani-themed in the location of our first episode. And we did - a Paraguayan restaurant! Two in fact, both of which it would transpire are owned by the same family. We only visited one, Sabor Guarani, and I got very excited about Paraguayan food...and the Guarani words scattered lovingly across the wall behind where I was sat.

"Where are you from?" the waiter asked as he came to take our order.

"We're from the UK. We've just started a year long trip. We're going to Paraguay, I've been learning Guarani!" (Can you tell I was excited?)

"Ahh! Qué bueno! But how have you been learning Guarani in England?"

Our Spanish began to creep in, but remained with weavings of English to keep Ashley in the loop.

"Online, mostly through Spanish, with a tutor, Duolingo…" I tailed off, "Che astudia avañe'ẽ" *'I study Guarani'* I said proudly, speaking Guarani for the first time to someone in real life who might actually understand me.

The waiter paused, "Sorry, otra vez, say it again."

I was going to have to step up my Guarani studies on the road somehow. Deflated, I slumped back into Spanish as we finished ordering.

"Do you have tereré?" I asked. Having heard so much about the essential Paraguayan drink since starting to study the language, I was confused not to see it on the menu.

His eyes widened with pleasure and surprise, "Sí, sí, we can do tereré for you!"

A few minutes later, the waiter returned with a huge leather-bound jug full of iced water; an equally leather-bound cup, full of yerba mate, the caffeinated herb mix that makes tereré; and with a bombilla, a metal straw with holes in the bottom to stop you sucking up all the herbs, stood bolt upright in the cup.

He poured some ice cold water from the jug onto the herbs.

"It's customary to share tereré. With one cup, with friends, everybody shares," and with that, our waiter took a sip from the drink he'd just served us at our table. I struggled for a moment to think of another restaurant in New York City where you could encounter a waiter sharing the drink he's just served you.

The tereré was strong, almost bitter, and tasted like it would be addictive were you to drink regularly. Nevertheless, in my utter joy at finding a Paraguayan restaurant, I smiled and enjoyed it.

We'd ordered a mixture of foods from the menu, also based on words I'd encountered from my Guarani studies so far: sopa paraguaya, mbeju, chipa, and some empañadas just in case we didn't like any of the new things. As it turned out, everything was delicious and it got us even more excited to get to Paraguay.

***

A couple of days after our visit to Flushing, we had arranged to meet Benny at YouTube Space.

In an attempt to encourage creators to keep creating, YouTube has established various YouTube Spaces around the world. With free snacks, workshops, and cameras for hire with more Ks of megapixels than the eye can probably see, they're slightly surreal places that echo elements of co-working spaces that have popped up in the past few years.

It's located above Chelsea Market, a modern food and drink stall setup with a hipster edge. One coffee shop had a whole menu board with just one item gracing it in simple white block letters: "COFFEE $4". Flushing this was not.

As the lift doors opened, we were met with hushed tones and fingers on lips from lanyard-wearing staff. A live recording was going on, right outside where the lift opens. Benny was waiting for us, and after our silent hellos so as not to disturb the live recording on the other side of the curtain, he showed us around the place before we headed to the room he'd hired for us to film in.

After recording a handful of other videos (you have to make the most of these reservations at YouTube Space when you get them), we recorded our very first interview for Language Stories. Affirmed again, it was happening.

I asked Benny what it was like being a language learner in New York City, and if it was easy to find speakers to practice with.

Benny told me how when he came to New York for his book tour a few years before living there, he found himself bombarded with all the languages he's ever studied and felt inadequate to speak them. Yet, New York, to Benny, is an inspiring city that makes you want to do stuff. He feels that that makes New York a great place for him to make a difference and that he can learn a lot from the people of New York to do that.

***

One of the things I loved about travelling in New York is that my phone package from the UK gave me free roaming data, so I could use my phone (and most importantly the internet) on the subway, in the street, in a Paraguayan restaurant just like at home. It was something I'd soon lose as we moved onto other countries, but something that proved useful one afternoon when sat on a subway train checking my email.

Ross Perlin, the contact I'd found at the Endangered Language Alliance, who hadn't yet replied to my email request for an interview, had replied! We were so close to the end of the week, that if I hadn't had data and had had to wait until I got home each night to check my emails, we wouldn't have been able to arrange to meet in the short timespan that we did.

Upon arranging to meet, we headed into Manhattan and decided to check out Times Square quickly before making our way to the ELA office. Good move.

Gathered around the entrance to one building were hundreds of screaming fans waiting for...someone.

As we got closer, we saw a handful were holding posters, banners, and lifesize cutouts of Luis Fonsi - yes, Luis Fonsi of Despacito fame!

It soon transpired that he was appearing on Good Morning America as a result of reaching a gazillion YouTube views on the music video for Despacito. A gazillion may not be the exact number. Although perhaps it will be by the time you're reading this. After we'd joined the masses for a few minutes, Luis eventually came out for a brief interview with the presenters and posed for photos with some fans.

It was exciting! We were about to start a year exploring Latin America, no doubt with Despacito leading the way of reggaeton that would dominate our ears walking down the street and sitting on buses. It felt like a sign of what to come. However, not wanting to be late for our appointment with Ross, we left Times Square pretty sharpish.

We met Ross at the offices of the Endangered Language Alliance (ELA), which gave us a chance to better picture some of the awesome work they do there. They host classes, regular radio recording sessions, and have a range of books to make even the most hardened language nerd weak at the knees.

As we spoke with Ross, it was inspiring to hear how committed Daniel Kaufman and himself were to the work they'd set out to do. Remember, it was the ELA that estimated that figure of 800 languages in NYC that had sparked my initial interest in an episode about this diverse city.

Ross described New York as a linguistic hotspot, but a different kind. The term linguistic hotspot is typically used to describe places such as Papua New Guinea, the Himalayas and other areas with a naturally occuring high number of different languages often due to their geography and political and social history. New York however, Ross went on to explain, is a linguistic hotspot founded on migration, change, and human density.

But how did this happen? What made New York the place that all these people and all these speakers of different languages want to live? Ross referred to the city as an engine of money, jobs, and opportunity. As you visit various stops along the train and metro lines, especially the 7 Line, it's clear that he's right.

***

There was only one interview left: Daniel and Freddie. After having to cancel earlier in the week, the only time we had left to meet and record the interview was the evening of my birthday.

You have to understand: this was August, my birthday is August. Living in the UK means that school summer holidays have always fallen on my birthday, and with the exception of one thirty minute private class just once, I've always managed to avoid working on my birthday too.

My birthday fell as our last full day in the city, and I'd been planning to play big tourist since our early planning back home - did I really want to work on my birthday?

If we were going to make this series the best it could be, I'd have to. Besides, I knew these guys, it wouldn't exactly be "work" work.

I agreed with Daniel to meet him and Freddie on our final night (my birthday) in the city at their place in Brooklyn. That meant we still had a whole day to explore and play big tourist before then.

We visited Macy's, the all American department store I can definitely say is like an overrated Debenhams; and Lush, the all British soap shop I can definitely smell 20 minutes down the road at home.

I'm always curious to see how familiar shops differ abroad. In typical Lush style, the woman working there approached me within seconds of entering the door, "Hi there! How can I help you today?"

"Oh, I'm fine thanks. Just looking." I responded in typical British what-I'm-really-saying-is-let-me-look-around-in-peace style. Little did I know at this point how closely we'd be followed in shops as we worked our way down the Americas.

"You're British?! Wow! Have you been to the Oxford Street store? I so wanna go!"

"No, I haven't!" I sensed this was the Lush shop equivalent of "You're British? Do you live in London?".

After deciding that the prices were a little higher than at home, and that we'd only been away for a few days and I probably didn't need anything new quite yet, we headed out to join the queue at the Empire State Building.

As a birthday surprise, Ashley had booked tickets for us to go up the Empire State Building, which provided some stunning views from the top.

Wanting to keep up our week's theme of international food when we weren't eating cheap with 3 for $1 bagels from Staten Island, I opted for Koreatown for my birthday lunch. We found a delicious vegetarian bibimbap in a small food hall and followed it up with a bubble tea (because no one can walk past a bubble tea stand empty handed) and a pastry stuffed with Nutella and shaped like a fish...because...birthday.

After a few hours enjoying Coney Island, it was time to meet Daniel and Freddie so we found ourselves heading back into the centre of Brooklyn. We had a brief whizz around the local supermarket with Daniel, and were impressed to see Daniel start to make tortillas by hand when we returned to their home. We were having Mexican, a popular food group in our own household, so much so we even served burritos and nachos at our wedding, yet we'd never attempted our own tortillas.

"You've got to have this type of flour or it just doesn't work," Daniel said as Ashley and I stood in awe, chopping peppers and onions.

'MASACA' the bag read, in big bold yellow letters outlined in green, an image we'd become familiar with as we travelled down through Central America.

In the interview, Daniel and Freddie told us how New York is the perfect location for an organisation like Wikitongues to be based because of its multilingualism. Yet Wikitongues doesn't stay static. With volunteers across the globe, it's an organisation that aims to support languages worldwide through providing oral histories uploaded to YouTube, and, most recently, working to create a Language Reclamation Toolkit to help communities keep their languages alive. Pretty cool.

And just like that, as we took our ferry back across to Staten Island that evening, our time in New York had come to an end. Had we made the most of it and filmed enough for our first episode of Language Stories? We'd soon find out when we began editing in our next stop: Montreal.

Canada

Season 1, Episode 2: Montreal: Beyond Bilingual

France is close to home. Having been there many times for camping holidays during my childhood, the place wasn't new and exciting. Whereas with Spanish, aged seventeen there was pretty much an entire pulsing continent to explore that gave me a buzz to keep learning; for French, I struggled for a while to find that.

I didn't feel the drive to visit Francophone Africa at that age, nor did I know much about other pockets of the world that spoke French. Yet there was one place that stood out to me: Quebec, and more specifically, Montreal.

Photos of Montreal looked like the kind of place I would love. A place that took the tasty French croissants and hot chocolate and merged it with the vastness of North America. A place that seemed different to home, yet still comfortable. A place I could live. Montreal oozed effortless chic more so than Kate Moss and I wanted to be part of it.

It wasn't until 2016, when I was invited to speak at the first LangFest event (then known as NAPS) that I got the chance to visit the desired home of my seventeen year old self. I loved it so much that when the second event came around and we'd be starting our trip just "down the road" in New York City, we figured it was time for a second visit a year later.

It didn't take much convincing Ashley as he'd found a marathon in Quebec City on his birthday.

Ahh, this is a point in the book I should probably explain something about Ash. He loves to run. It's kind of a beautiful story. When he finished university and went home to start looking for work (he's two years older than me and was part of the lucky bunch that left university right slap bang in the middle of the 2008 financial crisis) he began to visit his granddad every day. But he didn't drive. So he'd walk the mile or so down to his granddad's house and back again each day.

One day he jogged a little bit. The next day he jogged a bit more, and the next, until one day he ran the whole way there.

After a few years of casually running for fitness, going gradually further and faster, he entered his first organised run and has been doing so ever since. He's the fastest runner I know, and yes, I'm biased, of course, but he's an inspiration for me to run too. I tell you this because it will shape the story of this book as the year goes on.

Anyway, armed with me speaking at LangFest in Montreal and Ashley running a marathon on his birthday in Quebec City, we headed to Canada.

For a North American, the following may sound rather dull. We took a Greyhound Bus from New York City to Montreal.

But yes, everyone else! A Greyhound Bus! Like in the movies and stuff! Like what people do when they go coast to coast and stuff! A Greyhound Bus!

Ok, North America, you can come back now our awkward excitement has passed.

This Greyhound Bus was due to take a good 6 hours or so - the time it would take me to drive nearly the whole width of my own teeny-tiny pocket-sized country from Fishguard on the far coast of Wales to Great Yarmouth on the edge of Norfolk. They say Great Yarmouth is the new New York, so you know, pick which of the two journeys you choose to take wisely.

After being directed to about 7 different buses at Port Authority Bus Station in New York, a longer stop than expected in Albany when our bus disappeared with our luggage, and a lot of questions at the Canadian border about going to Cuba, we finally arrived in Montreal in the dark and made our way to our Airbnb.

Thankfully, it was Friday night, and we were conveniently located right next to a street full of food. Not literally food filling a street, but simply many choices of eateries. We found a poutine place with an Instagrammable menu. And if there's one thing New York had taught me, it's to go for the eating establishment with the menu designed for the 'Gram.

***

As for the Language Stories episode in Montreal, much like New York, we were fortunate enough to already know a handful of people, mainly from my visit to the first LangFest event the previous year.

We'd agreed to speak with Tetsu, and Joey and his wife Mariuxi, organisers of LangFest. On top of that, I'd become good friends with Kate, a volunteer on the previous year's event team who had offered to show me around her multicultural and multilingual neighbourhood the year before. Oh, and Kate also knows where the best croissants are hidden in the city...nay, maybe even the world. Don't tell the French.

We met Tetsu one morning at the venue of LangFest itself. After a few minutes awkwardly sat in the lobby of the Concordia University building we'd agreed to meet in, Tetsu arrived, beaming as always, wearing his LangFest t-shirt with a photo of Bella Devyatkina on it. Bella had gone viral online that past year after appearing on a Russian TV talent show showcasing her language skills...oh, and she was only five years old. Her and her mum were attending LangFest this year.

Appropriately, given the t-shirt, we wanted to speak with Tetsu about how he raises his own children multilingually. He is of Chinese heritage and his wife of Japanese; they live in Montreal, a bilingual city with French and English; and they hired a Spanish speaking nanny to bring the total of languages his little ones are learning up to five. How does he do it?

Tetsu uses what's known as the OPOL method, which stands for One Parent One Language. This means that he speaks in Chinese, his wife in Japanese, the nanny in

Spanish, and the world around them in French and English. OPOL is just one of various methods adopted by parents who want their children to be raised with multiple languages, and in Tetsu's case it's proved successful so far.

After meeting Tetsu, we set out later than week to interview Joey and his wife Mariuxi about their multilingual life. Joey has Italian heritage, and Mariuxi is from Ecuador and moved to the city as a young student keen to learn English and French. They met around that time and have been together ever since.

It was beginning to become apparent that Montreal isn't just a bilingual city, the topic we originally imagined for the episode, but rather, a *multilingual* city. The question is more often, "What's your *third* language?" assuming people can speak at least some English and French.

But of course, not all Montrealers do speak both English and French. There are communities within the city that speak only English or only French. For example, on my first visit, I ended up staying in what I soon discovered to be an English area of the city. One day catching the bus into the event I even witnessed some linguistic misunderstandings on a bus, which led to a passenger getting off enraged that the driver wouldn't speak to him in the language he wanted.

Towards the end of our week together in Montreal, before Ashley headed to Quebec City for his birthday marathon and I stayed on for LangFest, we met with Kate to hit the streets and interview people in her neighbourhood about languages.

It was a format totally different to what we'd done in New York and I was nervous about interrupting people's day to ask for an interview about language. Thankfully, Kate had some people in mind already - her local stationary and printing shop, owned by a family of Greek origin with customers speaking French, English, Yiddish and more; and also her hairdressers, where we spoke in Spanish, English and French with a hairdresser from Chile.

Feeling on a roll, we even asked a few taxi drivers parked up at a taxi bay if they'd like to speak with us. One agreed, and we learnt about how he uses French, English, and his native Haitian Creole in his everyday life.

Oh, and of course, after it all, we went for the best croissants in the world. I still can't tell you where because the French mustn't know.

Montreal and Quebec City were due to be the only places on this trip that spoke French, a language Ashley doesn't speak. Before we came away, he'd been learning Spanish in preparation for our time in Latin America. And funnily enough, the host of our Airbnb in Quebec City was a Colombian lady who didn't speak much English! So for a few days, Ash was on his own, having to scrape by in Spanish without me until I joined him a few days later when LangFest was over. I like to think of it as a trial run for him for what was to come in Latin America.

Originally, we'd wanted to use Quebec as a jumping off point for visiting the rest of Canada. Taking the train across this vast land and discovering languages along the way before making our way overland down through 'Merica. But, the states we'd be arriving at in the USA are some of the few with minimal Greyhound Buses! I know, rest of the world, we've been lied to by the movies! Upon realising that this would cost us nearly what the whole year would elsewhere, we soon abandoned the idea and started looking into flights from Quebec to Latin America.

Cuba kept coming up.

We hadn't really thought much about Cuba. Of course it's an island, we'd have to fly in and out. We weren't really looking to fly, we wanted to go overland as much as possible. But, it seemed Canadians had thought a lot about Cuba, a country not exactly best buds with the USA. A tropical paradise where Canadians wouldn't be mistaken for Americans. I guess it makes sense. It's the same reason the Irish visit...well, I don't know because I'm British, that would ruin it for the Irish if I knew, wouldn't it?

So Cuba was to be our next stop. But how did this fit into Language Stories? Some quickfire Googling told me that the vast majority of Cubans speak Spanish and there's not masses of other language communities on the island. Hmm...this was going to be tricky.

As it turned out, not having a language to make an episode about was to be the last of our worries.

Cuba

Season 1, Mini Episode 1: Chinatown in Havana

Cuba being home to multiple popular tourist resorts meant that flights from Canada to Cuba were a lot cheaper to said resorts than to Havana or other cities on the mainland a little further from the white sand beaches we see in travel agency windows next to the word 'Cuba'.

This meant that we landed in a pretty expensive resort area called Cayo Coco. Sure, it was beautiful but seeing as resorts weren't really what we were after, we planned to catch a taxi from the airport right out and off the resort island to the nearest town: Morón. Yes, There's a town called 'moron'. But thanks to the fancy Spanish accent, it's pronounced more like Mor-ON. So the town's not as dumb as you might initially imagine.

In fact, it was quite a nice introduction to Cuba. It was an easily walkable town with examples of everything you'd expect - vintage cars weaving their way around the dusty roads dodging horse carts and bike taxis, holes in the wall selling peso pizzas and ham sandwiches, street carts set up with colourful chilled drinks and huge avocados.

But judging by how keen our casa host was to get us a shared taxi to the beach back at Cayo Coco, it's clearly not expected that tourists hang around much in Morón. She looked pretty disappointed when we said we weren't interested and that it was too expensive (partly referring to the cost of the taxi and partly referring to the cost of eating, drinking and just being in the resort town for one day). She left a little disgruntled.

Five minutes later there was a knock at the door.

"There's a bus to Cayo Coco tomorrow morning at 8am, comes back at 4pm, costs 5 CUC each." Our host said in Spanish.

I translated for Ashley. Five CUC wasn't too bad. The CUC is shorthand for the Cuban 'Peso Convertible', aka the tourist dollar.

You see, Cuba has two currencies (or at least it did at the time we visited): the Peso Convertible, otherwise known as CUC, convertibles or peso; and the regular Peso, otherwise known as Moneda Nacional, MN or peso. Yup, they can both be known as pesos. They also look pretty similar too. So what's the difference? The CUC is pegged to the US dollar and is the same as 25 MN. Not confusing at all. Honest…

Anyway, back to Morón.

"Ok," I said, "5 CUC is ok. Where does the bus leave from? Do we need to reserve tickets in advance?"

"Parque Martí at 8am."

(We'd soon discover that pretty much every town in Cuba has a Parque Martí)

"No need to reserve, just show up and pay on the bus," she replied.

So dutifully, at 8 the next morning we were stood by a bus parked on the side of Parque Martí, shorts and shirts covering our swimwear, with our snorkel just poking out the top of our bag.

But there was no sign on the bus to say where it was going nor anyone actually stood by the bus.

Maybe we're early, I thought. Maybe Cuba time is a little more lax than UK time.

Two men showed up and inspected the bus much in the same way we had.

It turned our one was a local Cuban and the other (who didn't speak much) was apparently from Spain. The Cuban told us they were friends but it seemed more of a "Hey friend, let me be your local guide" kind of scenario than a "Hey buddy, fancy going down the pub tonight?" thing. Still, it was reassuring to know we weren't the only ones expecting the bus to take us to supposed paradise. Even more so given that one of us was now a local.

The Cuban told us that the bus driver was just over the road having a coffee and would be with us soon. And he was. Along with a flood of other Cubans all wearing a mishmash of white tops.

It soon clicked. This was a bus for workers at the resorts. We were fugitives. Sneaking into the place we were expected to already be staying judging by the pasty colour of our skin.

And that's no exaggeration.

There's a police checkpoint going onto the resort island to prevent Cubans who fancy a little sun, sea, and sand from entering unless they're working there.

We were ushered towards the back of the bus and told to sit on the right side - furthest from the checkpoint's view.

A few minutes after departing and the initial hellos, the woman opposite me thrust a white shirt into my hands.

"For the checkpoint," she said in Spanish, "so you blend in."

"What about him?" I asked, pointing to Ashley.

She flapped her hand dismissively, "No worries, he seems Cuban enough."

Bear in mind this was our first full day in Cuba - we were still pretty obviously not Cuban even if we tried. Like I said, pasty.

"Oh." I looked at Ash and shrugged.

The checkpoint soon approached and we were told to switch seats. As we did, the people we swapped with pulled the curtains closed.

Despite everything, we were ushered through the checkpoint without a second glance and could enjoy our day at the beach safe in the knowledge that...we had to do the same thing on the way back.

When we arrived, we walked down to the beach and could easily see why there were so many resorts here. The place was stunning.

We walked along the sand a bit before settling and taking it in turns to go in the sea and snorkel, still not (and probably never in any country) comfortable enough to leave our stuff unattended on the beach.

After a morning of tag teaming it in and out of the ocean at various points along the beach, it was soon time for lunch. Problem being that everyone else here eats in their all-inclusive resort buffets. This doesn't leave much demand for other restaurants, explaining the monopoly that one *ranchón* (restaurant) had across the whole beach.

And also explaining how the food was so lame. Vegetarian isn't really an understood concept in Cuba, a country living under rationing as recent as the 90s. There's a "Why would you not eat meat when we were deprived of it for so long?" kind of attitude, and understandably so. So we had to pay 2 CUC each for a plate of rice, chopped tomatoes and cucumber and hope it would keep us full until we got back to Morón.

We headed back to the beach for a few more hours of snorkelling with the fish before sitting and drying off in time for heading back to the bus.

This bit proved trickier than expected. There were a couple of buses, ready to take the workers back to the mainland, but none of them were willing to take us as tourists. The last thing we wanted on our first full day in Cuba was to have to pay full whack for a taxi back.

After running around the car parks of one resort thinking we saw the same bus that brought us in, we emerged from the entrance to spot a bus taking passengers on the other side of the street.

We ran across, waving our arms wildly, and tried our luck. One of the workers who spoke a little English was more than happy to practise his English with us and told us to wait for a moment while he asked the driver if it was ok.

Thankfully, it was. We got on, slipped our money to the driver and sat at the back on the far side of the bus, drawing the curtains mostly closed ready for the impending inspection.

Yet again, our bus was ushered through and we made it back to Morón, with slightly pinker thighs and, undoubtedly, a Cuban criminal record in the post.

Other than that day in Cayo Coco, memories of Morón itself are mostly of food. The queue at the bakery in the 'burbs that had ran out of bread and was currently whipping up a new batch mid-afternoon, the woman sat on a low stool not far down from there with huge avocados laid out on a cloth in front of her, the peso pizza hole in the wall cafeterias and conversations with the owners that followed.

Morón was a great introduction to what to expect from Cuba, so much so that by the time we got to Havana, the usual sights that would make a tourist grab for their camera were just part of the scenery to us.

But Havana was a long way off yet. Next up was Ciego de Ávila.

***

Ciego de Ávila wasn't really a place I'd wanted to visit when doing our initial planning, yet it seemed necessary as part of the journey from Morón to Trinidad, a cobbled, colourful, colonial town on the southern coast nuzzled by the Topes de Collantes mountains.

We had to take the train from Morón to Ciego de Ávila and then the Viazul tourist bus from there to Trinidad.

With the town being nothing more than a transit hub, we were initially thinking of stopping just for one night, but the transport times didn't quite match up so we opted instead for two nights. And were glad we did.

The town was a little bigger than Morón but still manageable on foot, which we liked. And the lack of big city sights allowed us a little time to check out the municipal museum and zoo once we'd confirmed our bus ticket out to Trinidad.

The zoo was more impressive than the museum, which was mostly a collection of what can only be described as "stuff", with minimal explanations, even in Spanish.

There were some ok-sized enclosures in the zoo, as far as zoos go in smaller countries. The lone giraffe and zebra had a decent roaming space. That said, not every animal got so lucky and the monkey cage (yup, cage is the only word to describe it) was saddening, as was the lion's concrete box. I know zoos are a controversial place to visit, but I have to admit that I find them an interesting insight into different countries.

After the obligatory tortoise/turtle pen, ever present at any animal attraction, the most impressive sight of our day at the zoo was a hippo eating.

Yes. A hippo, in the middle of Cuba, chomping through a pumpkin like you've never seen. He picked it up whole, punctured it with his tusk-like tooth and swallowed it whole. Just watching it was enough to make you gag a little bit.

And good God, I've never been so close to a hippo. Or a zebra. In a nation where it's illegal to have the Internet in private homes, they sure do trust you at the zoo.

In our short time in Ciego de Ávila, it felt like we walked the pedestrianised Boulevard about fifteen times. That considered, we hardly ever ate there, mostly on the hunt for places that charge in Moneda Nacional, meaning they'd be cheaper.

This led us to some interesting food choices in Ciego de Ávila. The first day, we headed out to the relatively new park that centred around a lake, making it a natural spot for 'The Floating Restaurant'. Of course, that's where we wanted to eat because, well, why wouldn't you?

The only trouble is, they had no menu on dry land before heading down the plank to reach the restaurant. It's a smart move because it means by the time you reach the restaurant, you're in it! And the trouble with that was it was a fish restaurant. With no vegetarian option.

But they did have prices in MN so we settled for a drink each and soon ordered another and a small dessert each, partly so as not to feel guilty for not ordering a meal, and partly because it was so darn cheap.

Still hungry, we headed on, inspecting the menus of the various restaurants along the way until we saw it. A restaurant in a plane. Well, *behind* a plane, technically.

A peek at the menu showed their prices in MN and after asking if they can just give us rice and beans with vegetables 'sin carne' (without meat), we sat down in the retro-styled restaurant and started watching the reggaeton on the screen as it competed with around three other reggaeton songs being blared from other places outside. A cacophony of the familiar 'boom chi boom chick' of the music that had become a part of our daily lives by now. Bizarrely, 'Tale As Old As Time' complete with the video of the ballroom scene from Beauty and the Beast interrupted the flow of the reggaeton at one point.

The waitress asked if we wanted a drink. I asked for a water and Ash ummed and ahhed as she offered a mojito, a daiquiri, a Cuba libre…

"Cuánto cuesta mojito?" he asked. I was impressed by the speed he'd started to use Spanish spontaneously.

"Un peso" the waitress said.

Remember the prices on the menu were in MN. One MN peso is around four pence in UK money!

"Bueno, mojito por favor!" Ash replied.

It wasn't until we got the bill that we discovered she meant one *Convertible* Peso. We were discovering the joys of two currencies. And we were wiped out of our MN supply.

You see, the other thing about the dual currency thing is that when you go to an ATM with your foreign card or you go to the CADECA (that's the money exchange office with a branch in every major town, including Ciego de Ávila) with your Canadian Dollars (not US ones, you'll be charged extra on top of your exchange rate), you're going to get given Convertibles.

So you have to ask to change a small amount of those into MN, around five CUC will last a week or so. Unless you order a 'one peso' mojito and pay in MN that is.

After restocking up on MN after the mojito, on the second afternoon, back in town, we decided to eat at a gazebo grill taking up one side of the road with a few tables and chairs spilling out into the road in front. They charged in MN, and we definitely needed to save some dinero after the pricey mojito the day before.

We went to sit at a table in the sun but they ushered us under the gazebo to the only table in the shade. The only table that was also covered in more flies than you could imagine. I can't even begin to describe it. The table was *absolutely* covered with flies. As in, less table cloth visible than fly. And the flies didn't move either when we sat down. Not shy flies.

Ash got brave with his Spanish again and asked to move back outside, she understood him and said yes of course. It was a pivotal moment in his Spanish progress.

But the rice and beans wasn't enough and we were on the hunt for dessert. We found it at Coppelia, a national state-run chain made famous beyond Cuba by the film Fresa y Chocolate back in the 90s.

Apparently at Coppelia in Havana, they have two entrances, one for each currency, and tourists are ushered into the CUC priced half of the parlour.

However, with Ciego de Ávila not exactly being a tourist hotspot, there was no ushering. There was an upstairs that could have been priced in CUC, but we didn't wait to find out and instead we queued for the downstairs and ordered five scoops each for a grand total of sixteen pence in UK money!

The thing about Coppelia, this being Cuba and all, is that the flavour board isn't exactly brimming with choice. The day we visited there were just three flavours on offer: chocolate, guava, and chocolate rice. We got a mixture of all three and did our best to get it down before it all melted into a guavary chocolatey mess. Then we paid sharpish. Then we left. Each branch of Coppelia had a queue most of the time we saw them, so it's a constant flow of people in and out eating their ice cream as swiftly as possible. And it works.

***

Our bus ride to Trinidad (the only daily departure time) left very early - 4.40am. And you have to be there thirty minutes before. So it was an early morning leaving for our next stop. And what a stop it was to be…

Trinidad was up there as one of the places I was looking forward to the most about Cuba. It just seemed like it would be my kind of place from everything I'd seen and read. But I guess this is why you have to travel - sometimes, places just aren't as you expect.

Trinidad isn't exactly a secret. For the first time in Cuba since sneaking onto Cayo Coco, we saw multiple foreign faces other than our own reflections. Not that that's a problem - we're tourists too so it's hypocritical to complain about tourists! That's not what I'm saying.

But tourism has definitely driven up the prices in Trinidad. It became harder to find cafeterias charging in MN, meaning our eating out each day was mostly restricted to restaurants geared towards tourists, charging in CUC. That said, we did find a great little cafeteria on our penultimate day in Trinidad - one that we liked so much we went back to for lunch the following day before getting the bus out of there.

So maybe I'm being a little harsh on Trinidad and we're just biased because it cost more than where we'd been to that point. Well, that and the breakfast lady putting a downer on the place.

The woman who served us breakfast every morning in Trinidad mentioned her daughter's quinceanera multiple times, noting to include that the people that stayed in another room gave her a dress that her daughter loved. One morning she went on to tell us that her mother has bone cancer and she was awake all night because of her mother's howls. Another morning when Ashley took his phrasebook and notepad to breakfast she asked him if he had a spare notepad for her. We paid her ten CUC to do our laundry and it came back smelling worse than before. On our final morning she told us that if we had any gifts for her we should give them directly to her and not the casa. When she realised we weren't going to give her any gifts, we found her promptly knocking on our door to tell us we had to leave before 9am because more guests were coming...check out wasn't until 11am, she just wanted to clean up early and get home.

Now I understand the dynamics of this to a certain extent. I get that being poorer than others in a country like Cuba is hard, especially in a tourist spot like Trinidad. I get that seeing people every single morning who can afford to leave their country and come to your country for a short time must be a temptation to ask for just a little help in varying ways. But I struggle with it because it doesn't solve any problems if we give her something.

If every morning that she goes up to serve breakfast, and new guests give her a notepad, a dress for her daughter, money for her mother's healthcare, then of course she's going to continue to ask for those things everyday. But it's not a solution. It's just plugging a hole temporarily and it creates a dependency on tourists who aren't there to be that solution.

I realise this sounds harsh but it's an unfortunate truth. We saw it in action later on our trip in Havana.

We were chatting to an American at a hole in the wall cafeteria waiting for our pizzas when a woman approached and asked us for money. Ashley and I politely declined but the American reached into his backpack and handed her a ziplock bag with a toothbrush, a small tube of toothpaste and other necessities. Seems like a good idea, right?

"I have four children, I need four more." she promptly replied in Spanish before even saying thank you.

He reached back into his bag and handed her three more, claiming that was all he had. She thanked him, asked where he was from and left.

Minutes later she returned, this time with a friend in tow.

"This is the guy," she said in Spanish as she pointed to the American, "Have you got one for my friend?"

He had to hand another ziplock bag to the woman's friend. I never did ask how many he was carrying.

I don't know what the answer to this problem is. I want to help people when I visit places but equally I want to help people in my own country too. If I walk past a homeless person in the UK but hand out ziplock bags to everyone that asks in Cuba, does that make me a bad person? On the other hand, is it right if I don't give anything to people who ask in Cuba? Is it right if I do give something, potentially creating a dependency on tourists for handouts? Is there a right or wrong answer to any of this? It's a sticky ethics issue that I don't know the answer to.

***

Most of our days in Trinidad were spent wandering the cobbled streets, enjoying the live music on every corner. But we did have one day out of the city.

I wanted to treat Ashley to a belated birthday gift - a journey into the mountains to visit a coffee plantation and cafe I'd spotted in a guidebook. I also wanted to visit the mountains to swim in a natural pool, go hiking, and do all that nature stuff. We booked a tour with Cubatur that had everything we wanted in one day! And it involved a "Russian truck".

The following morning we arrived at the office ready to go. And ready to discover exactly what was meant by the open to interpretation term "Russian truck".

It was a beast. It was a very high off the ground truck that was slightly too wide for the cobbled streets of Trinidad. It seated around sixteen people in the back, with open sides and a tarpaulin roof. And it was fun.

The roads up to the mountains were steep. Like, no way you could cycle up here steep. The Russian truck was a necessity.

We stopped at a viewpoint; the coffee place (which, to be honest, was slightly underwhelming); and a "farmer's market" (aka a stall by the side of the road), before pulling over to start our 3km hike through the forest via a waterfall and cave to our swimming hole before lunch.

I love this stuff. I'm not a huge fan of tours generally, but tours that take you through nature that you couldn't see on your own? I'm up for that.

The swimming hole was definitely a highlight. We stripped down to our swimwear at the side of the pool (there was even a little privacy space built if you weren't already in your kit), and hopped into the water, complete with tiny fish!

Interestingly, the tiny fish didn't bother you when in the water but when I sat on the dock to rinse my feet after getting dressed, they flocked towards me and started sucking on my feet! These were the same fish you get in those fish foot spas that seem to have disappeared in recent years at home due to hygiene laws. I'd found them in nature! No hygiene laws in nature!

The lunch was also impressive considering the tour details had said "light lunch". We were presented with plates of fresh fruit, rice, chicken, bread and more before heading back down the mountain in the truck.

That was undoubtedly the best day in Trinidad. We had initially planned to stay five nights but cut it down to three due to having done pretty much everything we wanted mostly in one day on the tour, and things being more expensive than expected.

That meant that we had time to see somewhere extra and unplanned before ending our trip in Havana and Viñales. We decided to add in a trip to Santa Clara, the town where Che Guevara's soldiers derailed a train full of Fulgencio Batista's supplies, an event that after the final battle in the town led to Batista fleeing the country. One night would be enough, just to see the Che stuff and try and understand the history a little more for ourselves.

But one night soon turned into five…

***

As we visited the only semi-close-to-the-centre peso cafeteria we'd stumbled across in Trinidad for the second time, bags in tow just before we headed to the bus station for our reserved and already paid for journey to Santa Clara, we were met with plenty of local customers telling us "Woah, you go to Santa Clara today, you won't leave tomorrow...the 'cyclón' is coming."

We looked at each other, a little wide-eyed in disbelief but equally feeling safe in the knowledge that surely the bus wouldn't run if it was going to be that dangerous?

Stuffed with cheese sandwiches and tamarind juice, we set off for the bus station, and sure enough, we got on the bus without even a muttering of the word *'cyclón'* from anyone working at the station.

The journey was pretty normal, nothing unusual. And even when we arrived in Santa Clara, all was normal.

We found ourselves a casa particular and settled in before heading out to explore the city and visit the Che Guevara mausoleum.

The town was pretty calm. With the exception of the crosses of brown tape on the windows of shops and restaurants to try and stop glass from smashing that appeared more and more throughout the day, you certainly wouldn't think a hurricane was imminent.

That night, the boxy, fuzzy TV in our room was playing constant footage of a weather man with a mighty moustache ensuring us of Hurricane Irma's route. It looked like we might get some rain from the edge of the hurricane but nothing too serious in Santa Clara.

The following day, our casa host moved us to another room, higher up and closer to the house, as she was worried about flooding in our lower than ground level room. We promptly upped sticks and shifted rooms.

Despite kind of not really believing it, we stocked up on supplies should we be unable to get out the following day.

The supermarket. Oh, the supermarket.

Thanks to casas particulares not generally (or in our case, not at all) providing you with cooking facilities, it's not exactly top of the traveller priority list to self-cater in Cuba. And besides, even if you chose to...well, the supermarkets.

The day before Irma hit was our first real venture into a supermarket in Cuba and what an interesting experience. Well, I say 'our', I mean 'my' - Ashley wasn't allowed to come in carrying a bag, and you had to pay to leave it at the *paquetería* (a hole in the wall outside where your bags are looked after while you're in the supermarket).

Being British and not being accustomed to paying to leave your bags outside a supermarket, we decided that one of us would wait outside. That burden fell on Ashley.

So I headed into the chaos and grabbed a basket. It was pretty busy and the queues were long and painful, but it was hard to tell if that's normal or just a hurricane panic buying frenzy taking over.

There's no fresh food in the supermarkets. Instead, you would buy fruit, veg and meat from a market. That means that supermarkets are reserved for canned and packaged food, a small selection of toiletries behind a counter, and washing powder. Lots and lots of washing powder.

It's not that the supermarket was understocked - the shelves were all full. It's more that the shelves were all full with lots of the same stuff.

All I managed to get for our hurricane rations were crackers, tomato puree, condensed milk, and water.

There were other products - tins of lentils and green beans for example. But for the equivalent of $2.50 per tin, I was happy to stick to our 70 cents tomato puree.

But my stressful and slightly saddening experience of the Cuban supermarket was to pale in comparison to what was about to happen. Irma was coming.

***

On our second night in Santa Clara, after the wifi (yes! We finally had the internet in Cuba for all of one hour!) electricity, and water had all been lost, we were awoken multiple times in the night, partly due to rain outside and partly due to the rain dripping into our room and onto the fridge, and consequently onto our food rations.

The following morning, we gingerly peeked out of the door to see as we expected from what we'd heard in the night.

It was still raining. It was still windy. And it was showing no signs of stopping.

Our host assembled a quick breakfast for us as best she could. We stood on the terrace, sheltered from the rain and it wasn't long before I was called to translate.

The second room on the higher level had a French couple staying in it. I sorted their breakfast drink order and we got chatting. They'd visited Cuba three times, each at this time of year, and this was the first time they'd known a hurricane to hit.

The front door to the casa was jammed shut with a wooden bar. It felt like the end scene of Beauty and the Beast. And there's no way we were going anywhere for the day.

It was a weird time. On the one hand, you feel foolish, imagining people shaking their heads at you back home saying "Well, it is hurricane season, what did they expect..." but on the other, it feels like you're completely in the way of the casa hosts, the locals, the country. After realising that there's very little you can do to help, you just want to disappear out of the equation. But you can't. Because there's no transport. There's no way to disappear.

Over the next few days, as an avocado tree fell in the garden, I translated multiple food orders, and we all got gradually more bored, we fell into a pretty numbing routine: breakfast, head out and walk the 2km to the bus station to see if they had any info on when we could leave, walk down to the train station to ask the same thing, and back to the room - disappointed that we were facing another day of doing nothing.

There were some positives - the forced time sat in the room meant I got to do some work on my planners for Lindsay Does Languages...but this was limited until the power came back. We also got to watch many of the films we'd downloaded on Netflix in Quebec City before leaving for internet-free Cuba...but besides The Breakfast Club, which I fell madly in love with, the other films we had downloaded (and on reflection, I don't know why) were the Sharknado series. So, you know, not exactly escapism in a hurricane.

Finally, on Monday (day four in Santa Clara), as the storm had passed and the town was beginning to cog back into motion, we struck gold when a guy asked if we wanted a bike taxi anywhere.

"No," I told him in Spanish, "unless you can bike us to Havana?! Ha! We need to get to Havana."

"Ahh, you want a colectivo?" he replied, offering us a shared taxi.

"Maybe…"

"Wait here, let me go get my cousin, he's a taxi driver!" he sped off to the right leaving us waiting on the corner of the main square.

"What's going on?" Ashley asked. The conversation had been in Spanish.

"Well, his cousin is apparently a taxi driver and he might be able to take us to Havana tomorrow. He's just gone to get him now."

"Is it legit?"

"I have no idea…ahh, I guess this is him."

We agreed he would pick us up at 8am the following morning, Tuesday, and it would cost $50 - $25 each. Not much more than the bus we'd been waiting to return to action for so long. We shook hands.

Sure enough, at 8am the following morning, a small white Lada showed up complete with two other Cuban passengers already, and definitely a different driver behind the wheel to who I shook hands with the day before. Nonetheless, the reggaeton-fuelled journey got us to Havana. Finally! And as our luck changed, the timing was perfect to catch a bus out that same afternoon to Viñales, the place in Cuba I'd most been looking forward to…

***

Viñales did not disappoint. From the moment we arrived and headed off the main street towards a casa listed in the guidebook as growing their own coffee, I knew this was the place I'd been waiting for. We stumbled into the garden of the casa, no one in sight until someone called us from across the fence. I never did figure out if we ended up in the spare room of the actual casa we were looking for or of a neighbour, but either way, we hit the jackpot. Walking all the way down and away from the centre street towards the hills rewarded us with the best views of any casa in the town. There was nothing interrupting our view between our porch where we had breakfast and the view of (in this order) dirt road, farmers' fields, lumpy hills.

Yup, lumpy hills. The Spanish name is *'mogotes'*, which translates as 'heaps', 'stacks' or 'piles', and couldn't be a more accurate description. It wasn't a mountainous landscape, more so one dotted with heaped hills here and there.

Heaped hills here and there makes for excellent nature walks, climbing, and caves. The latter being the main reason I was so excited about this place. I love caves.

Our first full day, we took an afternoon tour out to Santo Tomás, part of the second biggest cave system in the Americas.

Waiting on a bench outside a restaurant, as we were instructed to do that morning, we soon found ourselves in our first (and only) Cuban 'vintage' car! Although, from the longest air con unit I've ever seen and the 'MP5' screen, you wouldn't think this was a relic of the 1950s. The DIY wooden window winders might have had you realising it though.

Our driver took us and a young German couple to the cave entrance where we waited for the next tour to begin. It began with a walk up what would be fenced off in the UK - slippery branches and trip hazards aplenty led us to the entrance of the cave, where we were allowed, nay, encouraged and expected to go ahead while we waited for everyone else to join us.

The tour was more like our spelunking experience at Cheddar Gorge a few years before than your average cave tour with a boardwalk and floodlights.

Not that I'm complaining, like I said, I love a good cave. And to be honest, this was the most impressive of our trip to Viñales.

There was another that we visited the following day after hiring bikes from a friend of the casa. The cave (which involved a motor boat ride through it) was a little underwhelming, and closer than expected on bike, so we decided to ride a little further out seeing as we had the bikes all day and took ourselves on the 50km roundtrip journey to the coastal town of Puerto Esperanza.

It wasn't an overly easy ride, partly due to the sun beating down and burning my little hands and partly due to the potholes along most of the uphill roads.

However, we arrived at Puerto Esperanza, saw the disappointing coastline, ate a pretty decent $5 lunch, and started the journey back. At the time it wasn't my favourite day in Cuba. Looking back, it was a great experience. Ashley enjoyed it both at the time and after. In fact, a photo at the coastline of us and our bikes is still the background on his laptop desktop.

Preparing for our skin to peel, we settled in for the night to preserve energy for our final day in Viñales. We were going walking in those lumpy hills. On our own.

***

The following morning, we were keen to aim for a cave I'd seen on the map and read about where there was a swimming hole inside. Natural swimming?! In a cave?! Yes please!

The guidebook described it as "a doable hike" and our casa owner didn't seem too concerned when we told her our plans in the morning, so off we set.

The track was pretty accurate to the route on my map app until...the mud.

It got thicker and thicker and showed no signs of getting better. Yet we persevered...until my shoes got completely stuck in the mud, still 2km from the cave entrance according to the map app.

Disappointed and angry at my ruined shoes, we headed back, deciding to stop at a hut in the direction of a *'jugos naturales'* sign thinking we could at least get a drink from this journey if not directions or some water to wash off my now very muddy bare feet.

As it turned out, the hut we approached wasn't the place the *'jugos'* sign was pointing to, but nevertheless, a kind man came out with a small plastic cup of coffee for Ashley and a cup of water for me which he used to wash my hands. He even offered Ashley a cigar, which he politely declined.

I asked how we could get to the cave, he asked if we wanted to ride a horse, we said we didn't, he asked if we wanted to go by horse cart, we said we did, he said he'd show us, we agreed on a price (5 CUC each), and off we went.

After a quick stop at what turned out to be the place the *'jugos naturales'* sign *was* pointing to (which included a coffee tour for free that was much better than the place we'd stopped at on our Trinidad tour) we set off through the fields until we reached a tobacco drying hut and he told us to get off.

We had to walk the rest of the way. Mojito (yes, our horse was called Mojito!) was tied to a tree as we set off to finish our journey.

After crossing an unexpected bamboo patch, we met two guys who were waiting on the off chance that some tourists would arrive at the near impossible to reach cave. It was their lucky day.

We paid 2 CUC each and headed into the cave with one of the guides, our new friend waiting outside with the other guy.

The cave itself was pretty average but as we reached the end, we were met with a pool as promised, completely in the darkness were it not for the torchlight of our guide.

"It's this deep," he signalled with his hands, speaking Spanish, "There's no animals and it's 18 degrees. Enjoy." He sat himself down on a rock by the water's edge and rested his torch shining towards the pool.

This was it. This was what all the wading through the mud, the frustration of having to turn round and the changing of our luck for the day had been leading to. We took off our clothes to reveal our swimming clothes. In we went.

It was cold at first but soon felt comfortable and was all in all a pretty magical experience. It really stands out as the most memorable experience of our time in Cuba.

Given what a great time we'd had in Viñales, we were both quite sad to leave the following morning as we headed for our last stop: Havana.

***

Havana is an evocative city. A city so often cited as beautiful, special, unique. And it definitely is all of those things, but it's also gritty, grubby and very unashamedly real.

That is all of Havana except for where we stayed, Casa 1932.

A German couple asked us on the bus to Havana if we wanted to share a taxi into town from the bus station, about 6km from the centre. Great idea!

As we all got off the bus we were bombarded by casa and taxi offers. I opted to head for bags first, and arrange taxi second. But as I was queueing for the bags, the German guy tapped me on the shoulder to say he'd already sorted a taxi. Excellent!

Unsure of how much Spanish they spoke, I sat in the front of the cab so I could speak with the driver. We had a good conversation, not helped by my terrible decision upon hearing One Direction's 'What Makes You Beautiful' playing to translate 'One Direction' into Spanish and say it out loud. In a moving taxi, on a road, 'one direction' isn't a great thing to say out loud. He was confused to say the least.

Regardless, we chatted about music and after he complimented my Spanish, I told him how Shakira inspired my choice to learn it. As we arrived at our casa, he gave us his number and a cheaper price to get to the airport when we leave.

We headed into the casa. It was by far the swankiest of all the casas we'd stayed at so far. The whole place was tastefully decorated with 1930s art deco pieces. We were given the Lux room for two nights followed by three in the standard room. I'm glad we got to see the Lux room! Not only were we gifted with a TV, kettle and satin sheets, but there was also a book exchange in the room!

Aside from our accommodation, most of our time in Havana was spent wandering the streets looking for sights not affected by Irma a week or so before. The *malecón*, one of the main attractions, was completely shut off to traffic and pedestrians, so much so that police were standing every few hundred metres to stop people from walking on the *malecón* and risking it falling underfoot.

Havana was noticeably more expensive than other places we'd visited, as you might expect for a capital city, and CUC was definitely the prime currency here.

That said, it did mean we treated ourselves to Indian food in the self-proclaimed 'only' Indian restaurant in all of Cuba, Buena Vista Curry Club. It was definitely our most expensive meal in Cuba, and was actually pretty good Indian food. After weeks of cheese sandwiches and vegetable pizzas, it was worth it.

Despite the dominance of CUC in Havana, we planned to eek out the cash we had left by eating lunch at MN *cafeterías,* so headed to CADECA, the money exchange place found in every town across the country, one afternoon to get ourselves some MN.

We joined what we thought was the queue only to discover that Cubans have a...unique method of queueing. As we neared the front, four or five people stood up from the shaded steps nearby to join the queue in front of the young couple in front of us.

The young couple questioned it, only to be told that these people had been in the queue, they'd just been waiting in the shade. And here we were waiting in the sun like mugs. It turned out the couple were from Mexico and as equally baffled by this very Cuban method of queueing as we were.

A couple of days later as we waited for a wifi card at ETESCA thinking we needed to check in online to our flight, we saw the same queueing system with multiple people sat across the street waiting in the shade. We waited one and a half hours for that card valid for one hour of internet, only to discover that we couldn't check in online, nor could we book Airbnb for our next stop in Mexico while we were in Cuba, simply being shown an 'Airbnb does not allow bookings made from Cuba' message after going through the whole process. Cuba was beginning to get annoying. I can't even imagine how frustrating it must be for those who live here - the supermarkets, the internet, the dual currency...

But then again, maybe it's not that frustrating. All the Cubans we encountered were happy. Maybe when you don't know an alternative, the grass doesn't seem so greener on the other side. Because there is no obvious other side.

Our impromptu horse cart driver in Viñales told us that he didn't like going into the town because people only cared about money, it was too busy, he didn't like the pandering to tourists. And that was a one-street town.

Things are undeniably changing in Cuba, and they'll continue to do so. On the one hand this is a great thing, connecting a country to the rest of the world via the internet, giving people more food choices, and unifying the currency (something the government said they'd do back in 2013). But on the other hand, it's hard not to consider the downsides of this. I'm not talking about rolling your eyes seeing Coca-Cola adverts at every corner or tutting at a McDonalds opening up. I'm talking about the inevitable consequences that our horse cart driver already sees in Viñales. However Cuba moves forward, it's somewhere worth visiting now and in the future, as I'm sure the one thing that will remain is the sheer life that pulses through every inch of this island.

Mexico

Season 1, Episode 3: Maya Isn't Dead

Season 1, Mini Episode 3: You Know A Word in Nahuatl

If there's one thing every travel guide has failed to list as a highlight, it's natural disasters. Who wouldn't want to get stuck in a hurricane in Cuba? Definitely top of the list.

And if that's not enough, you should definitely opt for "stuck in a hurricane in Cuba and learning that the place you're going next is currently going through a series of earthquakes". It's really top notch fun.

Our brief glimpse at news during our quick liaison with the internet again just before Hurricane Irma hit in Cuba had shown us that while we were getting wet, Mexico was going through a series of earthquakes. As in, the same Mexico where we were planning to spend the following six weeks.

In a bizarre twist of fate, this led to us staying in one spot in Mexico, Mérida in the Yucatan, and using our time there to catch up on work after our time mostly Internet-free in Cuba and for me to open up enrolment on my course, the Online Teaching Starter Kit.

Mérida treated us well.

We had a great Airbnb apartment, a big supermarket just up the road, and even a running track just running distance away. Always a handy feature for a running track.

Spited by our lack of full Language Stories episode for Cuba thanks to the curious inspection of our filming equipment upon arrival, we were determined to make a great episode of Language Stories here during our extended time in Mérida.

And we were in luck! The Yucatan Peninsula is home to the Mayan language Yucatec Maya, and in Mérida, we were able to meet with some incredibly inspiring people who are all doing wonderful things to promote and keep the language in use.

I soon realised (as in, really soon) that my initial email I was using to reach out to people would need to be in Spanish. Of course. And formal(ish) Spanish at that.

After dusting off my formal written Spanish and crafting a well-polished email to invite people to speak with us for the episode, I began to click send.

At this point it was terrifying.

We hadn't yet started to publish the episodes and had no evidence to send to people to prove we were legit and demonstrate what we were doing.

And if people didn't respond here in Mérida, and as a result we ended up with less episodes, it would only get harder to find interviewees further down the line.

Thankfully, everyone I really wanted to respond responded. As I'd find out later in the year, there's always going to be some requests that get zero response, but mostly these are from language councils or government bodies rather than individuals doing amazing things with language, which is what I cared about getting in the series more so.

Firstly we spoke with Vicente Canché Moo, a name that kept coming up during my research online for Yucatec Maya advocates.

Vicente is a primary school headteacher and as well as encouraging young learners to study the language at school, he's been involved with countless other projects all with the aim of promoting and encouraging the use of Yucatec Maya in the region.

We met one evening as the sun was setting in Parque de las Americas, a large park north of the city centre, with monuments dedicated to each country in the New World.

When I asked Vicente the question "And what have you done personally with the language?" I wasn't quite expecting the length of his answer.

From creating textbooks and story books to audio and video resources, Vicente soon became an inspiration to me for the rest of the series, and for my own life and what I do with languages. The world needs more Vicentes.

When we finished the interview, Vicente handed me a bilingual book that he had written and had published in Spanish and Yucatec Maya. I was honoured and humbled.

The book has pride of place in and among my language bookshelf, and although I can't yet read a word of Yucatec Maya, it reminds me to keep going and to always aim for good, productive and positive work.

***

To say we knew *no one* in Mérida would actually be a lie. Back in Montreal, I was unbelievably excited when, upon telling a stranger about our year ahead over lunch, I was met with a "I live in Mérida, let me know when you're there!"

At that point, we had no idea that we'd be hanging around in the city for so long, yet I had remembered Carlos and asked if, despite not speaking Yucatec Maya, he'd be happy to be interviewed for Language Stories as a native of the region and language enthusiast.

He agreed and offered to take us to some cenotes one Saturday to film the interview. Let me explain what a cenote is and you'll soon see that taking Carlos up on his offer was a no brainer.

Cenotes are deep underground sinkholes that formed uniquely in the Yucatan peninsula as a result of the geography here. The land is flat and quite soft, which led to miles of underground water caves and passages beneath the surface. Due to their depth, cenotes are often the brightest, boldest blue hues, and due to their natural connection to the freshwater supply, they're popular swimming holes with locals and tourists alike.

We had originally planned to visit cenotes during our time in the Yucatan, but hadn't decided exactly where to go before Carlos offered to take us out that day. The ones within easy reach of Mérida as a tourist without a car are packed with tourists jumping from heights and swinging from vines with their orange life vests glowing as much as the crystalline waters beneath. Yet finding other more remote cenotes would have been challenging without local expertise and, perhaps more importantly, without a car.

I told you it wouldn't take much to see why we jumped at the chance for Carlos, a local with a car, to take us cenote spotting.

The thing is, however, that despite being so frequent, cenotes are sometimes tricky to find. We reached a town not far out of Mérida and Carlos pulled over outside a small shop to ask for directions to a good cenote.

Minutes later, he returned with a young boy. A young boy who had offered to spend his Saturday afternoon showing three adults in their late twenties where his best local cenotes were. A young boy who didn't ask for anything for doing so. A young boy who we were grateful for given that ten minutes later we were driving down a dirt track with corn growing dangerously close to the car either side. A dirt track we definitely wouldn't have found on our own.

The cenotes we visited were, as expected, beautiful. The first was much smaller than the second, providing a cool and calm introduction to cenotes. It was dark down there. The guy manning the place regularly lowered his head to the entrance and adjusted the mirror balanced on a rock outside to reflect sunlight down into the cave.

The second cenote was a lot bigger. As well as the main attraction, there were a few animals in cages as you approach, and the cenote hole itself was larger, deeper, and had a long set of metal steps leading down to a platform to enter.

As I tentatively made my way down the side steps into the water (I've never been one for jumping into water), I noticed lots of little black fish coming towards me and sucking gently on my skin. The Cuba fish were back! After a bit of swimming around, letting fish eat away my dead skin, and watching Ashley, Carlos and our young accidental guide swing from the rope into the water, we headed out to do the interview.

Carlos explained the contradiction to the typical expectation that Mayan languages are dead, that in actual fact they are very much alive and in use today. What has changed however, quite understandably, is the language itself. The Mayan languages spoken today are often very different from the Mayan languages spoken thousands of years ago. Carlos explained this is due to the influence of Spanish. He went on to tell us how despite Mayan languages still existing today, many people are beginning to use Spanish more for employment and education, potentially forgetting the importance of their indigenous languages. It's a fate, we'd come to discover from the rest of the series, that is not uncommon for languages across the world.

***

Our third interview in Mérida was with Mirna from Radio Yúuyum. Radio Yúuyum is a community radio station that goes live every Monday night to share stories, music, and discussion, as well as teaching, all in Yucatec Maya. With a small budget behind it, the success of Radio Yúuyum relies on the dedication of the team of volunteers working to promote and encourage others to use and engage with the language on a weekly basis.

We met Mirna by the cathedral in the main plaza and headed to a nearby coffee shop for our interview. Cold drinks and air con at the ready, we relaxed away from the Mérida heat outside to learn more about Yucatec Maya and Radio Yúuyum.

Mirna began by explaining that many people, even native Mayan speakers, will switch to speaking Spanish outside of their homes because, in Mirna's words, they don't think Yucatec Maya is really a language and they're kind of ashamed to speak it. Mirna went on to explain that one reason for this is the lack of Yucatec Maya in the media, something that Radio Yúuyum aims to help combat by producing radio shows in the Yucatec Maya language.

My search online that led to finding Radio Yúuyum was inspired by a fortunate afternoon early on in our time in Mérida glancing through a pile of local magazines left in our Airbnb. I spotted PatBoy, a local rapper who raps in Yucatec Maya. I made note of his name to find out more.

I almost didn't send the message. I mean, he's a rapper! I'm some random person getting in touch from England! He'd never speak to me, right? Wrong. PatBoy replied and agreed to meet.

Palms nervously sweaty and attitude a little edgier than usual, we hopped in a cab to a mall one rainy Friday evening to meet PatBoy. It didn't take much to recognise him, or for him to recognise us for that matter - him with his chain mirroring the images I'd seen online and us looking significantly paler than eveyrone else in the mall. We sat down to discuss what got him started with rapping in Yucatec Maya.

He explained that at first it was a hobby. He left school at sixteen and started working, but lost his job soon after. Being unable to get another job due to not being eighteen, as most employers preferred, he decided to give music a go. And why Yucatec Maya? Why didn't PatBoy rap in Spanish, the language we were speaking in right now? PatBoy explained how rapping in Yucatec Maya, he'd found himself getting closer to the culture and traditions of his Mayan heritage. He described music as a tool that can reach young people, and more of them too via radio, TV and music videos. He smiled at me, "That means a lot, right?"

By the time we were done, the rain still hadn't passed so we cabbed it back with our final interview for the episode safe and secure on our memory card.

I couldn't help but feel a huge sense of accomplishment. This was our first episode with hardly any contacts before arriving. Yet, we'd done it. We'd got people to speak with us. We'd met them and interviewed them. We'd learnt about the culture, the place, the language. We'd made an episode.

Belize

Season 1, Episode 4: Unbelizable!

This may sound strange for a native English-speaking language nerd travelling in a region that speaks mostly Spanish, but I was very excited to visit Belize, the only country in Central America with English as its official language.

Why? Partly because I love caves and Belize has some real good ones. Partly because I wanted to snorkel near The Blue Hole. And partly because Belize speaks English.

But, although we weren't there long, we'd soon discover that "Belize speaks English" is only part of the story.

My love for caves is shadowed by Ashley's love for running. Before we left home, being able to keep up running whilst we were away was one of the worries that kept Ashley up at night. I assured him it would be fine and thankfully, Mérida had been a good example of the fact that it would - we had a free running track near our place, Ashley found an unbelievable four races to take part in during our six weeks there (yes! four!) and to be honest, he was probably a little spoilt.

Keen to keep finding races, he found one in Antigua, Guatemala...up and back down a volcano. As you do.

The race in Antigua was a little earlier than we would have liked, which meant leaving Belize earlier than expected, which meant no on the ground filming or interviews for Belize. However, we did speak with Osmar and Timothy after our time there to discuss Spanish in Belize and Creole languages respectively.

Our time in Belize was short. I didn't get to cave to my heart's content or interview face to face, but I did get to snorkel.

I was never very sporty growing up. My teachers would tell my parents at parents' evening how I was great and very well-behaved but "could do better" in PE. "Her hand-eye coordination isn't great", they'd say. Sticks and stones may break my bones, but words? Well, they'll hurt for life and ever since my life has basically been one long quest to find my sport.

Don't worry, it's not a sob story. I actually really like it this way. I love trying things once and seeing if I'm good at it or, more importantly, if I enjoy it. So far, hovercrafting and caving are up there as things I've been good at and enjoyed, so you know, super easy sports to get into living in a city in the South Midlands.

Water sports, however? Well, that's a different ballgame, if you'll be a sport and pardon the sporting pun(s).

I'm a pretty strong swimmer, but, as we discovered at the cenote, I'm not a huge fan of jumping into water. This means that although I enjoy snorkelling, it makes the initial jump off the side of the boat a little tricky. Instead, I unglamourously climb down the ladder, flippers flapping and slapping on each step as I gingerly lower myself into the water, keen not to drown and die out in the middle of the deep blue sea.

I must have really been flapping and slapping like a good'un as the guides from our boat soon made their way over to me to quite literally hold my hand at each dive site. Irritating underestimation aside though, we saw some really beautiful stuff in the water - sea turtles, colorful fish, nurse sharks, and even a manatee!

After our boat ride back to the mainland, we had about an hour to explore Belize City before our bus was due to take us across the border and into Guatemala.

Belize City is a port city, so there's a very nicely done-up area where cruise ships will unload passengers for a few hours to walk around and experience a very small slice of Belize. This means that the port area where the boats from the islands arrive is that very nicely done-up area and as lovely as it is, I couldn't help but feel it didn't really reflect Belize City life for its residents. At one point, we crossed a bridge into what appeared to be a more realistic and lived-in Belize City, but swiftly headed back across so as not to be late for our bus.

Just like we'd heard on the islands, we heard some Kriol being spoken in Belize City too, in particular from a waitress in a cafe at the dock where we ordered a fry jack each - a huge greasy (and delicious) pastry stuffed with beans and cheese, and meat if you want. Highly recommended.

Donald Trump was talking about something behind a podium on the, muted, TV behind our table.

"Wat yu tink of Trump? He crazy crazy. Need a liddle smoke metinks!" the waitress told us, giving us no time to respond in between asking us what we think and telling us what she thinks.

Being in Belize was my first time experiencing a Creole language in real life settings and it was interesting.

It always feels rude to me not to say thank you to people in the language of their country when you're there - or at least to attempt to say thank you, even if it comes out sounding more like you're being rude because you pronounced it slightly off and consequently said something offensive.

So even when English is an official language, like in Belize, I can't help but feel that rudeness - like I'm not trying or making an effort. I realise that this is crazy. English is an official language in Belize! People do speak it and understand it!

But here's the thing - people don't speak it between themselves. Unless they have no common language (namely Spanish, Kriol, Garifuna, or German, among others) then Belizeans tend to not converse between themselves in English.

Whilst waiting to board our boat the day we went snorkelling, one of our boat men called to the other, "Yu say wat yu mean but d'yu mean wat yu say?"

I understood all the words, even the order made sense, but something about what he said still didn't sit with me as being fully understood. It was like a riddle. If I cracked it, maybe I'd get an extra ten seconds in The Crystal Maze.

But I didn't crack it. And that's the whole point of Creole languages: they are their own language.

Even if the words sound familiar, I don't speak Belizean Kriol, and with English being understood, I didn't need to feel uncomfortable that I couldn't, yet the language learner in me still did.

As Timothy explains in Language Stories episode Unbelizeable!, with Creole languages, you can learn them and you can learn about them, but with the historical context that comes with a lot of Creole languages, to use them, it's best to wait until you are invited to do so.

Guatemala

Season 1, Mini Episode 2: Star Wars: A Language Story

Season 1, Episode 5: Keeping K'iche'

After our brief foray into Belize, we headed into Guatemala with three things in mind: Tikal, Ashley's race up and down a volcano, and a Language Stories episode of some kind.

Guatemala is home to twenty-three languages beyond Spanish and so it would have been really easy not to know where to begin or which language(s) to cover for an episode. However, we had one lead: Dave.

Every year around May or June, there's an event called the Polyglot Gathering. The one that took place in Bratislava, Slovakia a few months before we left featured a talk from my friend Dave Prine called "Can learning K'iche' make you rich and save your life? (probably not but why take chances)". The title alone was classic Dave. He has a rather dry, sarcastic, almost British sense of humour (he's American).

I'd attended Dave's talk thinking I would be learning about Quechua. "K'iche' must be the word for Quechua in Quechua," I thought. Nope. K'iche' is the word for a completely different language from a completely different language family spoken in a completely different place. Not a language used in the Andes, but a Mayan language spoken in Guatemala.

Dave was my only lead for an episode about K'iche', but it was a start.

As we marvelled at Tikal by day, I'd be emailing Dave by night getting potential leads for other interviewees for the episode. None of those came to anything, but I did manage to find something that we hadn't yet been able to do.

Searching on Airbnb, I stumbled upon Carlos' listing: "Stay with a family in the Mayan countryside". It was a listing for a homestay experience without the flag-wielding guide nor the umteen stops at weaving workshops (no purchase necessary, but clearly very much preferred) or markets (seriously, we're not just being polite, you need to buy something here, this is how we make our money).

Instead it was a genuine family who wanted to share their home with travellers. I messaged Carlos to ask if he spoke K'iche' and if so, would he be interested appearing on film. He said yes on both counts.

Excited, we booked a two night stay with Carlos and family and a few days later were stood on a street corner in the town of Quetzaltenango waiting to meet Carlos, who'd come into town to travel the three bus journey back with us to his village.

Three buses sounds like a lot of effort and waiting around, but in reality, the buses in Guatemala are run by so many different private individuals that there seems to be plenty plowing the same routes, meaning you're never stood waiting for long.

Maybe you've heard the term 'chicken bus' before? Well, the chicken buses are the bigger, old North American school buses covering major local routes, and sometimes further afield too. Then supporting those routes connecting smaller places are a possibly bigger network of *'colectivos'*, minibuses or shuttle buses, that (much like the chicken buses) *always* have room for one more.

The chicken buses are easy to spot, and more often than not beautiful to look at. They're often painted in bright colours, patterns and designs , sometimes including a character or two - Mickey Mouse, a Simpson, El Chavo (a Mexican cartoon character beloved across Latin America). The destination adorns the top of the front of the bus in bold, creative lettering.

And when you see the one you want to take, you just...get on. This is the most counter-intuitive thing. In the UK, when you board a bus, the bus pulls over from the flow of traffic, handbrake on (probably), you pay the driver, he gives you change and a ticket, and as you sit down he pulls back out safely into the traffic. In Guatemala, not so. In Guatemala, you jump on the bus quickly as it tucks in slightly to the side of the road on the bite point before pulling off again as soon as your second foot has left the ground. You don't speak to the driver. Instead you just take a seat.

As well as the driver, there's a second guy working the bus who deals with payment. At some point, normally after the bus has stopped making many stops close together and has begun to drive a bit further without stopping every 7 yards, that guy will come round and collect payment from everyone on the bus. And, as I mentioned, the chicken buses don't seem to have a capacity limit. Sometimes, this means the money man will have to (somehow) wedge his way through the mass of bodies stood butt to butt and belly to belly in the aisle. Good luck getting off at the next stop if you chose to sit down.

Thankfully, our first chicken bus experience with Carlos wasn't quite that busy. Which was handy since our bags needed a seat of their own. That first chicken bus dropped us in a layby on the outskirts of town and a few minutes later we were in a colectivo heading closer to Carlos' place. Around ten minutes after that, we got off again and waited another couple of minutes for the final colectivo of our journey that dropped us by the side of the road at the top of Carlos' village.

We set off through the grassy trodden path down the hill towards Carlos' house. It's definitely somewhere we couldn't have found on our own. Carlos lives in a modest stone house. When you walk through the front gate, you emerge into a small courtyard with the house on either side. One side consists of two rooms for guests, the other side has a further two bedrooms (one for the family and one more for guests) and the kitchen. Against the back wall is the toilet, with a bathroom behind the main courtyard area. One of my favourite things however, was the young cow living behind the house, just visible from the back entrance to the courtyard. Next to the *vaca* was a huge wire-framed box storing a collection of drying corn on the cob. Red, black, yellow, white...I was beginning to learn the importance of corn in the region.

Carlos introduced us to his family - his wife, Carolina; daughter, Heidy; and son, Elicio - and it wasn't long before we were heading back out to explore the local town. Up on the road, we waited a matter of minutes before another colectivo (our fourth for the day at this point) pulled up and we hopped in.

It was interesting to see a smaller, less-touristy town in Guatemala, especially with a local acting as our guide.

Christmas was coming, a fact we were reminded of by the ever-there faint din of beeped versions of Jingle Bells playing from demo packs of LED lights as we headed through the market with Carlos while he bought food for dinner.

Once we had all we needed, he took us across to the church, a large building making its presence known as it cast a large shadow across the square in front of it.

"Are you religious?" Carlos asked as we walked down the aisle inside to take a seat.

"No, not really. I was christened but we're not religious," I replied in Spanish.

"Me neither. I think it's good that if people need it, they can be religious but I don't believe it myself."

As he replied, people crawled on their knees behind him down the centre aisle of the church towards the altar.

"Are they praying?" I asked, never having seen anything like it before.

"Yes. But I don't know why they do it like this! I've never seen this anywhere else."

As I write this down, I realise that it may look like Carlos was simply repeating and agreeing with me. I could tell that wasn't the case.

Despite learning that Carlos hadn't attended many years of school, something not uncommon for the indigenous population here from what he told me, he was clearly wise and had made his own decisions about life and aspects of it, including religion.

After lunch, we made our way back to the village, but not before a stop at the local bathhouse. Talk about off the tourist trail!

For a small fee, you get access to the three domed steam baths, with natural sulphur-scented hot water coming down from fresh springs nearby.

After a quick catch-up with the guy on the counter, Carlos walked us through to the first and biggest of the domes. As we made our way through the barrier, he explained a little about the place in English.

"Many people don't have hot water or showers or baths at home, so they come here. They bring their family and take a bath."

I looked at Ashley as we entered, slightly nervous about looking out of place as fully-clothed foreigners in a room full of swimsuited bodies. His glasses steamed up as the heat hit us upon entering the room.

Everyone turned to face us.

We looked around the room we'd just walked into. To our right, there was a big concrete whale head painted in shades of blue with a fresh stream of water flowing from its mouth. Ahead of us, a concrete path curved around the blue, warm water pool. The water was full of bodies soaking and washing and the path was covered in bags of clothes, puddles of warm water, and people drying themselves. Or taking off their clothes ready to get in. As it turned out, most people weren't swimsuited after all. They were mostly naked. And we were invading their bathtime.

I can't imagine how I'd feel if some tourists casually made their way into my bathroom while I've got my Lush bath bomb fizzing away and my candles lit.

Yet, despite the fact we were clearly where we didn't belong, people smiled at us and engaged us in conversation.

"Where are you from?"

"What's your name?"

"Hello!"

No one minded. If ever I need proof that the British are overly prude, this is it.

As we left, people by the door waved us goodbye with a smile, and we looked at each other slightly baffled by what had just happened, and frantically trying to find the words to describe what happened to everyone back home, a task made even harder for the fact we had no video footage to back up what we're saying like we normally would. You know, because of all the nakedness.

Our brief visit to the bathhouse was our last stop before catching the colectivo home to Carlos' place.

Whilst he helped Carolina with the cooking, we played with Elicio in the courtyard. It didn't take long to discover he liked football. And when he was bored of football, his favourite thing to do was show us around the farm behind the house, even though we'd already had the tour (multiple times from Elicio himself).

The following morning, after breakfast we got comfortable in the courtyard to film Carlos' interview for Language Stories. He had dressed smartly for the occasion and was wearing a traditional shirt and hat. Meanwhile, we hadn't washed that day.

Perched on a wooden chair facing Carlos, I started by asking him to give me an introduction to K'iche'. According to Carlos, 92% of people in the region speak K'iche', which they learn from their parents. I asked what he speaks with his own family. Sometimes Spanish, sometimes K'iche', and sometimes when they like, they mix it. Why? Because their children need to know so they can communicate with the generation of their grandparents. Carlos went on to tell us that his own parents can't speak Spanish very well, which means K'iche' is the connecting language between them and their grandchildren.

Elicio stood cautiously watching us for a moment as we interviewed. At various points during our stay, we found ourselves helping him with school work. On the language front, he's learning K'iche', Spanish, and a little English. Him and his older sister, Heidi, are smart and enjoy their education. Learning K'iche' shouldn't disadvantage them. *Being* K'iche' on the other hand unfortunately might. Various sources of data consistently agree that indigenous people in Guatemala are more likely to live in poverty or extreme poverty than non-indigenous people. In what's considered by some as one of the countries in Latin America with the most unequal economies (roughly 1% of the richest in Guatemala have wealth equal to the poorest 40%), something needs to change to ensure indigenous people, so key to the heritage of the country, aren't left behind any longer.

After filming our interview with Carlos for Language Stories on our second morning with the family, we went back out, this time to the laundry station, which was en route to the internet cafe where Carlos needed to go to check his emails.

Walking around the village, we'd already noticed various laundry shelters with handfuls of large concrete sinks. However, what we saw that day was completely different. The water came down from a natural spring again, much like the bathhouse (in fact, some people were cleaning themselves here as well as their clothes). Only this time, there were no steam domes. Instead, the water had been fed into three concrete pools for washing clothes.

It was clearly a very communal activity, and as someone who's used a laundrette about twice, I wondered how things would be different back home if we also had more of a communal aspect to as simple a task as laundry. There's definitely convenience in having a washing machine, or even a dryer also, in your own home, but with high levels of loneliness reported in the UK, could something like this be a simple contributor to a solution to that?

That said, the laundry place did have its downside. On the path away from it, you pass the pool that collects the used water...and the soap scum layer...and the plastic wraps from bars of soap and washing powder. It definitely wasn't the cleanest place to clean your clothes, unfortunately.

After our two nights with Carlos and his family, we caught the bus back to Quetzaltenango (otherwise known as Xela. I'll call it that from here) for another four nights before making our way back down the country to Antigua. Most of my memories of Guatemala are plagued with illness in one way or another. When I wasn't sniffing and moping around in bed, Ashley was. We tag-teamed our sickness.

At the time, it seemed obvious that we were feeling ill because it was colder than we'd been used to everywhere else we'd been before that point, but on reflection later down the line in Cusco, I discovered that altitude is not my friend, and wondered if that also played a part in being sick in Guatemala too. Xela has an altitude of 2,333 metres, which although being 1,000 metres lower than Cusco, is still pretty darn high up, and at that point, the highest place I may have ever been in my life.

That said, we couldn't lie around feeling sorry for ourselves for too long, we had another K'iche' speaker to meet and another interview to film.

***

Chichicastenango is a town not too far from Xela that's famous for its twice weekly market, and although we visited on market day, that wasn't the only reason we were there.

By the way, if you've noticed all those *'-tenango's'*, let me put your mind at ease with the question I know you've got because I had it too - *'tenango'* is the Nahuatl word for *"place of"*.

We were visiting the town for the day to speak with Juan from Galeria Pop Wuj, an art gallery in the town that also hosts K'iche' Maya classes from time to time. We met at a cafe almost impossible to find behind the market (seriously - this market really take over the town!) and Juan walked us down to the gallery.

He showed us around and as he did so, we passed numerous walls covered in art, piles of colourful shoes, glimmering shrines in a corner and on the roof where we met his brothers. Our tour of the gallery was accompanied by the sweet smell of Mayan incense that we'd become accustomed to from watching the Pok Ta Pok each Friday night in Merida. Memories unexpectedly came flooding back from the scent carried on the air.

After our tour of the gallery, we sat down at a table in a room full of art. Juan began to tell me about K'iche', including his thoughts on school, which were similar to what Carlos had gone on to tell us of his own experience at school: that teaching in Spanish devalued K'iche' and leads children to thinking it's less important. Nevertheless, Juan was what could only be described as a firm advocate for K'iche' language and culture.

Our only way to get to Chichicastenango on a Sunday seemed to be by tourist minibus, and apparently it wasn't a very popular time of year as there was just one other girl on the bus with us and the driver.

We met the girl again on a street corner at the agreed time and headed back across the winding roads to Xela. Until we weren't moving anymore. The traffic entering the city was static. We could have walked quicker. But what was slowing us down? A Christmas procession.

As we cut down onto a side street parallel to the main road where the procession was taking place, we crawled along beside it for a few kilometres, admiring the costumes and the music.

"Siempre hay procesiones en Xela!" *There's always processions in Xela,* the other girl on the minibus said, in part to our driver and in part to us. It turned out she lived here and had done for the best part of a year.

Seeing as we saw another procesion the very next day going past the central square in honour of a firefighter who had lost his life on the job, we were inclined to think she had a point.

***

Xela is quite high up the country on a map as well as quite high up geographically, which meant it'd be a long old journey to get to El Salvador or Honduras. To break things up, we opted for stopping in Antigua for one night.

We'd already been to Antigua early on in our time in Guatemala for Ashley's race up and down a volcano. I've been to support Ashley at many running events over the years, and I'm quite pleased with the routine I've made for myself. Take along a book, typically a language course, and get some good solid reading or writing done while he's out running. However, I wasn't well that day.

Instead of learning a language, I sat quietly underneath a tree next to what turned out to be an elderly Costa Rican lady there to support her son. I said goodbye (pura vida) and headed towards the finish line after about an hour and a half, expecting Ashley to be coming in soon. He was exhausted. I'd never seen him finish a race and look so tired. There was blood on both his knees.

Yet, on the walk back to our homestay, it was me who couldn't make it and had to lie down on a park bench in an attempt to muster up the strength to walk back. Like I said, not well that day. I'd spent the rest of our time in Antigua curled up in bed, so although we only had one night there this time round, I was hoping to be able to form some more memories of the place.

Arriving in the dark, not being sick, Christmas being closer...I don't know quite what it was but Antigua was sweeter this time. There was a sense of magic in the air. As we all tumbled out of the minibus, we were met with twinkling yellow lights covered every inch of the trees in the square in front of us.

We checked into our hotel and headed out into the darkness to find some food, by which point it was close to 10pm. The only thing we could find was a boutique Belgian frites shop, offering various fancy ways of cooking the potato, jazzy flavours, and snazzy toppings.

We got in just before closing time and walked back down to the square where the trees were covered with row upon row of string lights, twinkling in the thick blue darkness. We sat ourselves on a bench facing into the park. Chips have never tasted so good.

But we weren't in Antigua for long, our connecting bus to Copán, Honduras was due to pick us up at 4am the following morning.

And so, full of potato and salt, we soon made our way back to the hotel and settled in for our shorter than average sleep.

Honduras

One day in New York at the very beginning of our trip, sat in a cafe, we were discussing our plans for the year ahead: where to go, what to see, where *not* to go.

Ashley had a list of three countries he didn't want to visit: El Salvador, Colombia, and Honduras. Thanks, news.

To be honest though, I was quite grateful he'd said it and not me. None of the three were top of my list because if the news is to be believed, you will 100% definitely absolutely die if you go to any of those places.

So, naturally, we were about to board a bus to Honduras.

Thinking back, I'm not quite sure how we got to that point. I guess somewhere along the way, you begin to feel comfortable with being in a place and being closer to a place. I remember when I visited Myanmar for the first time in 2011. Before then I'd never had an interest to visit India, but having been relatively close to it geographically, I came away feeling "ready" to visit India. Maybe our time in Central America to this point had done the same for Honduras.

However, there were no obvious Language Stories that would be easy to find interviews for in Honduras, so it would be a short visit. We just went to Copán, 10km from the Guatemalan border for a few days. And it's a good job this was all we had planned.

***

Our minibus this time had just four of us: Ashley and me; a Polish guy; and a huge white bodybuilder guy from Zimbabwe with 'Rhodesia' tattooed up the inside of his right arm.

The Polish guy was travelling in the other direction to us, yet had already crossed through Honduras to Antigua the previous day from León, Nicaragua as it was apparently the only way he could get to Copán.

The Zimbabwean guy, who lived in London and also had a British passport, as, in his words, his "Zimbabwe passport is useless", was travelling around Central America for a few weeks after visiting in spring but going home early due to the excessive rain during the rainy season.

As we got out of the minibus at the Honduran border, the Polish guy was keen to point out that the entry fee was $3, $3 only, and we definitely shouldn't pay more. He was equally as keen to point this out to the immigration employee before even saying hello as he was called forward to the desk.

Next, the Zimbabwean guy was called forward to another desk.

I went forward next as Ashley waited in the queue. My desk was in between both of them - both of them who were now engaged in a language stalemate with both their immigration officers. I hopped between each side of my own immigration officer interpreting for the two of them, explaining that it's $4 at this border to the Pole and asking the Zimbabwean if he knew when he was leaving Honduras.

I'm still unsure how this happened but their immigration officers were like Statler and Waldorf from The Muppet Show whereas mine welcomed me with his arms raised, a friendly *"Bienvenidos a Honduras!"*, and a smile.

What I am sure of however is that the Pole's instant English-only insistence on the cost being $3 is why we all ended up paying $4 each.

Soon after the border we arrived in Copán Ruinas, a small town that thrives on tourism bucks from people visiting the Mayan ruins of Copán just a few kilometres out of town.

Of all the Mayan ruins we saw in the region, Copán is the one I'd recommend most for language nerds. The remains of Copán include many stones engraved with intricate Mayan glyphs seeming to bulge gleefully from the hard rock.

We left the stray dog who walked with us from the town at the entrance and went in. It was a joy to meander peacefully around the ruins enjoying a break from the hoards of tourists and souvenir stands at Chichen Itza, and the heavy rain at Tikal. We finally had a chance to enjoy a Mayan ruin in peace. Copán is a lot quieter than some sites in neighbouring countries. When I'd had my fill of marvelling at the glyphs in the rock, we left to head back into town.

"Mitch!" Ashley said excitedly as we left the front entrance. The dog that had followed us here from the town was still waiting for us. We'd called him Mitch on our walk down in the morning. He was a sturdy dog. We named him after the Mitchell brothers from Eastenders, a British soap.

"As if he's stayed there the whole time?!" I replied, equal parts overwhelmed by the cuteness of the stray, potentially rabid dog, and terrified that this may now mean we have to adopt him. Mitch walked with us all the way back to town and stayed with us for quite a while until eventually going off to meet his other dog friends. I have to say we were a little relieved.

Copán Ruinas itself is a small town, just big enough to handle the tourist numbers that come for the Mayan site. But, of course, as with all tourist towns, a small industry has developed of places to keep people lingering a little longer. I have two favourites from Copán: Macaw Mountain and The Tea and Chocolate Place.

Macaw Mountain, as the name might suggest, is a bird park built on a hill on the outskirts of town. We set off walking there one day, and eventually had to give in to a passing tuk tuk driver for a lift who ensured us it was "muy lejos", very far. We were doubtful as to how far. It turned out he was right. We would have taken much longer than expected on foot.

There were, of course, lots of colourful and beautiful birds in various large aviaries, but the true highlight of the visit had to be the chance to meet the birds and get a photo. As we marched down a steep slope, we came across a wide open space with some smaller aviaries and squawking parrots. A

Honduran man saw us and put down his wheelbarrow of foliage before gently jogging over to us.

"¿Foto?" he asked, mimicking a camera clicking in front of his face with his hands.

We looked at each other and nodded. Within what felt like mere seconds, three parrots were on me - one on each lower arm and one on my head. The man looked at me and told me to shake my wrist to make the bird open its wings.

"¡¿Qué?!" I replied, terrified the birds would flap away. He reassured me and I tentatively began to shake my wrists. Sure enough, the birds spread their wings and Ashley got snapping.

We swapped so Ashley got some photos too and then the Honduran offered to take one of us together with the three parrots. We thanked him and asked how much we owed him.

"Nada, nada. ¡Gratis!" he replied, shaking his head before emerging from his words with a grin.

***

My other favourite place in Copán was designed specifically for me, definitely. I like hot drinks but I don't like coffee or black tea. It makes for very convoluted "Are you sure? You don't want coffee? Tea? No tea? Just a coffee? No? No coffee? Really?" every time I visit someone's house for the first time and ask for a glass of water. No, my hot drinks of choice are all tea except black tea, and hot chocolate. And here it was, a small shop that serves and sells herbal teas and hot chocolate.

Sat out of the way, it would be easy to miss The Tea and Chocolate Place, especially as it only has limited daily opening hours, but it's worth a visit. Their hot chocolate is true Mayan style, even served in a traditional gourd. And their teas are everything I dream of finding in coffee shops at home when all I get is a limp teabag.

We sat with our drinks on the balcony overlooking the farmland of the owners where they grow a lot of what they sell. Beyond their land lay more green, flowing like a soft carpet into the horizon. It was well and truly one of my favourite places of the whole year.

For many, including us, Copán is all people see of Honduras, and I'm sure it's not a representation of what life is like for many Hondurans in their everyday life. However, even just those few days in a touristy spot is enough to make my ears prick up more now when I hear or see something about Honduras. And it didn't take long for Honduras to be in the news.

During our visit, the election happened, an election that many Hondurans believed to be rigged. So much so that they took to the streets. Protests filled the streets of the capital Tegucigalpa and the frequently labelled "murder capital of the world" San Pedro Sula (although in 2017 they were down to 26th according to Wikipedia) and blockades popped up across the country, blocking the roads with tyre fires.

It all sounds kind of scary, doesn't it? Until one morning, you're casually out running and come across one of these blockades in the small peaceful tourist town where you're staying. I wasn't running that morning, but when Ashley came home and showed me footage on his phone of the blockade he'd stumbled across outside the ruins, I was surprised to see no fear in his eyes.

"They were all very peaceful." he said, "Laughing and joking and saying hello to me!"

That afternoon, when walking through the town trying to find an ATM that would let us get some Lempira with any one of our UK cards, as well as meeting Mitch who followed us again for a good ten minutes, we bumped into the Zimbabwean guy again. He told us that no transport was leaving to go further into the country, and that the best thing to do was get out.

Thankfully, we'd already planned to do just that as it was just a flying visit. However, our minibus being full to the brim the following morning proved to us that he wasn't the only one who had decided to abort mission and get out of the country to avoid getting stuck with the protests and blockades.

We only had to travel 10km to the Guatemalan border...we could make that without there being a blockade at the border, couldn't we? Thankfully, we did, and we were soon out and on our way to El Salvador.

El Salvador

El Salvador. The name alone congers up images of death, violence and gangs. People escaping life there and risking everything to reach the United States of America.

So it must be awful, right? It must be as dangerous as Honduras and you're definitely going to get shot if you visit, right? Wrong. Well, sort of.

We spent just five days in El Salvador - three in the northern city of Santa Ana and two in the capital San Salvador. Of course, there's no way I can give a full and thorough analysis of the country and say it's totally safe and everyone there is living their best life. Obviously when so many people risk it all to cross the borders to the US, that's not the case. You don't risk everything to take a journey like that just for fun.

However, what I can say is that El Salvador intrigued me, more than most countries we visited during our Language Stories trip.

We left early morning from Copán and the Zimbabwean guy who was on our bus into the country was also on our bus out. Unlike our bus into Copán however with just the four of us, this shuttle was packed to the brim. We'd always planned to leave the day we did, but due to the election disruption in Honduras, more people were heading out of the country sooner than they had planned.

The Salvadoran border was odd compared to where we'd been so far. They stopped the van, had a look in and a brief glance at each of our passports (we're all still sat on the bus at this point) and then they sent us on our way. No stamp. No stamp?! What is this place, the European Union?!

As we entered Santa Ana a few hours later, it was clearly very different from the touristy glean of Copán. From the bus, Santa Ana looked dirty, loud, messy, crowded. Voluptuous Latinas sat on the back of mopeds, holding small toddlers in one arm and bags of shopping in the other. Stall holders stood on corners shouting prices and products in the hope of selling out their daily wares. Young men with oversized watches, flat peak caps, and reflective sunglasses held a mobile phone to their ear as they crossed the road without looking, confident the cars would stop upon their presence - a modern day Moses.

"Oh, I don't like this," said the Zimbabwean, "What a dump."

He'd previously told us he didn't like Copán when we bumped into him in the main plaza there one evening because it was too touristy. I was beginning to wonder where he did like.

"Look at that! Man, you don't even see that in Africa."

We sat in traffic and ducked and dived through the gritty gridded streets. Soon a voice piped up again from behind.

"Oh yeah, I like this place. It's got character. Yeah, this is my kind of place."

I'm still not sure what changed his mind. Either way his sudden change of heart made the bus smile.

Ashley and I were the final people the shuttle dropped off. We headed into our hotel to be greeted by a smiling face. The receptionist was a young man with impeccably clean clothes and hair. He showed us to our room. From his pride of the place, I wondered if he'd styled the rooms himself. The bathroom was fitted out with a copper shower head and taps and a stained glass sliding door between the bathroom and the bedroom, as well as many other features that wouldn't look out of place in an interior design magazine.

Not what you'd expect from El Salvador.

We headed out to explore. The main plaza was adorned with a towering Christmas tree and strings of LED lights, unlit the first time we saw them as it was daytime. There's not many sights in Santa Ana, but there is an abandoned water park. Not the type you see some urban explorer sending their drone into, just a small park with a few slides and a large crack in the concrete through the middle of the park.

It was eerie. I still don't know if it was an earthquake or just badly built, but El Salvador is one of the countries in the world with the highest concentration of volcanoes, and is often struck by earthquakes. Seeing this made that feel all the more real.

We weaved our way out of the city and to a mall on the outskirts in search of a supermarket to buy some food for breakfast. On the outside of the fence surrounding the mall, regular Salvadoran life continued ignoring the display of wealth behind them. The regular street vendors were present - the food stalls, the shoes, the knuckle-dusters...wait...knuckle-dusters?!

Yup. We had to look twice ourselves but there they were. Right there laid out on a tarpaulin on the pavement. Knuckle-dusters, switchblades, nunchucks.

Perhaps what you'd expect from El Salvador.

Quickly averting our eyes we headed up the stairs to the overpass and headed towards the mall.

The mall was reasonably sized with a Starbucks outside in its own unit! It was the first Starbucks we'd seen since Mexico. Out of curiosity, we entered to see how much Starbucks had adjusted their pricing for the local economy. Surprisingly, they had. And as it was now December, the Christmas drinks menu was in full flow.

Oh, and it was 30 degrees Celsius plus outside so that Christmas drinks menu included 'frappe' and 'iced' and 'chilled' in the titles. We had an unusual Christmas ahead of us. Embracing it, we decided to indulge ourselves in a half-the-price-of-the-UK Starbucks Christmas drink.

Not what you'd expect from El Salvador.

Breakfast, lunch and dinner filling shopping bags in our hands, and festivity filling our footsteps, we made our way back into the centre to our hotel, only to discover a

Christmas procession along the way. If Guatemala had taught us anything, it's that Latin America loves a good procession. Thankfully it was going in the same direction as us, so instead of having to wait patiently to cross it, we weaved through the pedestrians and phones in the air filming on the pavements and soon found ourselves walking alongside the front of the procession.

"Bienvenidos a El Salvador! Welcome to El Salvador! Where are you from? What do you have to say to everyone today?"

A microphone was thrust into my hand. I replied in Spanish.

"Actually, I can speak Spanish! I want to say thank you to everyone for welcoming us to your beautiful country and I wish you a happy Christmas! Thank you!"

Phew. Somehow I'd survived accidentally becoming part of a Salvadoran Christmas parade.

***

The following day we left the city for the Parque Nacional de Volcanes.

El Salvador isn't overly equipped for tourists. There isn't an abundance of "Tour, mister?" as you walk down the central tourist street. Partly because there's so few tourists that there is no central tourist street. That means that trips out to places like national parks are mostly done on local buses, which is great because they're super cheap! Everything seemed to cost a dollar in El Salvador. (Yes, an American dollar. They use the American dollar).

We headed to the bus station early and got our tickets before sitting in the station waiting patiently for the bus driver to call us through to the platform. Local buses mean chicken buses à la Guatemala as opposed to tourist-friendly shuttle buses. Chicken buses are a lot more fun on day trips when you don't have your big bags with you to worry about. This bus took about an hour and arrived at the park about an hour before the daily tour up to the summit of the volcano.

As we waited with a pupusa or two (I promise I'll explain the joys of pupusas soon) the shuttle buses soon began to arrive (where from and how I have no idea as the infrastructure was just not visible in the city) and our small group of about eight from the local bus soon swelled to around thirty.

At 11am, a guide showed up and walked us up to the entrance of the trail we'd be taking to the top of the volcano. He gave us the briefing in Spanish and English. This is where things got interesting.

In Spanish, the briefing designed for locals (who were all wearing jeans and would soon be casually cruising up the side of a volcano blaring reggaeton from their mobiles) described the hike as "*fácil*". In English, that means "easy".

The English briefing the followed however was much more advisory - wear sunscreen, take enough water and snacks, and - most cryptically - be prepared as the hike is "difficult"! Difficult?! But he just said it was easy en español?!

Determined to prove to our guide that this little white girl can also do the climb, I followed my running philosophy 'reasonable not wheezable' and set off. I don't know why I felt the need to prove anything to our guide though seeing as we never saw him again as he set off way ahead of everyone in the group.

But fear not! We weren't alone as we had a police escort armed with a rather large gun bringing up the rear. Apparently bandits sometimes target the trail and leave hikers penniless and cameraless and phoneless. But hopefully not sunscreenless, waterless or snackless. We'd need *those* things just to survive the difficult hike.

Thankfully, we had no trouble on our venture to the top, and rumour had it that there hadn't been any problems with bandits for a number of years now.

Not what you'd expect from El Salvador.

The view and sense of accomplishment at the top was worth it. Never underestimate me, oh Salvadoran guide. I may be a small lady who's clearly not from here or used to this climate, but just you watch me climb this volcano.

The volcano crater consisted of a steaming turquoise sulphur lake, which shone beautifully in the sunlight, and was no doubt a lot more beautiful thanks to the fact that the steam carrying the sulphur stench was blowing in the other direction.

After around twenty minutes at the top, we were told it was time to descent back down. Dutifully we all set off (all thirty of us) and began to make our way back down, accompanied still by the omnipresence of tinny reggaeton from the locals' phones.

Towards the beginning of the hike, there'd been a short section that involved walking down the side of the road the bus drove up. On our way back to the park entrance, a group of French tourists started a mutiny and declared by the side of the road that they were waiting there for the bus and wouldn't be going all the way back up the road to the park entrance. As is the human way, when one group of four or five people in front of you are stopped, you assume there's a good reason and you must stop too.

Well, Ashley and I decided to buck the trend and make our way back up the road to the entrance where we began. The hike wouldn't be complete if we didn't get back to the start! And we'd come so far! Never underestimate me!

Off we set, half expecting to start our own reverse mutiny if you will, only to look back on our way up the hill to discover no-one following us. Note to self: must work on mutiny-starting skills.

Feeling pretty proud with ourselves for actually completing the hike all the way to the end, we enjoyed the bit on our own back up through the woods to the gate where we started...until we realised that the gate we'd come in through was closed. Not just closed. But locked.

"Well, that's not good. What do we do now?" I asked Ash, "The last bus will be here in about...forty minutes. It took us at least half an hour to get back up to here. I don't know if we could make it back to the road."

"Hola?!" Ash shouted. No reply. "I think I can climb over the fence...."

"I don't know if I can...do you think you could go and get help?"

"What do I say?"

"Remember this: la puerta está cerrada. Tell them that."

"La puerta está cerrada...la puerta está cerrada....ok...I think I can remember that. Ok...I'm gonna jump over the fence."

Ashley bounded over the fence and I waited patiently. Then not so patiently. I began to think that I'd be living the rest of my life here. Right here in the Salvadoran countryside. Next to a locked gate that definitely wouldn't be opened again the next day for a new group of tourists to hike the volcano. And definitely with no option of walking back to the main road.

I peeked over the fence and looked downwards. Urgency took hold. I was beginning to think I could make it.

As I lifted my heel ready to take the plunge, I heard a faint motorbike in the distance. A bike soon appeared around the corner, Ashley following.

The confused guy unlocked the gate and after much gracias, we headed back across to the entrance to wait for the bus. We were the only ones that got on the bus from the entrance.

As the bus headed down the hill, only five others got on where the French mutiny had begun.

"What happened to everyone else?" we asked a Dutch couple who we'd been chatting to earlier in the day.

"Some got a taxi, the rest hitchhiked I think. Gradually people just disappeared!"

And that, I guess, is how you mutiny.

"You know the guy that opened the gate?" I asked Ashley on the bus ride home.

"Yeah, what about him?"

"He looked really confused. Was he expecting to see me there? What did you say?"

"I said 'estoy estudiando español'...was that not it?"

I laughed, "You didn't, did you?! You told him you're learning Spanish and then expected him to follow you to unlock the gate?!"

"Oh, I thought he looked confused..."

***

We picked our hostel in San Salvador as it was directly across the road from the Tica Bus station, where we needed to be at 3am to head to León, Nicaragua. It was a good choice as the chalkboard display behind the reception proved: "Pupusa class! $3. Tuesday night."

Today was Tuesday. We'd had five days eating a lot of delicious pupusas. We wanted to learn how to make pupusas. So we did.

And what is a pupusa? Imagine a little tortilla stuffed with any combination of cheese, beans, chopped vegetables, cooked small bits of meat...yum, right? Right.

Pupusa knowledge in the bag, El Salvador was growing on me. There was something very honest about the place. It had nothing to hide. Despite being the most Americanised country in Central America (the Starbucks, the Pizza Huts, and the US dollar bills to name a few), it certainly maintains its own secretly lovable unashamed character.

The American influence is on full display in La Zona Rosa in San Salvador, where our hostel was located.

I'm under no illusion on the safety of San Salvador. La Zona Rosa in San Salvador however, home to the majority of international bus terminals; foreign restaurants and shops; hotels; and streets like 'Calle Country Club' *is* rather safe. It feels odd. It feels like a façade. It feels sugar-coated. It doesn't feel like everyday life for the majority of Salvadorans.

Unfortunately (or fortunately, perhaps) La Zona Rosa was the only area of San Salvador we visited. Fortunately (definitely not unfortunately), the excellent Museum of Anthropology is there.

I've never been in such an honest museum, a museum where I've photographed nearly every single sign because I want to read it again later.

There was one exhibit in particular about immigration. The exhibit was the opposite of La Zona Rosa surrounding the museum. It felt honest. It didn't feel like a façade. It didn't feel sugar-coated. It definitely shared everyday life for many Salvadorans.

Rather than blame people for wanting to immigrate, legally or illegally, to the USA, the exhibit frankly outlined reasons why, quoting people themselves. Sharing what their life is like, was like, or what they expect it will be like once they cross the border. It told the truth.

It hurt my heart as I read the exhibit word for word, even holding back tears at times. The reality of life in El Salvador isn't La Zona Rosa, it isn't climbing volcanoes (easy or difficult), it isn't Starbucks Christmas drinks.

Real life in El Salvador is often hard. Gangs exist. They are real and they do impact the lives of Salvadorans, many of whom want nothing to do with them.

If I were in that situation, I can't say I wouldn't seriously consider risking everything to cross the borders, legally or illegally.

And the only thing that means I'm not in that situation is the fact that I happened to be born where I was - into the family and the country I was - and not in El Salvador.

Even just scratching the surface of the country has been enough to really make me sit up and pay attention when I hear or see El Salvador in the news, much like how the few days in Honduras had impacted me. That for me is one of the joys of travel: the connections formed, no matter how small, that can help us empathise with others living a life far different from our own.

That's not what I expected from El Salvador.

Nicaragua

Season 1, Episode 6: Nicaraguan Sign Language

Contrary to the last two countries, we were expecting to visit Nicaragua. It was on my list for Language Stories from the beginning thanks to my curiosity about Nicaraguan Sign Language. On top of that, it has sea turtles and I wanted to see them around Christmas time. And besides, it's a big country in the middle of Central America, it would have been hard to avoid. We weren't expecting to visit León however, and we definitely weren't expecting to accidentally visit on a national celebration day.

Our accommodation in León was quite possibly the worst of our whole trip. The Airbnb room was large, but the loud dripping from the shower was unstoppable. I politely mentioned it to our host to see if there was a simple fix. We spent the rest of the evening with men with spanners in our bathroom fixing the shower leakage.

Finally, the dripping was over and we were able to shower - quite the luxury after our long, long journey from San Salvador.

By the way, I say shower, let me clarify here. Our shower in León was a single pipe of cold water coming out of the wall. No shower head, no direction, no part of the pipe curving downwards to angle to water towards your head and body. Because let's be honest, showering while levitating to reach the horizontal water is kinda tricky.

Now I have nothing wrong with showering differently in different places. I do have a problem however when the pipe bursts out of the wall as soon as you gently turn the water on to reveal what is apparently too much pressure.

Our pipe-in-the-wall shower is now a hole-in-the-wall shower. With water bursting out and hitting the other end of the wall, much higher than my height.

After patiently getting very cold and a little bit damp, I decided I was clean enough and we set off to explore León.

León is a small student-heavy city in the north of Nicaragua. It was crucial during the Nicaraguan Revolution due to the high student population. If ever there was any doubt of students not getting enough tuition time for their fees, the amount of student protests across the world is proof. I mean, who's at every protest ever? Students. Always.

The central plaza of León (we were getting quite used to these central plazas by this point) was full of festive, and to be honest slightly garish, displays ready for Christmas. A towering papier maché woman stood on one side of the entrance to the town hall. A shorter, wider papier maché man in a suit with blonde hair on the other. It felt like a subtle Trump metaphor.

On one side of the plaza is the Museo de la Revolución, somewhere we'd had recommended to us, and somewhere that made us glad we visited León first.

The Revolution Museum costs a very small amount to be guided around the photographs and displays in a couple of rooms by a local, often someone who lived through the Revolution. In fact, half way through our tour, our guide lifted his leg to reveal a scar. His scar was caused by being shot in the leg during the revolution. Being so close to history made me realise how different my memories of the nineties are to someone such as the man guiding me round this museum. We'd soon discover just how relevant and important a role the revolution played to the Language Stories episode from Nicaragua.

As we headed back to our Airbnb that afternoon, our hosts were preparing a display out front of religious Christian paraphernalia surrounded by candles and tinsel and palm leaves.

"Qué está pasando?" I asked what was happening, pointing to the display.

"Today is La Gritería, and it's a big festival for Christmas. At 6pm tonight, people set off fireworks, then at 12am, 6am, and 12pm again. Tonight people come round asking for sweets and gifts to celebrate."

I translated for Ashley, "Kinda like Halloween meets Guy Fawkes Night, I guess."

When we were told people would set off fireworks, we naively assumed that would mean in a safe place, keeping the family well back, lighting and standing a safe distance back themselves, and happily watching the fireworks explode into lights in the sky from a distance. How wrong we were. At 6pm, we discovered that was not the case.

The banging began in earnest, and we headed out front (safely behind the fence in front of the house, I might add) to watch. Our Airbnb host family had fireworks too.

The male of the house headed into the road...the road with cars and motorbikes and people continuing their day, and casually lit a strip of firecrackers before walking away like he'd just caused an explosion in an action movie. He didn't even turn to look! He didn't even get to appreciate the lights he'd set off across the ground!

As cars dodged the neighbour's lit fireworks, our guy headed out again and lit a rocket. On the road. With cars driving past.

I keep repeating these events in my head because I can't get over it myself. Perhaps if I repeat it enough I'll begin to believe it.

Soon after the most dangerous fireworks display I've ever seen, strangers began approaching the house and saying something rhythmic and repetitive as they stopped and held their hands through the fence. The women of our Airbnb host family sat near the fence and laced the palms of the hands reaching through the fence with sweets.

"What are they saying?" I asked, after hearing the same sing-song rhyme a couple of times from different groups thrusting their hands through the metal bars.

"They say 'Quién causa tanta alegría?' And we reply 'La concepción de María.'"

Who causes such happiness? The conception of Maria.

"Wow, can we go try?" I replied, keen to get involved with this unexpected festival and keen to leave the family to their evening, which was clearly a personal time.

"Of course!"

So off we set into the night, swerving the streets through the masses of groups of people and gradually building the confidence to ask who causes such happiness when we saw a huddle of people at a gate, hands outstretched.

"Salt! I got a bag of salt! What am I going to do with this much salt?!"

Thankfully, not all the goodies given out were bags of salt. We headed back from our evening of festivities armed with sweets, salt, a box of matches, and a penny whistle. Certain they'd get more use from it than us and not really wanted to cross Latin American borders carrying a bag of white granular goods, we left the salt for our hosts.

***

Our next stop in Nicaragua was Granada, a place we were visiting for two reasons: Ashley had found a half marathon (I'd also signed up for the 12km!) and we had an interview lined up for Language Stories.

We were in Granada for two whole weeks. After such a quick dash through Honduras and El Salvador, and moving around Guatemala relatively quickly before then, I was in need of some work catch up time.

However, we couldn't find a decent Airbnb apartment for long enough in the city, which meant that after four days in a lovely apartment, we ended up in a private room in a hostel. It proved to us why we'd been paying slightly more for full privacy so far.

Our room was right at the back of the hostel, which meant although the pool (postage stamp sized, mind you) was right outside our door, we were too far back for the wifi to work. This meant I had to work in the dining area each day, laptop unplugged as there were no plug sockets. To top things off, the wifi was weaker the more guests signed onto it, which was a lot of guests considering the majority of our time there was spent with two World Challenge groups from Australia and New Zealand passing through at different times. Working in Granada was hard. The run went well however, as did our interview.

We were there to interview Tio Antonio, the host of Cafe de Sonrisas, a social enterprise cafe staffed entirely by Deaf and hard of hearing Nicaraguans.

As we walked up to the entrance, I suddenly realised that I wouldn't be able to communicate to the waiters why we were there. I whipped out my phone and quickly typed a message in Spanish, "We're here to meet Tio Antonio for an interview. My name is Lindsay." Thankfully it worked, and we were soon introduced to Tio Antonio, who instantly began the interview.

"Hola! Bienvenidos!" Antonio thrust out his hand to shake ours and proceeded to show us the weaving workshop, the office, the biggest hammock they'd ever made, the rabbits roaming the place freely, the tables and menus with images of the food. Ashley quickly grabbed the camera from the bag and started filming as soon as he could. Some interviewees are more cautious - waiting to be sat and ready before we begin. Others dive right into it before we even have the camera out.

Antonio told us of the suspected reasons behind a larger than average Deaf population aged between 20-35: the past. During the war, Soviet medicines were being used - the side effects of which weren't known at that point. Now people estimate that these medicines affected people's hearing.

"Tourists come and are initially surprised, but leave with their hearts full," Antonio told us towards the end of our interview, "But the beautiful thing would be if one day that wasn't a surprise."

Antonio himself is Spanish but moved to Nicaragua to set up the cafe despite friends thinking he was crazy for doing so. Now, after much hard work, the cafe is a success, and Antonio is keen to share his wisdom with other budding owners of cafes like this across the world.

"People ask me, 'Antonio, how much does it cost for you to help us set up something like this?' But that's the wrong question. We're not Starbucks, McDonalds...we're Cafe de las Sonrisas! Copy us. Do it. The important thing is that you do it."

***

Despite it being really close to Christmas, our days working in Granada were filled with what seemed to be a series of just three songs on repeat: Cómo Te Voy a Olvidar by Los Angeles Azules, Medicina de Amor by Raulin Rodriguez, and Me Rehúso by Dany Ocean. All with similarly annoying repetitive beats. Not quite a reggaeton beat you can get behind, but slower beats that made me feel a little bit seasick somehow. Listen to them and you'll see what I mean.

The good news was that these songs tended to stop by the evening when the night staff would arrive and either turn off the music completely or insist on their electro dance music playlists. (Do you want to stay at this hostel yet?)

One evening, about a week into staying at the place after a relatively productive day working (the World Challengers were out which meant the internet remained strong all day. Yay!) we were cooking in the kitchen and getting ready to settle down and eat when a Dutch couple rushed through the kitchen and to their room.

Minutes later, they were back and speaking to the staff at reception. There was an uneasy tension. We didn't know what was up, but you could tell something wasn't quite right.

"How long have you been cooking? Did you notice anything odd? Anyone strange going past?" the Dutch woman questioned me as I stood, spatula in hand.

"Err...I...don't think so. Why?"

"Someone has broken into our room and stolen $300 and a credit card."

My eyes widened. Without even replying, Ashley and I ran back to our room and unlocked the door, expecting our laptops, money, and cameras to be gone. Expecting our trip to be over there and then.

After a week in the place, we'd began to feel comfortable and had left our laptops out on the bed while we'd gone to cook. Before (and after) that day, we'd always locked everything away anytime we'd left a room, wherever we were staying.

We opened the door. Thankfully, everything was where we left it and nothing had gone from our room.

We locked everything away and locked the door. Checked it. And double checked it. And headed back to the kitchen.

"I'm sorry we ran off like that. So, wait, what happened?" I said to the Dutch woman.

"Well, we were in the restaurant and I got this text message from my bank saying they'd blocked my card because it had been used for petrol in Nicaragua. I checked and I didn't have that card with me, as I thought, so we rushed back here and found it was gone along with $300."

I didn't quite know what to say. As the evening unfolded (including the Dutch hostel owner WhapsApping photos from their CCTV to other hostels in the city because privacy laws are a little more laxed in Nicaragua than a lot of other places it seems) it transpired that this wasn't a one-off.

It's common around Easter and Christmas time according to the hostel owner that people will drive down from Guatemala and up from Costa Rica and check in with fake names and ID to hostels where they know foreigners go with the intention of stealing as much *dinero* as they can.

This particular occasion involved a male and female from Guatemala checking in, and the female ordering drinks and asking what there is to do in the area (aka distracting the lone staff member) all while holding her phone to her ear but not speaking into it.

Meanwhile, the male had gone into the Dutch couple's room and taken the cash and card, presumably on the other end of the phone with the woman at the bar so as she'd know when she could stop distracting the staff.

It's simply bad luck on the Dutch couple's part that the Guatemalan couple had been checked in to the room right opposite them.

We spoke to the Dutch couple quite a bit over the next few days after it happened and I have to admit, I don't think I would have been as calm and collected as they were had it been our room. They took solace in the fact that a Guatemalan child might be getting a better than average Christmas this year, albeit by illicit means.

As far as I know, the Guatemalan couple never got caught and they got away with the cash, although the card had been instantly blocked.

From that day on, we've always been what some might describe as overly cautious when it comes to locking things away, but when you've been so close to it it's the only way to react.

***

Granada wasn't our last stop in Nicaragua. Way back in Mexico, we had to plan ahead for Christmas and New Year to ensure we'd be set and not sleeping on the streets. We'd settled on San Juan Del Sur, a beach town on the southwest coast of Nicaragua for Christmas, and Monteverde, one of my favourite places in the world, in Costa Rica for New Year. We'd also booked an overpriced tourist shuttle online to be sure we'd make the journey between the two when we needed.

We took the journey from Granada to San Juan Del Sur by public bus, which involved a change of buses in the transit town of Rivas.

The first bus was fine, nice and spacious. The second bus however was a little busier. We boarded the bus as it sat still in the station at Rivas waiting to fill up with passengers before leaving. There weren't many seats. Ashley had to stand, but next to him was one empty seat. With a lone child sat by the window in the seat next to the empty one.

"Hay alguien acá?" I asked him if anyone was sitting in the empty seat.

"No hay" he replied, shaking his head. I smiled at the child, thinking it odd he was travelling alone, and sat myself down.

As the engine switched on, a lady made her way through the mass of people now filling the aisle to where I was sat. Without really saying much, perhaps presuming I wouldn't understand her, she indicated that she was sitting where I was. She had used her lone child to reserve her seat. As you do.

When I say there was a mass of people in the aisle, I mean it. There was really no wiggle room. If she wanted me to get up, I had nowhere to go! There wasn't even enough space for us to switch places.

"But where should I go? There's no space to switch places," I said to her in Spanish, slightly annoyed that she didn't seem to be budging on her decision that I should move because she reserved her seat with a child.

"Fine. Move up," she answered, perching herself down next to me without giving me a chance to move up.

Tightly, the three of us now sat on a seat for two. No one happy as we were all now seperated from the people we were travelling with.

Then it began. The child started crying. No, scrap that - wailing.

Now, he was a small child - easily lifted, and I offered multiple times for him to be carried over me so at least one pair of us would be next to the person we came with, but no. That didn't happen.

I think it's fair to say they underestimated my level of Spanish as I understood every word when the child started crying "I don't want to sit next to a foreigner! She's not allowed to be here!" and the mother responded with, "I know, dear. She's very rude."

Well! Now I'm staying put out of stubbornness!

But soon the crying got too much. I couldn't take it anymore. But I also couldn't move. I'm pretty sure a photograph of me that day would have qualified to be placed next to the definition of "trapped" in the dictionary.

I fished around in my tote bag on my lap. There had to be something I could do to stop this child from crying and insulting me. Finding a scrap of paper, I drew four lines to make a noughts and crosses grid.

"You know how to play?" I asked the boy, politely in Spanish, "You pick circle or cross and you have to get three in a row. What do you want to be?"

He quietened down but pretended to ignore me. I looked to his mother for some help. She smiled.

"Are you listening? Do you want to play?" she said to him. He shuffled to face out the window.

"Ok, I'll play with mum. Mum, do you want to play?" I said, picking up the signals from the mother than she'd be up for co-operating if it meant getting her son to stop crying.

"Yes! I'll play!"

"Noughts or crosses?" I responded, happy to be making progress on Operation Silence That Child.

"Noughts"

We played a game of noughts and crosses, dragging it out as long as we could, gradually peaking the boy's interest. By the end of the game, he'd completely turned back around from looking out of the window and was ready to play. We played another game, this time me vs mum and son. I let them win.

They got off before we arrived in San Juan Del Sur, and things must have gone well as I got a smile and a wave, which was more from either of them when we started our journey.

***

San Juan Del Sur was a place that worried me as a decision for where to spend Christmas. It sounded too touristy, too backpackery, too...not what we wanted. However, it didn't disappoint.

The first thing we did after arriving in the small town was go on the hunt for a place to take our sea turtle tour with.

One thing I wanted to do on our trip was see sea turtles laying their eggs or hatching on the beach, it would depend on the season where and when we managed to do it. You see, I kinda love the turtle family. I say family because in British English we use three words: turtle, tortoise, terrapin. At home I have a tortoise, her name is Gonzo and she's probably going to outlive me. What a star.

Missing Gonzo and not yet having reached the Galápagos Islands, Nicaragua, and San Juan Del Sur in particular, promised to be a good spot to see sea turtles. It didn't disappoint.

We headed out on our first evening in the town as the tour guide said there would be less to see if we went out on Christmas Eve as we'd originally planned.

It was honestly one of the most magically nights of my life. There was just Ash and me, and a young northern British couple along with our guide. And there weren't many more people out on the beach - just one other group of around six people. We couldn't have asked for a better night.

We arrived and headed down to the beach where we saw both mama turtles making their nests and laying, and little baby turtles hatching - at one point from underneath the front flippers of a laying turtle!

I wasn't sure how we'd improve on our unexpected highlights of Nicaragua for the rest of the year. But, of course, Costa Rica was next.

Costa Rica

Everyone has a place. Regardless of when, how long, where; we all have a place that's special because it was the first "big", far away, exotic, far different from home place we went to. Maybe you don't have that place *yet*, but you will.

For me, that place is Costa Rica.

And ever since my first visit in spring 2008, I'd been dying to return. To see the village where I'd lived with a family, worked in a school teaching English, and used the internet cafe until it shut down due to "illegal activity" in my last week of being there. To see the tourist town, La Fortuna, nextdoor to my village and witness how different things were now that the key draw of Volcano Arenal had stopped its active daily fuming and lava trickles. To see more of the country that had made such an impression on me all those years ago.

Costa Rica didn't disappoint, I mean, how could it? It's Costa Rica! To ensure that Ashley would leave with the same warm and fuzzy connection to the place, I opted to start our time there in the cloud forest town of Monteverde, a relatively short shuttle bus ride from San Juan Del Sur where we'd spent Christmas in Nicaragua. Christmas at the beach and New Year at the cloud forest? Yes, please!

Only I'd forgotten how variable and chilly the weather can get up in the clouds, which meant we may as well have jetted home for New Year if we were just there for the weather. But we weren't. We weren't there for Language Stories either.

I'd initially considered making a Language Stories episode about Costa Rica based on my time there, asking and attempting to answer the questions: do you need to spend time in a country to learn a language? Is immersion really all it's cracked up to be?

However, I decided on reflection that I wanted to keep Costa Rica my place, my memories, and I didn't want to be asking around the people I hadn't seen for ten years if they wanted to be interviewed. I wanted to speak with them sans camera. So we did.

We already had plenty of film and episodes to be editing together, so instead we opted to use Costa Rica as a chance to catch up and get up to speed with the current episodes we had in the works. This meant that our time there would be purely ours, aside from work, to enjoy and for me to show off the place to Ashley.

There's something you may already know about Costa Rica: it's pretty pricey. And on top of that, Monteverde is a tiny town with a lot of tourists. This meant that finding an Airbnb or apartment to ourselves wasn't really happening, which meant private room in a hostel it was for us in Monteverde. The hostel that proved once and for all, we're too old for that.

Our room was at the front of the small hostel, with a large single-pane window facing out to where smokers would gather...and the smoke would filter through to our room. Yet we couldn't sit outside of the room in the common area to get bits of work done on our laptops because things were going missing.

After cooking for ourselves one evening, we placed a tub of leftovers in the fridge for lunch the following day. When we returned ready to take our lunch out on our adventure the next day, our tub was gone! You have to understand, not only had someone taken our food but our tub was a fancy collapsible tub! The kind that would make Tupperware fans glisten with envy.

I told the owner immediately that someone had taken our food. He casually got up, took a look in the fridge, and called someone on his mobile phone. When he hung up the call, he opened the freezer door and there was our tub of food, semi-frozen in an empty freezer.

"Why was it in the freezer?" I asked, relieved yet perplexed.

"The cleaner put it there," he shrugged, indicating he was as confused as we were.

A few days later, a young American guy came downstairs to report that $80 had gone missing from his wallet. His wallet that he'd left lying on his bed in a dorm because, in his words, "You can trust travellers".

After a visit from the police, who ensured we knew they were Costa Rican by the 'Pura vida' they said on arrival instead of 'hola' (I'll explain in a moment), it soon transpired that the cleaner had been caught stealing before, possibly also why she'd earmarked our tub of food - if no one missed it, she'd take it home after a day or two.

She was instantly fired. We were a little sad. She made eggs in the morning and Ashley had gotten quite used to practising his daily egg vocabulary he'd learnt from Cuban breakfasts.

Aside from the cold, smokey, theft-ridden hostel, Monteverde was the good introduction to Costa Rica I'd hoped for Ashley.

We trekked through the Cloud Forest, did a coffee tour (which changed his life and means we now have a rather large coffee machine sat on our kitchen counter), and purchased ponchos.

But alas, soon it was time to leave the coffee hills of cloudy Monteverde and make our way down the mountain to my home from home, La Fortuna.

When I initially selected where I wanted to go for my first Costa Rican trip teaching English, I had the choice between 'urban' and 'rural'. I picked rural because I'd grown up in a small town and figured rural would be easier to adapt to than a bustling Latin American city. I wasn't expecting rural to be right beside one of the biggest tourist sights in the country.

La Fortuna (which means The Fortune, as you might have guessed) is a small town at the foot of the Arenal Volcano, which is just around the bend from Arenal Lake. Oh, and there's a waterfall down the road in the other direction too. What I'm trying to say here is that it's a well-named town. They really are fortunate when it comes to top notch nature.

Except for in 1968 when the volcano erupted, causing damage to many buildings in the town and surrounding area. However, in true 'pura vida' style, the inhabitants soon turned their fortune around with the arrival of tourism. The volcano was still active and people came from further and further afield to see an active, yet not overly dangerous, volcano. When a volcano is regularly spouting smoke, ash and sparks of lava, it's often considered less dangerous than when it's dormant and could technically explode at any time.

During my three month stay in 2008, the volcano was still active, which meant as well as many attractions in the town to keep me busy on weekends, I had a spectacular view from my window and on my walk down to school each weekday of an active volcano showcasing different plumes of smoke. Some evenings I would sit on the front deck in a rocking chair and watch the night falling, casting the volcano into silhouette. I was incredibly lucky.

It was a truly magical time and I realise this sounds like a huge cliché but it changed my life entirely. Before I left, I had a place reserved for me to begin university a year later, mostly because I'd changed schools at sixteen and the sixth form I'd gone to shouted the word 'university' at every chance they got compared to the hushed whisperings of the word to a select few (not including me) at my previous school. If everyone else is doing it, is this what I had to do to have a good life?

Costa Rica showed me that there's other ways to live your life. There's other things that matter beyond going to university and following the expected path.

Costa Rica showed me that I didn't need the people around me that I previously thought I did. People may treat me like a doormat or underestimate the hell out of me, but if those voices aren't there, I can do anything I put my mind to and I'll do it well.

Costa Rica showed me that home isn't always where your house is. I can adapt, I can travel, I can grow.

When I came back, I turned down that place reserved at university. I looked for other ways - ways that meant I could adapt, I could travel, I could grow. I found The Open University. I studied, worked, travelled, started Lindsay Does Languages, bought a home, and finished my degree 100% debt-free. None of that would have happened without Costa Rica. I'm eternally grateful.

When a place has that much impact on you, it sticks in your memory. Every street, every crack in the pavement, every face, all in vivid 3D. When we arrived from Monteverde in La Fortuna, it felt like I was walking on top of the map inside of my brain. In ten years, shops and cafes had sometimes changed names and hands, a handful of new buildings had appeared, but the town remained mostly the same. We ate a casado meal in a cafe close to the centre (ironically, a cafe I didn't remember) and waited until check-in time had passed for our accommodation. It felt beyond strange to be back, like I was a Sim living a fake reality in my memory.

The next day we'd arranged to meet the family I stayed with all those years ago. Despite hosting many volunteers like myself over the years, they had remembered me and we'd been in loose contact through social media over the years.

It felt easier to speak Spanish to them than to anyone I'd spoken with over the past four months. The words left my lips like soft butter without barely crossing my mind twice. I didn't care if I made mistakes. I just spoke Spanish. I knew they would understand me.

Ashley introduced himself in Spanish, to some confusion around his name. For the rest of the day he was known as "...hhhHAsh", much to everyone's amusement.

After a few hours at the house, which looked mostly as I remembered except for the addition of a new dog, we visited the grandparents' house.

I was fortunate enough to not be alone in my stay. Staying with one set of grandparents for the majority of my stay were two girls both a few years older than me - Hannah from the UK and Bree from Australia. Normally at least once a week, the family would visit and we would get a chance to share our stories from the week in English.

I was surprised when even the grandparents remembered me too! The grandmother took my hand and showed me her new enviable garden. Papaya trees overlooking a rice paddy, coconut trees dotting around the land as casually as a birch at home, lettuce growing in hand cut bamboo hangers. It was impressive.

Possibly the biggest change though was that the family now owned a fast food restaurant in the next village. After our trip to visit the grandparents, we stopped by and got a demonstration of how they batter the chicken freshly each time before heading back to the house to say our goodbyes.

It was a great day, and only amplified when a few days later on a bike ride, me and Ashley ended up back at the fast food restaurant to grab some lunch not expecting the family to be working, only to find they were! So we got to meet twice!

"Diez años y después dos veces en algunas días!" said the father, "Ten years and then twice in one week."

And just like that, it was time to move on. But no doubt to visit again, hopefully in less than ten years.

***

Our next stop was Uvita, inspired by one of the daughters of my Costa Rican family who showed us Google Images of the 'whale tail' beach there. But first we had to get to San José, and the bus times didn't match which meant a night in San José and an early bus the following day to Uvita.

Back in El Salvador, when the Zimbabwean guy was declaring to the minibus how he wasn't a fan of Santa Ana, an Australian girl he'd made friends with piped up that it was like San José in Costa Rica - the "necessary evil before you get to the nice bits". I disagree. San José is basically Nottingham. But more on that later.

However, arriving in the dark and having to walk through a bustling market to get to our hotel, San José wasn't doing itself any favours in the "I'm really a nice city despite what people say" rankings. We also had to leave early the next morning so never really saw San José at its best until we returned from Uvita four days later. Uvita wasn't quite what I expected. It's a small town but it's quite spread out with a busy main road running through the centre.

We were staying in a room at an Airbnb up from the main road. We headed up there, still relatively early in the morning because of our super early bus from San José and knocked on the door...and waited...and waited...and knocked again...and waited...until finally a dreadlocked head poked over the fence.

"Hey, hola. We have a reservation." I told the head, mostly in English, his appearance not striking me as Costa Rican.

"Wait a moment, let me come and let you in." the head replied in English, not with a Spanish accent.

The dreadlocks belonged to a Serbian guy travelling with his girlfriend, who was Hungarian. They'd just started an open-ended trip and were planning to make money to fund it by doing odd jobs and video work. He had recently taken some new photos for the owners of the place we were staying, which was his first job. They also communicated between themselves in English, which fascinated me, but it's the kind of thing you can't ask strangers about.

But it wasn't just them sharing the house with us. We were soon introduced to an Irish guy in his mid-40s who instantly clocked Ashley's Hoka trainers he'd purchased at the volcano race in Guatemala.

"Hokas! Are you into running ultras?"

"Oh, well, not yet. I've just run marathons so far."

I can tell it's not a conversation for me when the word 'just' is used in relation to running a marathon. I've run a marathon too, and I'd never say I'd "just" done it.

As I was trying to drift from the conversation, another guy emerged, this time with an English accent, Essex to be precise.

"Oh, hello. Welcome!"

The pair had met each other working on an eco farm further inland and had decided they'd had enough of that and wanted to come and work on the coast instead for a bit.

So basically, everyone staying at the place was working there in some way. I couldn't help but wonder if it was legal. All of them had the same tourist visa on arrival we did. They discussed visa runs to Texas various evenings, they were working in Costa Rica and getting paid (or at the very least compensated with board and food), and yet I couldn't imagine them being referred to in quite the same negative light as Latin Americans who'd made their way north.

Despite its size, when you do manage to find your way to the beach at Uvita, you're in for a treat. The sand expands out in front of you and the ocean peacefully laps up to it. At some points not so peacefully, making waves big enough to surf, attracting a bronzed surfer crowd. Not only does Uvita boast watersports but it's also home to whale watching and turtles at certain times of year. The real highlight though if you visit outside of prime animal time, like we did, is the 'whale tail' - a stretch of sand that leads outwards into the ocean meeting a rocky patch in the shape of a whale tail.

Yes. It's hard to believe but this place where whales actually come has a whale tail formed naturally flowing out from the beach into the sea. It sounds like some futuristic Dubai-inspired "let's build an island" plan, but it's true.

Go on, Google it right now. Type "Uvita whale tail" into your phone. I'll wait. Of course, when you visit, you don't get to see that view you've just Googled unless you rent out a helicopter. However, as you walk out onto the sand connecting the rocky tail to the beach, you suddenly realise you're somewhere pretty special. You look to your left and there's sea. You look to your right and there's sea.

Some places photographed, you can clearly see what you'd actually see if you were there in real life, Chichen Itza for example. When you visit in real life, there's nothing new that you haven't seen before. The whale tail at Uvita on the other hand? It's impossible to capture exactly what it's like to be there in a photograph.

Uvita is very well located. That main road I mentioned? North it leads right up the coast past Dominical and Manuel Antonio before meeting the Nicoya Peninsula. Go south and you'll be heading towards the wildlife-packed Peninsula del Oso, but not before you pass through Palmar Norte and Palmar Sur.

Unknown to most, the Palmar area is home to all that Ashley somehow knew about Costa Rica before we arrived: the Costa Rican Stone Balls. Not the official name given to them by the tourist board, I'm sure. I'd never heard of the stone balls, but when we were figuring out where we'd like to see in Costa Rica, Ashley threw out the words "stone balls" every single time.

"What's so special about these stone balls?" I'd ask.

"I dunno. I just know it's a thing. I saw it on TV or something."

Seeing as Palmar was just a short bus ride away from Uvita down the main road, we decided one day to make the trip to find out exactly what these stone balls were all about.

There wasn't much information online, but before we went, I did find out that there are various sites and the stone balls at Palmar Sur, where we were headed, were at a site called 'Finca 6'. Knowing we were likely to be offline, I searched and marked 'Finca 6' on my map app and we headed out.

We caught the bus just fine, we reached Palmar just fine, we got off the bus just fine.

"Right, it's a little walk from here, maybe 1.5km?" I said to Ashley, looking at my map app as we left the town. It was Sunday and the town was empty. It felt almost like a film set of a Western after production is over. I was half expecting Clint Eastwood to come around the corner in a Stetson, a cigarette lazily hanging from the corner of his pursed lips, the first few bars of The Good, The Bad and The Ugly theme to start pounding softly in the distance. Unsurprisingly, that didn't happen. As we headed out of the town, I soon began to realize that Finca 6 on my map wasn't the site of the stone balls at all, and instead referred to the name of an area of the town.

"Oh..." I said, "Hold on a minute."

A lady was walking up the hill from the Finca 6 I had marked on my map.

"Excuse me, we're looking for the stone balls. My map says Finca 6 is here." I said to her in Spanish.

"Stone balls? Hmm...This is Finca 6, but 'stone balls' you say?"

That wasn't the response I was hoping for.

"Yeah, the stone balls? There's a few different sites...they're just...balls...made of...stone...?" I didn't really know how else to describe them.

"Oh, the stone balls! Let me ask my friend. Come with me."

Remarkably from my minimal additional description, she now seemed to be on the same page. We followed her down the road she'd just walked up. She was no longer walking in the direction she'd been heading in before we met, she was simply helping us. Another woman approached us pushing a bike.

"Hey! Do you know where the stone balls are from here?"

"Woah, from here?! Wow, a way. Are they walking?" the lady with the bike replied, not to us.

"Yes, my map got it wrong!" I said in Spanish, shrugging.

"Let me call my husband. He's a taxi driver, he might be free to take you there."

"Ok, thanks," I said, as I turned to translate to Ashley.

These stone balls had better be worth it.

We followed the woman with a bike to a bus stop where she waited with us for fifteen minutes until her husband arrived to take us to the actual stone ball Finca 6.

"You know, when they found the stone balls and opened the site a few years ago, they did lots of work with schools here. My son is on a photograph in the museum! When you walk in, there's a photo on the right of three boys looking at some rocks and stuff. The middle one - that's my boy." she said proudly as we chatted while waiting for her husband.

And just because that part of the story isn't example enough of how ridiculously helpful and friendly everyone was in this town, when we arrived at the stone balls site, the taxi driver called inside, "Is Miguel working?"

He turned to me and said, "Miguel is my friend. When you're finished, just tell him you're ready to go and he will call me to come and pick you up."

"Ok, thank you," I said as I handed over the fare for this leg of the journey, slightly astonished at how much our luck had turned around.

Sure enough, the woman's son was on display as soon as you walk into the small museum room. I took a photo to show her husband when he picked us up.

The good thing about the stone balls is that it's a very new tourist thing in Costa Rica and as there's plenty of other things to keep tourists busy, it's still a very peaceful place to walk around. We were even able to sit and have lunch staring at some stone balls completely undisturbed. Ok, I realise the term "staring at some stone balls" doesn't exactly sound too appealing. You have to believe me when I say it was relaxing.

The bad thing about the stone balls however, is that they are, quite literally, stone balls. If you've ever been to any garden centre with a display of water fountains for sale outside that includes one of those rolling balls spinning in a flow of water or a solid stone ball squirting water from a hole in the top, then you'll have a pretty good idea of what to expect. In fact it could be argued the garden centre display is more impressive. I mean, don't expect rolling balls or flowing water from the Costa Rican stone balls.

Our pleasant and enjoyable yet slightly underwhelming time at the stone balls site was coming to an end at the final spot, a clearing with the most stone balls of all the stone balls site, when suddenly we heard a rustle in the trees behind us. As we turned around, we spotted a monkey tail moving through the leaves and branches. It wasn't long before we saw another monkey, and another. Suddenly, stood still surrounded by the stone balls, we found ourselves also surrounded by monkeys. And for a few moments, we were alone in the Costa Rican countryside with more monkeys than we could count.

We enjoyed it as long as we could before our necks got sore and one of the few other tourists approached the clearing, and we headed back to the museum and reception for Miguel to call our taxi driver.

***

After our time in Uvita, we caught a bus back to San José, where we'd be spending the next few days before heading down to Panama.

We were arriving in daylight. Maybe this would be a good chance for San José to show Ashley just how nice a place it can be! It was San José's time to shine. It rained.

When our Airbnb host eventually arrived with the keys, things began to turn around. We were the first people to stay in the apartment and the building was newly built. The hosts had thought of everything.

But we weren't there to stay locked up in an apartment, so it wasn't long before we headed out to the centre. Here's where Nottingham comes in. Go to San José, sit down on a bench at the side of the theatre, and tell me it doesn't feel like Nottingham. Or, if you've never been to Nottingham (a small city in the Midlands, England) then maybe just enjoy San José for San José. It deserves at least a little attention.

We had a coffee experience booked in San José that we'd found on Airbnb with a guy called Juan who owned a coffee shop, that he described as "a bit like a speakeasy". If you didn't know where the coffee shop was, you wouldn't find it. It was super secret. And very cool.

I said earlier that the coffee tour in Monteverde was the reason we now have a large coffee machine in our kitchen, but perhaps it would be more accurate to say it's thanks to Juan. So thanks Juan (and Costa Rica in general) for making my husband even more obsessed with coffee. Regards, a non-coffee drinker.

Panama

Season 1, Mini Episode 5: The Panama Canal

Central America is wonderful. It's compact and easy to get around; full of adventure, beaches, volcanoes, and jungle. However, this does mean that if you're travelling through from one end to the other, by the time you get the the other end you've seen and done a lot of the "stuff" - the coffee tour, the volcano climb, the beach, the sea turtles, the colourful colonial town. This meant that by the time we were ready to arrive in Panama, we opted to keep things simple and spend our one week there entirely in Panama City. Besides, the biggest attraction is the Canal, which can easily be accessed by day trip from the bright lights of PC. That's what the locals call it. Definitely didn't just make that abbreviation up.

We arrived in Panama City very early in the morning on a Tica Bus from San José. The border check had been the most rigorous and patronising one we'd had. It involved everyone taking all our bags off the bus and standing in a room together with the border guard telling us how to fill out a form, which, I kid you not, started with "Where it says name, write your name".

So you can imagine we were glad to finally arrive in Panama City, not least because I'd discovered online that the biggest mall in the Americas, the Albrook Mall, has a Lush, and after months of travel, we were in need of some new shampoo bars. However, Lush isn't open at 4am, neither is the rather modern and shiny underground train network. So after an hour of waiting in the lower mall of the bus station, we headed across to the underground for opening time at 5am with our crisp, fresh from the ATM US dollars. Yes, Panama is the second country in Central America to use the US dollar.

After months of colonial towns and bustling bigger cities with more market than mall, the shock of suddenly being on a metro was bizarre, especially when you could see chicken buses parked underneath as you cross the bridge towards it. As we'd soon discover, Panama City is like that - contradictory.

There's huge malls with global brands priced the same if not higher than they would be in the US, yet there's also much cheaper shops in the centre selling (probably counterfeit) goods for less than half the price.

There's the business district full of high rise offices glistening blue, yet there's also the old town full of overpriced ice cream and keyring shops.

There's the gourmet corner shop with organic gluten-free dairy-free milk alternatives, yet there's also the cart on the waterfront selling shaved ice and syrup.

I understand this exists everywhere. Wealth alongside poverty, modern alongside classic. But in Panama City, it felt like a different kind of divide. More of a canyon between the two sides of life, and good luck jumping across to get a taste of that wealth because there's no one to catch you if you fall.

Eventually, we found our Airbnb, located right on the front of the Cinta Costera, with stunning views from the living room out across the water. To the left, we could see the shimmering blue of the office towers and in the distance to the right, the old town. In front of us was the Cinta Costera itself, a long stretch of road with plenty of space for pedestrians, cyclists, runners, and the free gym equipment either end to entice them there. It was a spectacular view. And one like none we'd seen during our time in Central America.

We spent most of our time in Panama City between working, eating, and malling (I'm a mall rat at heart), but we did take a day to visit Miraflores Lock, the Panama Canal site closest to Panama City. I say closest to, the country is so narrow that it takes just two hours from Panama City to reach Colón on the Atlantic side of the canal.

I have to be honest, and I hope I'm not alone in this. Sometimes I feel guilty for how I leave a country in my memory. With Panama this happened. I arrived on the high of Costa Rica, and we'd be leaving in a week to go to the Galápagos Islands, something I'd always wanted to do. Panama was very much a not-so-tasty filling in a sandwich of gourmet bread. Panama was never going to be given a fair chance to be remembered as fondly. Someday I'll go back and dig a little deeper and learn more about Panama.

Ecuador

It was happening. We were sat on a plane about to land in Guayaquil, our gateway on the Ecuadorian mainland to the Galápagos Islands. You have to hand it to Ecuador, they do a pretty good job of caring for the islands. A very limited number of airlines are permitted to land there, they have to fly out of only two airports in Ecuador: Quito and Guayaquil, your bags are checked, you have to pay a $100 fee for your permit to enter the islands...it's all very thorough.

And before we knew it, my dream had come true and we'd arrived on the Galápagos Islands. It was a truly incredible five days, although you could spend a lifetime and never really experience it all.

We spent the whole time on just one island, Santa Cruz. Many people choose to visit multiple islands on cruises or boat day trips, but we stayed put mainly because the thing I cared most about seeing was the giant tortoises, which you can do lots of on Santa Cruz, and a lot less of on a boat.

We paid numerous visits to the Charles Darwin Research Centre near town, and tortoise ranches in the centre of the island, both of which are home to more tortoises that you could dream of. We only planned one visit to the tortoise ranches in the centre of Santa Cruz island initially, but ended up sneaking in another visit on our last day because where else can you see giant tortoises in the wild? Not many places.

On our first visit, we caught the bus to the nearest village and walked the remaining few kilometres up the hill, turning down to the left when we saw the rather large carved wooden tortoise sign.

"This must be it, right? I mean, the sign is shaped like a tortoise and it says 'El Ranchero de Tortugas'," Ashley said as I looked quizzically at my map.

"Yeah...but that doesn't make any sense. The map says it's further up and then down to the left. But I guess...the sign is shaped like a tortoise and it does say 'El Ranchero de Tortugas'. Let's try this way."

After another kilometre or so, we found ourselves at a fork in the road. By now I was beginning to empathise with Alice making her way through Wonderland, except we didn't have the joys of a Cheshire Cat to help us make our decision.

In front of us were two signs; one pointing to the left with a tortoise carved into the top of the sign and another pointing to the right with a tortoise carved into the bottom of the sign. Not an easy decision. I didn't want to miss any tortugas! We eventually chose the left one, as the map said it was a little closer to that ranch. Along the way, we saw multiple tortoises by the side of the road, some even on the road. In many ways this was more special than the ranch visit itself as it was so unexpected and we were the only people out there. We'd seen a handful of shells rising among the grasses from the bus window on our journey from the airport to town but up close it was magic.

That said, the ranch itself was awesome too. Both ranch sites were similar but took slightly different routes around their grounds past mud baths (which were very popular with the tortoises), wooded areas, and open plains. It's a very special place.

We did do some none-tortoise-related activities, I should add, like Tortuga Bay. Yes, I'm aware that tortuga means turtle/tortoise but there were none on our visit. A long walk out of Puerto Ayora leads you to a greystone path through a slightly ethereal landscape with cacti and twisted twigs and dried branches battling for space either side of you. This bit felt more like Prince Philip battling thorns to reach Sleeping Beauty's castle. This path eventually brings you out at Tortuga Bay, a long stretch of beach that appears to have been given the wrong name judging by the number of iguanas calling the place home.

Have you ever seen an iguana swim? The first time it happens you almost want to point and laugh. They look silly. They swerve and wiggle their way off shore and into the shallows swinging their back legs from side to side with what can only be described as sass. But they look silly. Someone needs to tell them.

Considering the islands are known for their history of educating us about evolution, you'd think that the iguanas would have evolved to swim with a little more strength and dignity, yet here they are giving bad Shakira impressions a run for their money.

But iguanas aren't the only inhabitants of Tortuga Bay. If you're lucky, you'll get a glimpse of a sea lion chilling on the sand. And even better animal encounters await if you're taking a dip. One afternoon as I attempted to snorkel, a pelican landed right next to me. I slowly raised my head and turned to Ashley on the shore as the huge bird flew away.

But the thing about the Galápagos Islands is that just as you think you've found the most special place, they've got somewhere else up their sleeves and around the corner.

From the dock in Puerto Ayora, as well as boats for day and overnight trips, there's a small boat that will take you a few minutes across to another side of town, from which you can walk to Las Grietas canyon, a natural gap between the rocks where you can swim up and down and see plenty of fish, and even lizards on the rocks at the far end if you're lucky. There's just nature everywhere.

But, of course, our time in the Galápagos had to come to an end eventually, and after five of the most memorable days of my life we made our way back to the mainland to see what the rest of Ecuador had to offer.

***

Flying into and out of the Galápagos Islands, you have two choices: Quito or Guayaquil. Seeing as we were planning to work our way down to Peru, it made sense to land in the most geographically south of the two: Guayaquil. Although Quito is the capital of Ecuador, Guayaquil is the largest city. Yet, despite that, it still has a relatively small city vibe to its streets. In our experience, everyone we encountered was incredibly friendly.

We arrived from the airport bus at a huge transport hub, slightly bewildered at how to get where we wanted. Tram? Bus? Taxi? We opted for tram, which was more complicated to a newbie than it seemed at first glance, but thankfully a young woman was there to help us out and set us on the right track (pardon the pun).

Following the instructions to our Airbnb, we asked the man in the shop next door as instructed to ring the host for the keys. In fact, he asked us.

"Hola! Hola!" a thick Chinese-accented Spanish voice came from the man walking towards us, carefully avoiding stumbling over the boxes of goods that lined his shop.

"You go here? You go here? Where you go?"

The streets were loud with piercing drills from construction on the pavements and bass-filled reggaeton from speakers positioned at the threshold of multiple shop entrances to entice customers in. I could barely hear the man. We understood each other eventually and after watching him make a quick phone call, were informed our host was on his way.

"Hola! Bienvenidos! Come, let me show you the apartment." a broad-shouldered Latino showed us upstairs, drowning out the street noise fractionally more with each step, "Did you find the place ok?"

"Yes, no problem. The instructions were great!" I replied as we entered our home for the next four days.

It was a small, newly-fitted room, with the bed taking up most of the space, a table and chairs at the end of the bed and the kitchen units flowing around the edge of one side of the room. The bathroom was through a closed door behind the table and equally as compact. There was an efficiency to the place that made you feel like you'd stepped into an apartment in the Ikea showroom.

"He is a good man downstairs. He helps to let me know when people arrive and I come and show you around. The Chinese are good people. Here, we are in Chinatown, so there are many."

That explained the Chinese writing on a handful of the shops outside. That said, it was minimal compared to most Chinatowns we'd experienced. The Chinese shops and restaurants blended into the fabric of the area, still very much alive with Ecuadorian-owned businesses. The Ecuadorian ones were easy to distinguish - they were often the ones with the reggaeton on full-blast outside.

The apartment was only a ten minute walk a few blocks down to the Malecón 2000, a coastal boardwalk with shops, restaurants, a cinema and parks built for the millennium. Despite being nearly twenty years old at the time of our visit, the Malecón still stood out as a sign of modernity in Guayaquil, where many of the repetitive-looking gridded streets are showing signs of wear: chipped paint, derelict doors with one or two graffiti tags sprayed haphazardly upon them, bags of rubbish thrown idly into the gutter. That's not to say it was a dirty place though. The bin lorries came round each evening, reminding residents to bring their bags of rubbish kerbside with a sinister ice cream truck-esque tune that wouldn't have been out of place in a film adaptation of a Stephen King movie.

Other places stood out too like Parque de las Iguanas, a park that much like the name suggests was full of iguanas roaming freely; and the impressive cathedral. From one end of the Malecón, you look up to see a paintbox of colourful houses sat on the hills. We never made it up there but the neighbourhood Las Penas is often recommended as a pleasant stroll through what I imagine to be cobbled streets and art galleries. However, I was more than happy with the view from a distance on the Malecón.

For the majority of our time in Guayaquil, we were working, with daily runs along the Malecón and occasional coffee shop trips. Despite the noise of our street, including three guys drilling up the pavement tile right outside of our apartment stairwell for a full day and a half, we quite enjoyed our time there. Staying in a lot also allowed us some time to figure out what we wanted to do with the rest of our time in Ecuador and how we'd get down to Cusco in Peru.

As we were figuring out our plans, I got a message on Facebook from my friend Mariuxi, who featured in the Montreal episode of Language Stories. A native to Ecuador, she lives most of the time in Montreal with her husband, Joey, and then spends some time each year back in Ecuador. She had just arrived and would be staying a few months, and wouldn't let me leave Ecuador without staying with her!

Mariuxi's house was in the town of Manta, further north from where we wanted to be heading. But we couldn't turn down the offer of seeing more of the mainland with a native. It was a great decision, and so our plans were coming together...even if we still hadn't figured out how we'd get to Cusco from higher up in Ecuador than planned.

We started by making our way up the coast and booked two nights in a brand new Airbnb on the coast near Montañita, a busy surfer town, the kind of place where people stay a little longer than they originally planned. We weren't too keen on visiting Montañita, however, the place we'd found was a couple of villages down and would allow us to break up the journey. On top of that, the host had agreed to pick us up in Guayaquil - three hours from her coastal home!

***

We left the noisy street of our Guayaquil apartment, excited to be heading somewhere a little more peaceful for a couple of days. Sure enough, around the corner was the car our host had described on our messages and she was waiting for us. We got in the car and thanked her profusely for her kindness.

"No importa, no importa! Don't worry about it! You're my first guests - I'm not sure I'll be the same after ten or twenty, but for now, I want to make a good impression." I appreciated her honesty. She had a warmth about her.

"Now, try on these boots. If they don't fit, we can change them now in Guayaquil."

As well as offering to pick us up three hours away, our host had also asked in our messages for our shoe sizes, mentioning that it gets muddy on the walk up to her house and she'd check she had some welly boots for us to borrow.

"Are you sure? It's very kind of you." I replied.

The shoes fitted and so off we went. But not before grabbing a bag of coffee beans from her favourite hole in the wall coffee bean roaster, more than enough to get Ashley involved in the conversation and practising his Spanish.

They bonded more over coffee when we stopped off at a supermarket on the way too. After getting enough food to last us for a few days, we grabbed a drink and small lunch before setting off on our journey.

Keen to try out his Spanish on a fellow coffee connoisseur, Ashley asked if the drink he'd just bought and taken a sip from was a typical americano in Ecuador.

"Why? What did they do? Is it not good?" she started to stand, as if ready to complain to the staff.

"No, no it's nice! It's just interesting that americano is different in every country."

"Ahh I see," she replied calming down and sitting back down.

"I think he only put one shot in it. Maybe he did it differently here then." Ashley replied, still sipping his coffee.

"Hang on..." she stood up fully this time, heading to the counter, Ashley's drink in hand.

"What do you think she's saying?" Ashley asked me.

"I'm not sure. Is she complaining? This is awkward…" I replied, my British blood getting the best of me.

Minutes later she returned with a new cup of coffee. "Try this." she said proudly, putting the cup in front of Ashley.

"Ahh, yes, that's better!" replied Ashley after taking a sip.

It was becoming clear by now we'd found ourselves a very independent, strong-willed Airbnb host. Our conversations on the journey confirmed my suspicions.

She told me that she had been married for many years, living in a gated community in Guayaquil with a maid and a chauffeur, until her husband left her unexpectedly and she had to raise her daughter alone. She got a job, worked hard in her own business, and recently retired and built her own house up on a hill in a small village by the coast. It was almost a movie plot: big city woman leaves everything behind for a new life in the country.

Three hours and many conversations later we arrived, and sure enough, it had rained and the car couldn't make it up the hill, and neither could we without wellies. Ten minutes later, we'd walked our way up and were shown upstairs to our apartment space. We were the first guests ever to stay, which meant lots of removing plastic covers from things and tentatively using them. But other than that it was an incredible two days.

Our host was keen to show us the local area and took us out to Montañita and other local beaches and sights along the coast. Our view was incredible, with hills in one direction and sea in the other; our host was regularly supplying us with snacks and drinks; and our outdoor table was a lovely place to eat. In the evenings, fireflies sparked sporadically in the greenery of the slope beneath our window. As we turned out the lights, we noticed some even made their way into the room.

It was the only place we were provided with (and needed to use) a mosquito net all year, and we'd wake up every morning with bugs dotted all over the outside of the net. Yet, despite the net, as we left with our host on our last day to take us to our bus to Manta, she noticed the rash that had formed behind my ears and under my eyes. I'd noticed it too that morning but was hoping it would be discreet. Obviously not.

This meant I met Mariuxi with very puffy eyes and no explanation why. "Hi, nice to see you again! Please excuse my eyes."

I still don't know if it was bug related or something else, but either way my eyes remained puffy and dry until half way through our three weeks in Cusco.

***

We arrived by bus in Manta, which isn't really a popular foreign tourist spot, so were grateful that the driver had remembered to remind us we were getting off here. The bus station was brand new, yet someone somewhere along the line had forgotten to include the free public wifi, now basically a human right. I'm kidding, of course. About the second bit. There was no free public wifi. Instead, I had to buy the cheapest drink I could from KFC to get the password for access to their network so I could contact Mariuxi.

She came to meet us and that night we sat on the beach and drank fresh coconuts. Halfway through our coconuts, she suddenly remembered something and reached for her phone.

"Oh! This is the best place for French baguettes and cakes in Manta. I have to call them to get some." We'd already got a jar of Nutella from the supermarket. Mariuxi was a true Montrealer.

"Oh no! They are refurbishing and won't be open until the holiday weekend. You're staying until then, right?"

"I don't know. We didn't want to overstay our welcome but weren't sure about transport options on the holiday weekend."

"Yeah, it'll be busy. You can stay as long as you need.."

It turned out we'd arrived at Mariuxi's place a couple of days before Carnival.

In the UK, this is the time of year when we eat pancakes. Shrove Tuesday, or Pancake Day, is traditionally a means for clearing out our cupboards before Lent before Easter. In Ecuador, however, the pancakes are replaced by aerosol cans of spray foam that no-one is immune from being struck by. Not struck by the can itself, I should add, but hit by foam, most often sprayed alongside an accompanying "Wahheeeyyy!" from a passing vehicle.

Mariuxi explained how the tradition used to be that people would throw water instead of the foam, but for health reasons (aka, where the heck is everyone's water coming from because potentially not everyone is buying securely sealed bottles) water being thrown was now banned in her city.

Oh, and tourists aren't immune. Everyone plays the game, even if you don't want to, or even if you've arrived expecting a relaxing holiday and you don't even know what the game is. So instead, we were hit multiple times by this foam as we walked around the city of Manta. It's not as bad as it sounds though, as the foam doesn't make a mess, or leave a stain, and it disappears very quickly once it's landed on you.

When we made our way down to Cuenca with Mariuxi to see her friend Fany for the day, suddenly, the foam festival had changed. As well as our now typical foamings, we were getting watered in the street too!

Cuenca is a highlight for many tourists to Ecuador. It's a pretty, calm town in the south of the country that draws many foreign and local tourists for its tranquil setting. And it's easy to see why. The cobbled streets lead down to a river, with lush green banks begging for picnic blankets to be laid out on them.

But Cuenca was to be our last stop in Ecuador. The following morning, we headed back to the bus station and back into the total contrast of Guayaquil ready for our flight out of Ecuador and down to Cusco.

Peru

I get it. Quechua would have been an obvious choice for a Language Stories episode. I agree. However, our time of arriving in Peru clashed with co-hosting the first Women In Language event. Women In Language was an idea I'd had many months before as a way to celebrate International Women's Day. The idea was to showcase the phenomenal range of females doing awesome things with languages across the world who don't always speak at other language events for one reason or another. It could be that they'd previously been too shy to put themselves forward, it could be that they live too far away and couldn't make it to previous offline events, or simply, it could be that they had no idea that language events existed.

When I told Kerstin Cable of Fluent Language and Shannon Kennedy of Eurolinguiste, they were more than up for sharing hosting duties for the event, and we ended up with a long list of people we wanted to hear from. So long in fact, that the initial one day event to celebrate International Women's Day turned into a four day online live event spanning International Women's Day to British Mother's Day. It was a huge success. But in order to make it a huge success, I needed to be able to work easily, without the pressure of missing whole days of work to long bus journeys or trying to do too much at once, including fitting in Language Stories interviews for Quechua.

Although we'd be spending three weeks in Cusco, home to many Quechua speakers, the Language Stories episode on Quechua would have to go.

Another reason for dropping the episode was that we would have to take some days out to visit Machu Picchu and other local Inca sites. How could we visit the region and not go to Machu Picchu?! Despite its popularity, I can honestly say, I've never encountered a more difficult to visit place. Machu Picchu is a long journey from Cusco. Yet as there's no roads to the town of Aguas Calientes, the town at the foot of the Wonder of the World, many people arrive in Cusco and make the journey to Machu Picchu from there in various ways.

I knew there was the option for a train, however, at the time we were visiting, that involved a substitute bus to take you to another train station to start the journey. The trails and hikes were mostly closed as the authorities close the Inca trail during the month of February (when we were there) to give the trail some time without many many feet pounding its soil each day. I started searching online for other options, only to be met with a bombardment of blog posts:

"17 Ways to Get to Machu Picchu" - I don't want 17! I want one!

"How we got to Machu Picchu for $1." - Good for you, now tell me how else you contributed to the local economy on your trip?

"Walk along the train tracks to Machu Picchu." - Nah, I'm alright, thanks.

It was mind blowing. Until one day as we were walking back to our apartment after having been shopping, we saw a sign outside of a tourist office: MACHU PICCHU BY CAR. By car? This was new. We headed in for more information.

"So, you get picked up from the main square, you travel by minibus here...stopping here for lunch, all included, here...and here," the guy told us pointing to the map as he spoke, "Then you have to walk two hours until you reach Aguas Calientes. Hotel, dinner, guide meets you that night, all paid for. Next day, you go up to Machu Picchu or if you like also Huayna Picchu. Then walk back along the train trains and the minibus will be there at 3pm. Bring you back to Cusco."

"Ok..." I said, it seeming too good to be true, "And what is included?"

"Transport, food - lunch, dinner, breakfast; hotel, tour guide, Machu Picchu ticket..."

"Including the ticket to Machu Picchu?!" I was intrigued. We'd already been to the ticket office and that combined with getting a train ticket from another office seemed an overly complex procedure.

"Yes, you just let me know if you want Huayna Picchu too and I will get your tickets."

"Ok...and how much?"

"$100 or $115 with Huayna Picchu."

"Really?! Ok…" I wanted to say 'wow' but I also wanted to keep my cool for fear of our guy suddenly changing his mind and putting the price up. Every other tour option we'd seen was $200 minimum.

We booked our trip, including three other day trips around Cusco of other Inca sites and crossed our fingers we hadn't just been scammed. But I got a good vibe from the guy having had our conversations in Spanish.

The following day was our first tour, the City Tour, covering the major Inca sites within a stone's throw of Cusco. Our guide was incredible, and told us in English (but, interestingly, not in the Spanish translation) that the condor, puma, and snake idea was actually a projection of Catholic beliefs onto the Inca system, going as far to call it "bulls**t". How true that is, I'm still not sure. And considering by his lack of translation of that bit into Spanish, I wonder if it's perhaps an uncommon opinion.

We're not used to having a tour guide, and after three days of following a man with a flag and being taken to numerous workshops and having three demonstrations of the same local liquor on the bus, we were flag-toured out. That said, the sights themselves were more than worth it. Like watching an advert on a YouTube video to see what you really came for. The sights of Ollantaytambo, Moray, Pisac, and the Maras Salt Mines stood out to me as truly memorable, jaw-dropping places.

Moray showcases the Inca farming terraces in what looks like at first glance a perfect crop circle. Pisac is the remains of a town, with various buildings and terraces over a vast expanse. Ollantaytambo is a collection of terraces and building remains clambering up a hillside, looking down on where the modern town sits today. And the Maras Salt Mines are a beautiful patchwork of salty squares delicately placed on the side of the valley, the views from the bus to that one are phenomenal. But of course, we hadn't visited Machu Picchu yet! Surely that would be the site to take the crown?

We woke up early, and got ready to walk into the centre of Cusco, where we'd be meeting our group for our trip. After a few hours of breathtaking views over the mountains and listening to an array of podcasts to accompany the journey, I suddenly turned. We'd been rising up and up constantly the entire journey - Cusco was already 3,000 plus metres above sea level - how high were we going?

I'd not been too badly affected by altitude sickness in Cusco. A little breathless walking up stairs but that was it. No need for an oxygen tank. Until now.

I felt hot. Then cold. Then hot again. I was sweating. I was cold again. I lost control of my muscles and fell onto Ashley, still conscious enough to know not to fall onto the unsuspecting German girl sat next to me on the other side.

I'd been focusing on the audio in my ears. The Unpopped podcast. They were talking about the Spice Girls. That's all I remember. Ashley turned it off. I wanted him to turn it back on to give me something to focus on but I couldn't get the words out to tell him.

I couldn't speak. I couldn't control my muscles enough to sit up. I couldn't breathe normally. I panicked.

After what felt like a lifetime but was probably three minutes maximum, I was suddenly thrust back into real life, feeling somewhat normal again. I could remember what had happened but I couldn't explain it. Was this altitude sickness?

I tried to look out the window, my eyes squinting and my vision blurred slightly. We were going down the mountain. I'd had altitude sickness. As if to confirm my doubts, seconds later I was sick into a plastic bag. Yup. I had altitude sickness alright.

Our Machu Picchu experience was so far not looking good. After a second speat of altitude sickness overcoming me, we soon stopped for lunch. Just in time. I'm not sure how much more I could have handled. Nor the poor German girl next to me.

Lunch wasn't exactly appetizing. When nothing would taste good, bowls of soggy pasta with overcooked vegetables don't exactly go down a treat. But I knew I had to eat something. I survived the rest of the journey without being sick or being hit by another bout of altitude sickness.

When we arrived mid-afternoon at Hydroelectrica, it was raining heavily. Thankfully we just had our little backpacks to carry but we only had two flimsy ponchos and one umbrella between us.

Not being given any guidance as to what happens next, I asked our driver where we should go.

"Just over there," he said, pointing loosely towards the end of the car park, "You'll see train tracks. It's easy, just follow the tracks. The guide will meet you in the main square in Aguas Calientes."

We knew we'd be walking for two hours but no-one had told us it would be *on* train tracks, exactly how we didn't want to get to Machu Picchu. There seems to be an arrogance to doing something like that in a different country. I'd never do that at home, so why here? However, at this point, we had no choice. We were two hours walking distance from Aguas Calientes, and it would be dark in just a few hours. Off we went.

The walk wasn't too bad. It was mostly flat, what with being besides the train track, and there were multiple minibus loads of people who'd been dropped off at the same car park taking the same route, either expected or not.

When the trees cleared now and then, the views surrounding the track were spectacular. Mighty green hills towered over the crashing, brown river flowing fast cutting its way through the landscape.

We powered through and made it to Aguas Calientes, dutifully making our way towards the main square, where we waited in the rain for others in our new group. After being taken to our better than expected hotel, we headed out for dinner and our pre-Machu Picchu info talk from our guide. The dinner was, much like lunch, not exactly a highlight.

To make it to the top of Machu Picchu and meet our guide at the entrance, he explained, we'd have to set up around 5am, and wake up even earlier. We swiftly left the restaurant and got to sleep as soon as we could for our 4.30am alarm. After taking a quick shower and grabbing our breakfast bag from reception the following morning, we left the hotel for our dark walk to Machu Picchu itself.

There is a bus that takes tourists up the steep hill to the entrance. However, we'd come this far on our own feet as much as possible in February when many trails are closed, there was no way we'd be catching the bus at the very last hurdle. Besides, the bus wasn't included in our tour package price.

Proud of ourselves for leaving on time, we found ourselves stalled at the gate leading up towards the entrance. People were beginning to form a line and despite being told to leave early enough to make it to the top in time for our guide to start as soon as the site opened, we were left waiting at the gate for thirty minutes, which it turned out didn't open until 6am. 6am soon came, and like the start of a race, we all set off up the hill.

I have a philosophy for exercise. I enjoy it, but I'm not one for overdoing things or sweating excessively and breathing heavier than looks or feels comfortable. I like to think of myself as a sensible exercise role model. Reasonable not wheezable. No matter what pace, we'll finish this race.

So it was very enjoyable for me to see guys who fancied themselves as the macho type (but weren't really) power past me, shirtless, only to catch them up as I casually walked past them sat wheezing sat on a tree trunk besides the trail. See ya at the top, boys.

The walk cuts right up the hill, crossing the snaking road for buses numerous times, and takes about an hour at a reasonable pace. And you'll know when you reach the top. The number of people is unbelievable, or possibly as expected if you're expecting more people than it looks like would fit into a delicate wonder of the world.

That said, the Peruvian government came under fire not long before our visit for allowing too many visitors to the site. Nowadays, they're experimenting with visitor number caps, morning and afternoon time slots, making guides compulsory, and as we'd found in Cusco trying to get here, it would seem they're also making it as difficult as possible to get there too. Maybe that'll help.

Soon enough, we found our guide and our group and were on our way in. Despite being promised an English-speaking guide, we had one who only spoke Spanish, which meant I was (self-)allocated interpreter for Ashley, whispering into his ear so as not to disturb the group.

We made our way up, showing our tickets and into Machu Picchu itself and....it was foggy. You couldn't see a thing beyond a hundred metres in front of you. The altitude sickness, the walking in the rain, the bad food, the early alarm. Worth it?

After about an hour of following our man with a flag, he said, "Who's climbing Huayna Picchu?"

I raised my hand, "Nosotros."

"Ok, you can go now to the gate for that, where we just were."

"Ahh, ok, adios!"

We left and I explained to Ashley why.

"But it's only 8 o'clock...isn't our ticket for Huayna Picchu at eleven?" he replied.

"Yeah, it doesn't make any sense to me either but we finally don't have to follow a flag around. We're flagless! Let's go and check the gate for Huayna Picchu and then if it's closed we can just walk around on our own tour I guess."

Sure enough, it was closed, with a note that the next opening would be at 11am. We spend the next few hours exploring Machu Picchu on our own, meeting llamas close-up and taking lots of mist-filled photos of the place.

At quarter to eleven we headed back to wait on the rocks by the Huayna Picchu gate and have a snack before heading up. We needed to be fast. The walk up and down should take an hour each way, plus with the two hours back to where the minibus was picking us up at 3pm, we'd have no time to mess around.

As soon as the gate opened at 11am, we signed our names and started the quick trek up the mountain to catch the view of Machu Picchu in its entirety. Huayna Picchu is the mountain in the back of the typical Machu Picchu shot so often in books and on Instagram. Even in real life it looks super far away and very high.

Yet somehow, we made it up faster than most in around forty minutes. As soon as we reached the top we turned around to see, briefly through our poncho-tinted haze...mist.

"Well, we'd better get the camera anyway." I said to Ashley, both of us tallying up all the "bad" stuff that had happened on our Machu Picchu trip.

And then, unbelievably considering our luck so far on the trip, as soon as Ashley's camera was out, the mist cleared showing Machu Picchu in its full glory for a few lingering seconds. It was spectacular. No one else was around, and then as soon as the next people reached our platform the mist covered the sight again.

We headed back down, as quickly as possible on narrow steep stairs and paths with a flow of people coming in the other direction. Thankfully, we made it back in time to the minibus and didn't get caught in the rain again on the two hour trek back along the train tracks. We waited around until finally, everyone had arrived and we were to start our journey back to Cusco.

This time I was prepared. I had bought some coca candy to suck and help deal with the altitude sickness. I have to be honest, I'm a bit sceptical about the whole coca helping with altitude sickness thing. I'm sure there's been some research into it all, and I, of course, respect the traditions of the locals. But I can't help but feel it's an excuse for visiting foreign tourists to go home and say "Guess what? I basically did cocaine in Peru! I'm so badass!".

I have absolutely zero interest in doing cocaine (or any drug for that matter), or in pretending I'm badass because I sucked a little candy sweet that's mostly sugar. But the altitude sickness on the way to Aguas Calientes was enough to make me buy a bag of sweets to at least help me to feel like I'd *tried* to help. Whether they work or whether it's the action of sucking hard on the sweet, similar to what some people do when a plane takes off and lands, I don't know. But somehow I didn't get altitude sickness on the journey back.

The mist clearing at the top of Huayna Picchu? No rain on our train track walk back? No altitude sickness? Our luck was changing!

And then our minibus broke down. In the dark. An hour from Cusco.

Remarkably, the different minibuses all cooperate and help each other out. They are going in the same direction and to the same place, after all. Gradually, our minibus load was split between passing minibuses kind enough to stop who had a seat or two here and there.

We finally arrived back at our apartment in Cusco around 10pm. I was terrified. I ran straight into the bedroom, checked the drawers with our tech and our bags with cash, and relieved, made my way back to the main room.

"Oh...thank God! Everything is ok." I breathed a sigh of relief.

"What do you mean?" said Ashley.

"I got a text from the Airbnb host that I spotted when the bus broke down. You know when the Airbnb messages come through as a text? It just said: 'Hi Lindsay, I just wanted to tell u that unfortunately our neighbor told us that there's a problem...'. DOT DOT DOT! That's all of the Airbnb message that the text message showed me! And there was no Wifi out there so I couldn't log on to check the whole message. I honestly thought that we'd been robbed. 'Unfortunately our neighbour told us'?! And we're not there?! What else could it have been?"

"Wait, what was it then?"

"I've only just read the whole message - 'Our neighbor told us there's a problem with the cable tv.'! That's why I ran to the bedroom - to check that our tech stuff was still here."

"Why didn't you tell me?"

"Because the bus had just broken down and we were stood by the side of the road in the dark! It made no sense both of us then having to deal with worrying about this on top of that! I was planning out how I'd do Women In Language and everything...figuring out the best place to buy a cheap laptop...then do we replace stuff here or in Paraguay in two weeks? Do we get stuff delivered to get someone to bring to the airport and pick up in the UK on our way to Asia? I dunno. I was putting things in place. It was scary! Like Nicaragua all over again with the Dutch couple!"

"Aww, you could have told me! But, I totally get why you didn't. That makes sense."

As soon as we got back, it was non-stop getting ready for the first Women In Language event, that had grown way beyond my initial idea of a one day celebration of hearing females doing interesting things with language into a live four day online event with almost thirty speakers and over three hundred people in the audience. It was a huge success...and it was lucky it wasn't a few days later.

On our last weekend in Cusco before heading to Paraguay, it was threatening rain all day. The sky was grey and heavy with rain just ready to burst. Eventually, it did, and before we knew it, there was water dripping, slowly at first, but then in full force, through the light fixtures in the kitchen and the bathroom.

Frantically, we stopped cooking and turned off the hob, grabbed all the towels we had, found basins to use to gather the water, and tried not to panic. We were the first guests here and the place was flooding! What do we do?!

I took some photos of the water dripping from the lights to send to our hosts, and got one back of a hail-covered sports pitch, where they'd been when the storm hit. The field had been evacuated and the game postponed. Upon seeing the photos, our hosts apologised and explained that this had never happened before. Thankfully, the light in the bedroom wasn't affected, as this was right above the bed and would have soaked right through to the mattress.

So after an eventful evening collecting water, emptying basins down the sink, and putting them back to catch the next drops, we were able to get a good night's sleep on a dry bed before heading to Paraguay.

Paraguay

Season 1, Episode 7: Guarani in the Heart of South America

Of all the places in Latin America we were due to visit, Paraguay was top of my list of places I was looking forward to. It's not quite like the rest of the region, I mean, nowhere is really, each country is unique in its own ways, but Paraguay stood out to me for a number of years before finally visiting.

In Paraguay, they speak Spanish, but also the indigenous language Guarani. And it's not like the expected story of "Oh, Spanish came along and now the indigenous language is struggling for survival." Not quite. Of course, Guarani has had its struggles for survival in the past, and still does, but the present is a different story to most languages in similar situations. Estimates suggest around 90% of the population speak Guarani *and* Spanish to some degree.

When we arrived then, bright-eyed with my "mba'éichapa" (hello, how are you) on the tip of my tongue, I was delighted to see everything around us at the airport in three languages: Guarani, English, and Spanish. This didn't last long however, and the conversation with the immigration officer happened in Spanish with barely a second glance at the fact I greeting him in Guarani. On the other side of immigration, signs resumed to regular international airport mode of English and the one most popular language spoken in the country of the airport, in this case, Spanish.

We paid a visit to the cash machine and casually withdrew a cool one million guaraníes (yes, the money is called Guarani too, and yes, it's a very high currency), and headed over to a small cafe booth to get a bite of breakfast before facing battle with the inevitable onslaught of overpriced taxi drivers each vying for our attention.

As we sat down on the high coffee stools, the terere culture soon became apparent. Much like their Argentinian neighbours, Paraguayans love drinking yerba mate. The main difference however, is that Paraguayans commonly drink it cold rather than hot. And it's not just a beverage for sipping in your back garden or in a cafe on a warm afternoon, oh no. Terere is a drink that must be with your person at all times...or that's how it seems at least with the number of flasks sat next to waiting passengers, either taking up a seat next to them or on the floor by their feet. Some flasks even guarded empty seats solo, a sure sign that their owner would be back and has probably nipped to the toilet or to check the departure board. Accompanying each terere flask is a small cup with a metal straw (called a bombilla) at least half full of yerba mate leaves. It was what we'd seen at the Paraguayan restaurant in New York at the beginning but amplified.

As we sat with our coffee and tea, instant signs we weren't from here, other passengers and airport staff came to ask the barista to top up their flasks with fresh water, which he calmly obliged to each time.

Once our out-of-place drinks were consumed, we headed out to face our least favourite bit of arriving anywhere for the first time: the taxi drivers. There's no bus from Asunción airport, and although I'd read somewhere that you can walk out to the main road and hail a taxi for half the price, we weren't really into the idea of that in the rising heat of the day, so instead, our only choice was to make a deal with a taxi driver waiting outside the airport.

Via our messages, I'd asked our Airbnb hosts how much we should expect to pay for a taxi from the airport and he suspected around 120,000 guaraníes. So when the first guy quoted us 120,000 guaraníes, we were quite happy with that and ready to hop into his car. And then something remarkable happened.

The taxi driver held my phone looking at the address and discussed directions with the other drivers all waiting for passengers. A few minutes later, he handed my phone back and did something I'd never had happen anywhere.

"100,000 guaraníes. Not 120,000. It's only 100,000."

"Qué?" I couldn't quite believe what he was saying to me. A taxi driver lowering a price?! Outside an airport?! Unheard of!

"Yes, yes, is it ok?"

"Of course! Let's go," I replied, beginning to pick up my bags and head towards the taxi before he changed his mind.

Baristas giving free terere top up water? Fair taxi drivers? Paraguay was off to a good start.

***

I didn't know what to expect from Asunción. There's very little written about Paraguay, especially in the way of tourist guides, and especially compared to its much larger neighbours Brazil and Argentina. Even Bolivia gets its own travel guide, but Paraguay? Often part of multi-region guides and nothing more. So I hadn't had much of a chance to read about Asunción for myself before arriving, which meant I'd had plenty of time to build it up in my head as a jigsaw of all the places we'd so far visited in Latin America.

I was expecting a handful of Cuban architecture, with a pinch of Salvadoran grit, and a squeeze of San José's hustle and bustle. I couldn't have been more wrong.

As our taxi drove closer and closer to our Airbnb, the houses got bigger, the cars fancier, and the cobbled streets more cobbley. Every second house had a booth out front for a security guard, who often sat calmly, arms resting on lap, hat just covering the eyes so as to catch a wink of sleep without being too obvious (it was obvious), and terere flask and cup resting by the chair leg.

Eventually we found our place, and after being introduced to our hosts, made our little apartment our own. Our accommodation in Asunción was one of my favourites. It was a reasonably sized open plan bungalow in the back garden of our host's house. Oh, and it was beautifully designed.

After dropping off our bags, we headed out to discover the local area. Ashley had found a park on the map that he wanted to scout out for running, and there was a shopping mall nearby that might have a decent supermarket where we could buy food.

The park was lovely, but the shopping mall was the big surprise. International brands sat besides local big names all surrounded by marble floors and skylights. In one shop, I noticed a large sign behind the counter displaying the minimum wage that staff would be paid there. It equated to roughly £10 per day. Nothing in that shop sold for that price.

There was no supermarket, but there was a food court, so eager to get our teeth into the Paraguayan treats I'd read so much about (and we'd tried right at the start of the trip in New York) - chipa, sopa paraguaya, and chipa guazu - we decided to eat there. Yet, there was no Paraguayan food available without meat (meat is also pretty big on the menu in Paraguay), so bizarrely, we ended up eating Japanese food on our first day in Paraguay. Another unexpected twist to the Paraguayan tale so far. Paraguay was *still* off to a good start.

"I'm gonna speak to that guy that served us in Guarani again when we finish," I said to Ashley, as I sipped my miso. I was keen to try out my lingo, despite the complete lack of signage in the language since leaving immigration at the airport.

"Yeah? What are you gonna say?"

"Well, when I paid, I said thank you in Guarani and he was all like 'Oooh, wow!' so I'm gonna say 'Thank you, the food was delicious'."

"Ok, do it!"

I did. It was well-received. I'd just spoken Guarani to someone in real life for the first time. And it was well-received.

That first week however, I didn't get to speak too much Guarani. You see, the thing about Paraguay is most people, especially in cities, are bilingual to at least some degree and the more populated the place, the more Spanish is spoken over Guarani, at least in public.

From what everyone told me who I met and spoke with about this during my time there, it seems a pretty common tale that Spanish is the language of the street - the public facing language, and Guarani is the language of the home - the private, more personal language.

After our first week settling into life in Paraguay buying a box of terere mix from the supermarket, exploring the local Parque de la Salud, and getting some work done, it was time for me to go back to school.

I'd booked for a week of lessons at IDIPAR, the only language school in the country that teaches Guarani to foreigners, but certainly not the only *school*. Guarani is taught across schools for local children in the country, despite the fact that it is primarily a home language. There is an immense and apparent pride for their language, and rightfully so. Paraguay is the only Spanish-speaking country in the Americas to have an indigenous language on a par with Spanish in terms of recognition. It's quite remarkable.

But it wasn't always this way. The Triple Alliance War saw Paraguay face Argentina, Brazil and Uruguay and lose an estimated 90% of their male population. This would have easily been the demise of Guarani, with men from other countries breeding with local Paraguayan ladies. As it turned out, it was the mother that helped to save the language here - speaking Guarani to their children. Down the line, the dictatorship of Alfredo Stroessner, commonly referred to as El Stronato by locals, from 1954 to 1989 saw indigenous populations suffer massacres and slavery. Yet, despite various setbacks in history, Paraguay remains a rare case where the local indigenous language has been raised in profile and seen as an identity marker by the wider population rather than crushed almost completely by a colonial or "bigger" language coming in.

Back to my first day at school and I was glad to discover that I'd been given the afternoon slot - four hours of lessons starting at 1pm and ending at 5pm. This meant I could catch up on a bit of work in the morning, grab an early lunch and head into the centre for my lessons around 12 o'clock. Despite their frequency, the bus into the centre took a variable amount of time depending on how many people wanted to get on and off on any given day. The bus rule in Paraguay seems to be: flag a bus down like you would a taxi...despite numerous stickers on each bus stating otherwise.

The other surprise about the buses was how the price changes each day. There was a range of around three different bus types for my route - one with a fancy turnstile and excessive barriers and bars all over the place (that one cost 3,000 guaraníes); one with no turnstile, no bell, sometimes not even a string to pull to tell the driver you're getting off (that one cost 2,000 guaraníes); and one somewhere in between the two that cost 2,200.

I soon learnt from observation that you get on the bus at the front, pay the driver, sometimes get given a ticket and other times not, then sit down and pull the string or ring the bell when you want to get off, and exit through the door at the back of the bus.

The first day I took the bus into the centre however, I didn't have as much luck. The traffic was really busy and after fifteen minutes of waiting, no bus had come with the right number or destination. I was beginning to panic - I'd definitely be late now and there's not much more I hate than being late, especially on the first day of something new.

Paraguay didn't have Uber or anything similar that we knew of either so we couldn't even run back home and hop on the wifi to call a taxi. Instead, we had to wait it out and hail a taxi, remarkably difficult considering how easy it is to get a bus to stop by the side of the road. Eventually we got one, and I arrived around twenty minutes late on day one. Great.

I'd been imagining walking into a room full of eager Guarani students looking and rolling eyes and tutting at my tardiness. However, as it turned out, I was the only student in the afternoon Guarani classes that week, which meant I got my teacher all to myself.

We started with the alphabet. I knew the alphabet. I was beginning to wonder if this was a mistake. I soon realised however that for the first time of all my time learning Guarani, I had a genuine speaker right in front of me. I decided to enjoy it and not worry if I was repeating anything I'd previously taught myself.

Ashley had shared the taxi with me to head into the centre and get some film footage for Language Stories and had agreed to meet me outside the school at 5pm. Sure enough, there he was as I left the school on day one, waiting outside, keen to tell me about the cafes and places he'd discovered in the centre.

Not sure where to pick up the bus yet having not caught it on the way in and seen where it would drop me off, I opted to pay for a taxi back, slightly disconcerted that a taxi there and back each day would almost double the cost of my lessons in the first place.

Still, it proved to be a useful decision as upon telling the taxi driver why we were here, he helpfully pointed out a bookshop, El Lector, that stocked Guarani books, and willingly listened to my basic Guarani phrases, practised now on my fourth person in real life (I'm including the passport officer, it totally counts).

***

On day two, I left a little earlier, eager not to make the same mistake and miss the bus by just a few minutes. Almost as soon as we reached the bus shelter, the bus came down the road, my arm went out, and much easier than the taxi the previous day, I was on my way. This time solo, as Ashley was staying behind to get some work done.

Cities always look different by bus. You're higher up than when you're walking or in a car. You see people get on and off the bus and can't help but wonder where they're going and why. You're detached from the city, watching from afar it seems until you step off and are instantly in a different place, like you've walked through a portal.

I wasn't sure exactly where to get off, so I stayed up front and asked the driver to tell me when we hit the right street, which he did. I'd obviously ended up on a pretty speedy bus as I arrived much earlier than the day before. Thankfully, there was a bakery on the corner of the street where my school was. I headed and, on the hunt for chipa.

Paraguayan food isn't exactly as well-celebrated as its neighbours Argentina or Brazil. You may find an Argentinian steak house or Brazilian restaurant in a city near you but there's not even a Paraguayan restaurant in London as far as I know. Of course, there's the two Paraguayan restaurants I found in New York but that's a little far for me. If I'm going there, I may as well fly to Paraguay.

However, I think that deserves to change. Paraguayan food is really good. You love those Argentinian steaks? They're all about meat here with hunks of cow flung across barbeques. There's a whole range of foods that can teach you some Guarani too like chipa guazu, vori vori, and kiveve. And, of course, you get to wash it all down with a shared terere.

The bakery was full of various Paraguay style breads and cakes. I opted for four chipa and a handful of crispy bread rings, I later discovered are called rosquitas, which were similar to something we'd had in Ecuador with Mariuxi. I saved some of my snacks for later to share with Ashley and headed into the school before 1pm.

My teacher had seen me leave with Ashley the previous day and asked where we were staying in the city. When I explained how I'd had to get a taxi, and asked if the bus picked up in the same place as it dropped off that afternoon, she told me ..."No." and instructed me on where to get it instead.

Following her instructions to the letter, four hours later, I found myself stood outside a shop and a small cafe by the side of the road, with no bus shelter this time or even any kind of indication that you'd expect a bus to stop here. As more and more people gathered, I soon figured that this must be a place to wait for something, surely it had to be a bus.

Sure enough, moments later, a bus pulled up with the right number on it and I got on, heading home after a successful first day using the Asunción buses. Hooray!

I was ready to enjoy the rest of my week and my little school and bus routine. A few hours of work in the morning after a quick run around Parque de la Salud, then a bite to eat and off on the bus to school, heading back in rush hour to be home in time for dinner before a glance at my notes and writing a few sentences in Guarani before bed.

The next day however, Wednesday, would be a little different. A few days after arriving in Asunción the week before, we'd discovered that a huge concert was coming to the city the following couple of weeks - exactly when we'd be there! We booked tickets for two of the three nights, keen not to miss the chance to see The Killers and Gorillaz and many other bands in what was quickly becoming one of my new favourite places.

The first of those concerts? Wednesday night. The plan was to head straight to the venue after my lessons at the school in the afternoon and meet Ashley there. Having no working phones meant that we were relying on good old fashioned Planning In Advance!

My lessons finished on time, I caught the bus minutes after arriving at my newfound bus stop from the day before, and settled in, glad to have found a seat.

Until I started to notice the road we were heading up didn't look much like the one I'd grown vaguely familiar with over the past couple of days. When we passed a huge graveyard, I checked my map app on my phone.

Oh no!

I'd got on the right *number* bus but not the right street direction. You see, (not so) logically, the number 30 had two routes, because it would definitely be too difficult to give each street route a seperate number.

Thankfully, I'd spotted just in time, and squeezed my way off through the now sardine-tin-esque packed bus as we waited in traffic at the huge graveyard.

If I crossed the road here, I could make it to the street I needed to be on in around fifteen minutes walking fast. And I did! I wove my way through the streets at record pace and was grateful to find a bus stop (this time we're talking an obvious one with a bus shelter) right where I joined the road I should have been on. Now all I needed was the right bus.

As time was wearing on and I could flag down a bus from anywhere (hopefully), I decided it best to just walk up the street, turning back every time I heard a bus to see if it was the right one. A few minutes later, a number 30 bus appeared in the distance. I held out my hand as it approached and instantly regretted it. The bus was packed. I spent the brief journey holding on firmly to the door bar with one hand and my other hand flat against the glass of the open back door. There was no way I could pay the driver if I tried. After a few painfully slow minutes stopping and starting, I hopped off the next time the bus stopped, figuring I could get there quicker myself walking.

I reunited with Ashley soon after outside the bike shop where we'd agreed to meet (so he'd have somewhere to look around. Just in case I was late. Worthy plan.) and we headed into the venue.

Asuncionico was held in an outdoor field space on the outskirts of the city near the Parque Ñu Guasu with three stages and numerous food and merchandise stalls (including one with terere, naturally).

We grabbed a veggie burger from a stand by La Pink Cow, a restaurant I'd found on Instagram but been unable to find in the city centre, and we had a great evening with everyone crossing their fingers the rain would hold off, which thankfully it did.

There's not many cities across the world where I'd feel safe walking home at 2am, but Asunción had become one of them and so we did. Most of the way there were other people making their way back into the city by foot from the concert too, and when we got close to the neighbourhood, the security guards were still sat peacefully in various booths outside some houses so we felt safe. We shared nods of acknowledgement with some of them we were getting familiar with.

***

After another couple of days at school, it was time to leave the city. Ashley had found a trail running race in the nearby town of San Bernardino. I'd booked us two nights in a cabin at a campsite run by a German and Swiss couple.

When we eventually got on the right bus (Can you tell buses are fun in Paraguay?!), we were on our way to the affectionately nicknamed San Ber.

Paraguay is a landlocked country, which means no beaches. Well, no *sea* beaches at least. There are however a number of beaches to be enjoyed on rivers and lakes. Most of the country (that's not the dry El Chaco) is bordered by rivers, and the Lago Ypacaraí proves itself to be popular with Asunción folk on the weekend and during holidays.

It's also popular with German speakers. And, yes, some Nazis may have been known to flee to South America, including Paraguay after World War Two, but that's not why Germans come now. Although when we asked a couple of Austrian travellers at the campsite (where we were the only non-German speaking guests) why Paraguay, this little known country in South America, is so popular with German-speakers, they had no idea. Still, it does mean that San Bernardino gets its fair share of German bakeries and Bavarian restaurants, so there's not too much to complain about.

We caught the bus from Asunción to the town of Altos, unable to go directly to San Bernardino despite its popularity. I guess most people that make it out here have their own cars. After a brief stop at a supermarket to stock up on supplies so Ash would be suitably nourished before his run, we started walking towards where our campsite was - somewhere in between Altos and San Bernardino.

Along the way, I spotted some colourful decorative parrots and flowers at a stand by the side of the road. As we got closer and a man came out of the house behind the stand, I soon discovered they were carved out of light wood and painted by him. And this being Paraguay, a place where tourists aren't exactly commonplace, they were a fair price. I purchased two.

Our campsite was beautiful, tucked away along a dirt track, a stone's throw from where Ashley's race was due to start the following morning. The views were spectacular, the owners and guests were all friendly, and our little cabin was lovely. We couldn't have asked for more.

The following morning, we woke up early ready for Ashley's race. After getting fed, dressed and ready to go, I picked up the extra cushion I'd thrown on the floor before sleeping the night before to place it back on the bed. Suddenly I leapt back in shock.

Underneath the cushion I'd just lifted was a huge millipede, curled up, barely moving, but still looking ready to pounce and transform into a beast twenty times his size and eat my head.

"What do we do? Pass me my shoe, I'll kill it." I said to Ashley, braver than I was feeling.

"You can't kill these things, they could be poisonous." Ashley replied.

"What?! That's all the more reason to kill it!"

"Yeah, but if you don't kill it first time, what if it gets angry and bites you with its poison? We're miles from anywhere, you can't get much medical help quickly here."

After a little more convincing I agreed to leave the millipede at peace and we set off on the long journey to the start line. I use the term "long journey" sarcastically. It took us mere minutes.

Like I mentioned, many Paraguayans living in Asunción have a second home in the countryside, especially around San Bernardino and Lago Ypacaraí. The starting and finishing point for the race was clearly one of these homes. The views across the lake were even better than from our campsite further up on the other side of the dirt track road. I sat there enjoying my Guarani courses on Memrise taking in the view while Ashley had fun on the trail run. But before that, something happened.

"Hola! Hey, you're from England, right?" a guy said as he approached us with a camera in hand.

"Yeah we are." said Ashley.

"Did you know we've never had anyone from England compete in the race series? You're the first person ever!" he replied, smiling.

After a little more conversation, he asked if he could interview us for the Facebook Page. I said yes as long as it could be trilingual.

I introduced us in Guarani, Ash introduced himself in Spanish and then with a little English to wrap up, we'd just been interviewed for the first time on a trip when we'd interviewed so many others ourselves!

An hour or so later, I headed over to the finish line to wait for Ashley coming in. One guy sped in, followed by another, followed by...Ashley! He came third!

As exciting as it was that Ashley had come third in a trail run which, he said, involved climbing over fences, dodging spiky plants, and balancing his way through muddy patches, it did mean we had to wait around for the prizes to be awarded. They played Animals by Martin Garrix. Multiple times. Then finally it was time and Ashley was invited up to the podium to collect his trophy! I was glad we'd planned a stop in London on our way to Asia if only to drop that trophy off.

Multiple Paraguayans asked for our photo as we began to leave, something that hadn't really happened elsewhere in Latin America, or in Paraguay in general.

Dizzy from our newfound fame, we eventually headed back across to the campsite for a late breakfast, which we hoped would still be served seeing as we'd had to leave too early to enjoy it before the race.

We headed up the path as the German lady owner headed down to meet us.

"How did it go?!" she asked before spotting the trophy. She gasped, "Ohhh! Did you win?!"

"Yes. I came third! First in my age category too," Ash replied.

"Wow! That's amazing. I must get a photo!"

I leaned into Ashley, so used to it after being asked to each time at our encounters with the cameraman and camera phones at the race.

"Oh no, just the winner." she said, brushing me away with her hand in the air.

"Oh, ok." I stepped aside to let her take a photo of just Ashley, my newfound literal trophy wife fame over sooner than it had begun.

After breakfast, we made our way into San Bernardino itself to see what it was like for the first time. We started to walk down the dirt track towards the main road to catch the bus when a pick-up truck pulled over and offered us a lift to the end of the road.

Waiting at the bus stop at the end of the road, the guy who'd filmed us pulled up on his moped.

"Where are you going? Asunción?" he asked.

"No, just into San Bernardino. We're just waiting for the bus."

"Let me call my friend, she's probably going that way, maybe she can give you a lift."

She did give us a lift. Paraguayans are beyond nice.

San Bernardino was a pleasant town, which you could tell gets busier during holiday time. We stopped for an ice cream, me not being able to resist a *paleta* (ice lolly) since Mexico, and headed back after a couple of hours.

It had all been an enjoyable respite from our millipede friend who we hoped by now would have got bored and made his way out of our home for the weekend. We'd even given him extra time to leave after spying him still there when we came back at breakfast. Tentatively opening the door we saw him, right where we'd left him, casually chilling by the wall.

"What do we do? Can I kill him now?" I asked.

"We don't need to kill it. We just need a way to get it out...I spotted a broom outside. Let me check."

Sure enough there was a broom resting outside our cabin, clearly for situations like this.

I stood on the bed as Ashley shooed our visitor out of the room. That millipede would give Galápagos iguanas a run for their money the way it was moving its hips as it wiggled and shimmied out of the room. And it was gone. Hooray!

Before we arrived in Paraguay, I was a little worried that Ashley wouldn't like it, or worse, that *I* wouldn't like it. I'd built it up so much because of my affinity with Guarani and the fact it would be the last place we visited in Latin America. That day when Ashley won his trophy however, I knew he'd fallen as in love with the place as I had almost on arrival.

***

We were glad to be back in our apartment in Asunción, where we'd left most of our luggage, and spent Easter there along with our second trip to Asuncionico (this time it was Gorillaz), before venturing further afield to Encarnación. Yet another adventure with the buses ensued, and eventually we got there so I won't go into detail. Long story short, it was a mission. If you'll pardon the pun. You see, the reason we were going to Encarnación was just that: missions.

Encarnación is the third largest city in Paraguay after Asunción and Ciudad del Este. Because Easter made travel difficult, we only had the time to explore one of these other big cities. We opted for Encarnación as we could visit the Jesuit Ruins at Trinidad, which would be helpful for the Language Stories episode. The Jesuit missionaries played an interesting role in the history of Guarani. In their efforts to convert locals, they wrote down Guarani, a language that had previously been primarily an oral one.

Encarnación has a similar vibe to a British seaside town in terms of holiday-ness, but very different in terms of the lack of donkeys and sticks of rock and arcades.

Manchester is the third largest city in the UK. Encarnacion is not Manchester. It's probably more like the size of Lincoln, at least in terms of population. That smaller population means it's walkable, calm, and quite different to Asunción. It also acts as a great base to explore the south of the country a little more. We took a couple of trips out from Encarnación. The first to the Jesuit Ruins at Trinidad, supposedly one of the least visited UNESCO sites in the world, as planned.

Having researched the history quite a bit for Language Stories, it meant a lot to visit the Ruins for me, and in some ways, I found it more moving than other larger better known sites in Latin America, like Machu Picchu. For one thing, I didn't have to walk along two hours of train tracks in the rain or suffer a bout of altitude sickness to get to Trinidad, so that was a bonus.

Our second trip out from Encarnación was to the Argentinian town of Posadas on the other side of the river (I told you rivers are borders here). We left as early as we could and took the train across the bridge to Argentina, because there's not many opportunities in life when you can "pop" to Argentina, so why not? We knew we wouldn't have much time, but were planning a stroll of around four or five hours to see the city before heading back to Paraguay for a cheaper dinner. Only something happened.

After lots of extended glances at our passports and our significant lack of luggage (I'm pretty sure my Guarani "hello" to the Paraguayan officer is what finally got us stamped out and on our way), we were free to enter Argentina on the other side.

We made our way towards what looked most like the centre of town and took a quick glance at our phones to check the time.

"Oh...hang on a minute...when did we leave?" I asked Ashley.

"At 10 o'clock, right?"

I thought for a moment, "I think we've gone forward an hour…"

After a quick check at the world time zones on my phone, we discovered that yes, we had indeed gone forward one hour as we crossed the border. Allowing time for the border that had been a lot slower than expected, we had a grand total of two hours in Argentina.

We laughed it off, walked around a bit, and looked for a coffee shop. Since Costa Rica, Ashley had developed a hobby to order simply 'a coffee' in each country and see how things differ from place to place. Not 'an americano', not 'a latte', just 'a coffee'.

So we were on the hunt for an Argentinian coffee. And we ended up in Cafe Havanna, a cafe we'd already enjoyed in Paraguay, but as it turned out is actually an Argentinian brand, so it totally counts as a coffee in Argentina.

We returned back to Asunción on one of the best buses we travelled on all year - I'm talking USB chargers, plugs, working wifi, snacks, water, huge reclining seats...very jazzy. When we arrived back in Asunción, we only had a couple of days left before the start of our journey to Singapore.

From Asunción to São Paulo to Lisbon to London to Kuala Lumpur to Singapore, it was always going to be a long journey. But we didn't quite expect what happened next.

The 89 Hour Journey

It all started so well. We arrived at Silvio Pettirossi Airport in Asuncion in good time; checked in to be pleasantly surprised that our luggage would go all the way to London despite our fight to São Paulo being operated by a different airline; and relaxed, enjoying for the last time the sight of terere flasks accompanying each family.

The flight to São Paulo went without a hitch and we even got given an unexpected snack and a drink. So far everything was much better than we'd expected.

Knowing now that we didn't have to check out at the airport in São Paulo to get our luggage, on arrival there, we followed the signs to transfers and looked for our flight on the board. And that's when it happened. Cancelled.

Just one flight cancelled on the board. And it was our flight.

What happens now? Our luggage was somewhere on the runway, there was no staff member from the airline due to fly us to Lisbon and London (I'll name and shame them, TAP), and no other member of staff knew where to send us.

"Excuse me. Our flight is cancelled. Where we go now?" I stumbled out in broken Portuguese, already weak after years of gathering dust in my brain, and now even more so after nine months of Spanish.

"Errr.." the lady leant forward on her desk curving her neck towards the departures board.

She was giving away entries to a holiday giveaway, not exactly likely to be a regular member of airport staff or to know where to send me but there was no one else to ask.

"Where is the TAP office?" I asked again, trying to help her by being more accurate with my questioning.

"Terminal 3. Straight down and you will see signs."

"How far?"

"Fifteen minutes walk, maybe."

"Ok," I replied, already walking away and translating for Ashley.

There was no TAP office where she'd said. I asked at another desk where the staff directed me back to where we'd come from initially. We were going round in circles.

Finally I asked a man in a hi-vis jacket who was carrying a walkie-talkie. He told us to wait by a desk on the other side of the room and someone from TAP would be here shortly.

There were already four passengers waiting by that desk, who all looked equally as frustrated and nervous as we probably did. Three women were travelling together to Italy and would miss their connection from Lisbon to Rome and the man travelling alone would miss the same connection as us to London.

Where were the TAP staff?!

After what felt like an eternity, a woman in a typical airline uniform arrived with a tight skirt and tailored jacket topped off by her perfectly straight bob. She was soon followed by a man wearing a waistcoat. He had short tight curls and it was clear from their body language that she was his superior and he was her dogsbody.

There were false hope rumours that the three Argentinian ladies might be able to get to Rome on an Alitalia flight leaving that night and that we could travel on British Airways to London, also leaving that night.

Now I'm writing this in retrospect, I don't know why they told us this. It was clear that they had no power to get us on those flights. Yet at the time we all clung onto the slightest hope that they might. Until they told us we'd be leaving the airport.

"Don't worry, TAP will pay for everything. Your food, accommodation, travel costs, phone calls, anything you need."

"But...I don't want accommodation, I want to get to London. We *need* to get to London, we have a connecting flight. Never mind food, accommodation...will TAP pay for a new flight if we miss our next one because of *your* cancellation?"

"Yes, yes. When you arrive in London, they will sort everything for you."

We had no choice but to believe her and follow our group of now around ten lost transit passengers to immigration, luggage collection, and finally a coach waiting outside for us all.

"How long will you be staying in Brazil?" the woman asked me at the immigration booth.

"I have no idea. We're with them. They cancelled our flight."

"Oh, I'm sorry. Welcome to Brazil." She stamped my passport with the stamp we didn't want. She was the first person to apologise.

When we arrived at the hotel, it was chaotic. Queues of families, couples, businessmen and women, all with equal floorspace of suitcases and luggage stood in line at reception, many of us looking longingly towards the dining area, wondering if our dinner tonight was paid for.

I looked at Ashley, "I miss Paraguay."

Our room was probably the best hotel room we had during our whole trip so far, and the food was good so we tried not to complain too much. Besides, there was still a slim chance we could leave early and be put on another British Airways flight direct to London the following day, meaning we'd *just* make our connection with Malaysian Airlines to Singapore.

The only problem was that our booking with TAP was to end at London Gatwick and the British Airways flight landed in London Heathrow. This wasn't a problem for us, in fact it was an advantage - our Malaysian Airlines flight connection departed from Heathrow! However, TAP was obliged to take us to where we'd paid to be taken: Gatwick.

We'd experienced a similar situation years earlier when travelling with Ryanair to Brussels. Due to a small aircraft crash at Charleroi, we'd been redirected to Brussels Airport (2km from the centre) and not Charleroi (36km from the centre) where we were due to land. Despite now being much closer to the centre, where I would guess from what passengers were saying is where 90% of passengers were going, the staff wouldn't let us exit the plane because they were contractually obliged to take us to Charleroi. We sat on the runway for two hours, meaning by the time we finally landed at Charleroi, it was too late to head to our accommodation (it was an Airbnb and he'd messaged saying we couldn't arrive that late) and we had to spend the night in the airport.

So we had no choice. We'd be going to Gatwick. They were never going to get us on the British Airways flight to Heathrow. But that didn't stop us from trying.

First thing in the morning, we headed down to reception to join the queue of equally disgruntled passengers waiting for the one phone continually connected to TAP. After what felt like an eternity it was our turn. I picked up the receiver.

"Hello?"

"Hello ma'am. How can I help you."

"Hello. We have a connection in London that we're now going to very likely miss. We need to get to London as soon as possible. We're meeting family in Singapore that we haven't seen for nine months who have travelled there especially to see us."

It wasn't exactly a lie. Ashley's mum had booked a trip to Southeast Asia before we had decided to head out to the region. She extended her stay by a few days at the end of her trip to meet us in Singapore when we arrived.

"I know, ma'am. Everyone is very busy."

"Yes, I understand. Are there any flights to London from São Paulo today that you can put us on? Yesterday we were told we might be added to a BA flight leaving at..." I looked up at the clock behind the reception desk, "...2pm? I think?"

"Ahh yes, I can see that on the schedule. I'll see what I can do for you and your husband, ma'am."

"Ok. Thank you. Obrigada. And how will we know if you get us on that flight? Will you call the hotel? Email us?"

"We'll inform the hotel and they'll call your room. Then you'll be taken to the airport for check in for your flight."

"Ok, excellent! So if it leaves at 2pm...then we should expect a call by what time at the latest?"

"I'll be back in touch with the hotel before 11am for you, ma'am."

"Thank you so much! Obrigada! We'll be waiting!"

Feeling quite successful and pleased with myself, I passed the phone to the next angry passenger behind me as I turned back around to Ashley.

"We have to wait here 'til 11am. They're going to contact the hotel, who'll call our room if they manage to get us on that BA flight."

"Ok, cool. That's good news, I guess. So will they email the hotel or call or what?"

"I dunno...he just said 'contact'."

"But, hang on a minute. How are they going to do that if that person is just constantly on the phone to other people? And does the hotel have any other contact with TAP?"

"Good question." I replied, the self-satisfaction beginning to fade.

We headed back over to the reception desk.

"Excuse me, are TAP emailing you confirmation when they get flights confirmed?"

The man behind reception looked confused, "No, no emails."

"Oh...err...fax machine?!" we asked, checking each other up and down to be sure we hadn't been transported back to 1987.

"No. We only have this phone for TAP."

We couldn't believe what we were hearing.

"So you only have this one phone line of communication with TAP? How are they supposed to let you know when they get us all on new flights when the phone is constantly in use?"

The man shrugged, "I'm sorry. I don't know. We're doing all that we can but it's up to them to get you booked up and out of here. I know it's a difficult situation."

It wasn't his fault. We thanked him and left for our room with a small glimmer of hope that we might get that call before 11am. We never did.

At 11.30am, we headed back down to reception and despite the current lack of queue for the phone, realised after thirty minutes that the guy currently holding it was doing just that - holding it. He wasn't letting that phone in the hands of anyone else until he was booked up and out of here. We headed for lunch instead of waiting, and after eating, he was still hogging the phone. This was getting ridiculous.

"Excuse me, what happens if we leave and go to the airport? Is there a TAP office? Someone we can speak to there? Because..." I signalled to the man at the other end of the reception desk with my eyes, "nothing is happening here."

"You can catch the shuttle to the airport at any time. You're free to leave, but as far as I know, TAP will only pay for your food and accommodation here."

"That's fine. We can sleep in the airport. We don't want them to pay for accommodation, We want them to pay for a new flight! When is the next shuttle?"

"Another ten minutes from now."

"Perfect."

We were ready to leave, flightlessly heading to the airport.

The queue at the TAP office in the airport wasn't much different. Some savvy travellers presumably from our cancelled flight were already there, their children swinging from luggage trolleys, their bags dumped in front of them in the queue, and their arms wearily resting upon the raised handles of their suitcases.

After at least an hour and a half in the queue, finally it was our turn. As it turned out, we *had* already been booked on a new TAP flight that was due to leave very soon, too soon in fact considering our arrival time at the airport. It's always nice to be informed of these things well in advance.

We were given new tickets for the next flight and informed with great confidence that our connecting airline (Malaysian Airlines) would sort us out getting to Singapore if we headed to *their* office at Gatwick as soon as we arrived and showed them the piece of paper we'd been given from TAP as evidence of our cancelled flight.

"So we arrive in Gatwick and go to the Malaysian Airlines office, show them this piece of paper and they'll put us on a new flight?"

"Yes, yes, exactly." the lady replied, attentive enough to be believed, but still rushed enough to make me believe this was a line to get us out and the next passengers in.

We were due to arrive in Gatwick at 11pm on our new flight. There was no chance the Malaysian Airlines office would be open until 8am at the earliest the following morning, which would no doubt be another day of stress and being a responsibility no one wanted to take care of.

"This is a piece of paper. What is this?! Like a Gentleman's Airline Code?! "Not a problem, fine sir! Cancellations happen, we shall cover your mistakes, my friendly airline friend!" It doesn't seem right." Ashley said as we walked away from the TAP desk towards check in.

"I feel like we should ring Malaysian Airlines as soon as we get the chance. Maybe when we get to Rio? We have a few hours and we won't have our luggage or anything to worry about."

Oh yes, I forgot that bit. We now had *three* flights between us and London, not just two. São Paulo to Rio de Janeiro, Rio to Porto, Porto to London.

We arrived in Rio and after grabbing some food, sat down in the quietest spot we could find (read: two seats right in front of an eternally grinding coffee machine) and called Malaysian Airlines. This proved to be a good move.

The man on the phone told me that if we didn't make our originally booked flight (departing just eight hours from then, there was no chance we would make it) then we'd be charged a £100 or more "no show fee" per passenger. Yup.

"What?! But it's not our fault!" I protested, my patience having been chiselled at heavily over the previous forty-eight hours or so.

"That doesn't matter. If you've booked a flight, you have a responsibility to be on that flight otherwise we charge you a "no show fee"."

"But...you still have the money we paid for the original tickets. It's not like you could have sold those tickets! This makes no sense!"

I explained our situation and how we wanted to be put on the same flight out the following day, allowing us a whole night to get from Gatwick to Heathrow.

"Ok, let me check the system. You will have to pay for the flight changes but it'll save you money because you've let us know so you won't have to pay the "no show fee"."

"Good?" I questioned, unsure of what is good service with an airline by this point, "Well, we've got this piece of paper..."

The hallowed piece of paper, so keenly promoted by TAP as our 'get out of jail free card' when it came to getting on a new flight to Asia meant nothing to Malaysian Airlines.

"No, there's no such agreement between airlines."

We knew it.

It cost us over £400 each to rebook our tickets, well over two thirds of the original ticket prices we paid when we'd booked them six months earlier back in Mexico. We had no choice.

"And what if, worst case scenario, the flights we're about to get on to London are also cancelled? Do we have to rebook again? And pay again?"

"Yes, but let us know so we can avoid that "no show fee" again."

"Oh, good." But not really.

***

Thankfully our flight from Rio went ahead without a hitch and remarkably, ten hours later we were in Europe. I've never been so happy to be on European soil.

"Costa!" Ashley near shouted as we made our way out of the arrivals gate.

Sure enough, there was a Costa Coffee right there, serving Pastel de Nata too.

"What's a flat black?! I've gone away for a year and coffee has changed!"

I smiled at his reveling in his newfound coffee knowledge.

"It doesn't say what beans they're using, what roast they are...nothing! Take me back to Martinez!" Ashley said with a jokey edge.

Cafe Martinez had become his favourite coffee shop in Paraguay due to their range of beans on display, the variety of methods to prepare the coffee, and the table service. Swanky stuff.

After a coffee at Costa, a stroll in the undeniably fresh Portuguese April air outside, and hours waiting and charging phones and the iPad on rotation, it was time for our last flight of this leg of our journey. London, baby!

Just as I'd never been so delighted to "feel" myself in Europe as we arrived in Porto, I felt a different kind of comfort at Gatwick.

When I went to Costa Rica at eighteen, I couldn't help but notice how big British number plates were when I returned after three months away from seeing them everyday. Nowadays, I always make a note to look at number plates when I arrive back home and see how big they look. They still look bigger than everywhere else.

My mum was waiting for us at Gatwick and kindly drove us to Heathrow, where we enjoyed another Costa together (this time with a sandwich in place of a pastel de nata) and dumped bags of Guarani books, a Paraguayan trail running trophy, and other things we wouldn't need in Asia on my mum to take home for us.

The next half of the journey was remarkably simple compared to the previous three days. So I won't write much about it. We went from Heathrow to Kuala Lumpur, and from Kuala Lumpur to Singapore. Seamlessly.

And just like that, 89 hours later, we were on the other side of the world.

Myanmar

After a brief stopover in one of my favourite places in the world, Singapore, with Ashley's mum, we were ready for yet another night in the airport. It has to be said though, Singapore's Changi beats Heathrow hands down. I don't think there's many airports I'd rather spend a night in out there.

Across the three terminals, as well as the expected shops, restaurants, and cafes, Changi Airport is well known for its elaborate garden displays, children's slide, and no doubt its own water park or something similar by the time you're reading this. So much so in fact, that it often tops lists as the world's best airport. It's hard to argue with that fact.

Our flight left early in the morning and Ashley's mum left late the night before (hence why we were staying at the airport and not heading back into the city for a mere few hours with all our luggage).

Around 4am, we woke up and checked in. I then began to doubt reports of ease of ATM access in Myanmar, which lead to us getting hundreds of US dollars from the currency exchange just in case. We were running very low after El Salvador, Panama and Ecuador all using the dollar.

The last time I visited Myanmar was in October 2011. The country was going through a period of hope-filled change. I sat with my hotel owners in Bagan watching scenes of political prisoners being released after years of arrest for speaking out against the government. With language being a barrier, I looked to them, their eyes transfixed on the small television set in the corner, smiling broadly as they watched the BBC World News. I gave them a thumbs up with questioning eyebrows. They gave me firm thumbs up and glorious wide grins in return, confirming that this was a good thing. Myanmar was about to bloom.

"About to" being key in that sentence.

There were no ATMS in the country. You had to bring crisp, clean US dollars to exchange for the local, much dirtier and tattier Kyat.

There was no internet in hotels, only in a small number of internet cafes, and even there it was too weak of a connection for a Skype call - video OR audio.

There was no e-visa. Visiting meant a visit to the embassy and a few days wait in Bangkok.

It was an eye-opening two weeks for me. I hated it at the time. I got ill, and spent about ten days of the trip in and out of illness, even vomiting on a lady's doorstep at one rest stop on a bus journey.

Yet, despite not enjoying most of my days when I was there (I say 'most' because there were a couple of great days I enjoyed at the time), on reflection it was one of my favourite places from that entire trip. I knew I had to return if we'd be making the long journey from Paraguay to Southeast Asia.

We arrived early at Yangon International Airport, in a terminal that was definitely new compared to where I'd arrived last time, with our printed confirmation of our e-visas in hand. We also arrived slap bang in the middle of the Thingyan Water Festival.

In various countries across Southeast Asia, they celebrate their New Year around March/April time with a 'water festival'. This involves getting wet, perhaps unsurprisingly.

Water stations, often sponsored by big local businesses, set up shop at the side of the road with large sound systems, a stage, and an elaborate hose system ready for spraying passing cars, pedestrians, and pickup trucks full of already soaked Burmese with water. Oh, and tourists aren't immune from getting wet. We weren't sure how far into the city we'd have to get before we noticed the signs of the water festival. As it turned out, the answer is "not far".

Minutes after getting into a taxi and leaving the airport carpark, we were driving through a small cluster of wooden houses when children ran out with buckets of water that they threw over the taxi. We kept our windows up, happy to play along safe and sound in the dry confines of the taxi.

After another few minutes weaving through the narrow neighbourhood lanes near the airport, we emerged onto a bigger road...a bigger road that was absolutely jam-packed with traffic. No one was moving. The entire right lane of each side of the road was loaded with white pickup trucks, and each pickup truck was full of soaked Burmese of all ages, smiling and enjoying themselves despite the traffic waiting to get to the next water station.

Some trucks had their own supply of amo - in other words a barrel of water and a selection of buckets and bottles to scoop the water out and onto other cars, pedestrians or truckloads of people.

"Ok, so I think we might, maybe, just maybe...definitely get wet." I said to Ashley, as I turned round to him from the front passenger seat. I smiled as I said it, trying to remain positive, knowing this was his idea of hell.

After at least two hours for what should be no more than a fifty minute journey, the taxi pulled over and the driver pointed across the street to the sign for our hotel. He couldn't get any closer because the street was full of pickup trucks, hoses, and people just trying to go about the daily business getting a little wet in the process. Needless to say, our attempt to cross the road and stay dry was fruitless and we got wet instantly.

On this side of the road, there was another narrower road in front of us, both sides of the streets covered with older Burmese ladies selling fruits, vegetables, fresh fish, whole chickens, herbs, spices. Everything displayed openly in various coloured plastic baskets on the ground. Shoppers filled the street space between the sellers, moving aside for passing motorbikes every now and then. There was a grubby looking stairwell to the left that looked like it must lead up to our hotel. Thankfully, the food on the streets seemed to make an unspoken no-go zone as far as the water festival was concerned, which allowed us a little time to contemplate if this was the spot we'd be spending the next few nights in.

"Where you stay?" a passing man asked.

"Ocean View 2?" I responded. Many hotels here expand and keep the same name, numbering their new branch to distinguish it instead.

"Ahh yes yes." he replied, pointing towards the stairwell and nodding his head.

"Thank you! Chay zu bay!" I was overjoyed to get a chance to use my basic Burmese again.

The hotel was simple but better than the stairwell would have you believe. After settling in, we were hungry and eager to explore, so headed out with plenty of waterproofing for phones, cameras and the like.

It was fun at first, however, the celebrations meant most restaurants were closed. Eventually we found a new, slightly-expensive-for-Myanmar place serving good Asian dishes. We ordered all the vegetarian dishes on offer (which wasn't as much food as the word "all" might imply) and had a good first meal in the country, sitting on the plastic layers placed on top of each chair by the staff to welcome wet passers by in. After heading out again, eventually we got soaked, and had no option but to head back to the hotel for a moment's peace. Ashley instantly stripped off and got to work washing his clothes in the sink.

"Look at that!" he exclaimed at the opaque brown liquid streaming from his clothes as he wrung them.

"Eww...well, that's gross."

"Where is this water coming from?!"

A lot of the water was being poured down necks from freshly opened ice-cold bottles of mineral water. That was quite refreshing. Some of it was coming from lukewarm bottles of water - not as refreshing. Some of it was coming from street puddles - I decided it wasn't fun anymore when I saw some toddlers lifting a pavement slab to fill a bottle. But most of it was being drawn from the main supply. Chunks of pavement lifted and resting at an angle on top of where they should sit plush allowed for hoses to be attached to taps on the main water pipes. I have absolutely no idea who pays the water bill after Thingyan.

"It'll dry off. It's quite hot in here. And then tomorrow, you can wear the same clothes and only get one set dirty I guess until we're out of the water festival and get a chance to wash them properly?"

It was hot. Over 40 degrees Celcius most of the day. The water festival just so happens rather conveniently to fall at the end of the hot and dry season before the rainy season arrives, gradually increasing until it often causes flooding a few months down the line.

***

We'd be flying out of Yangon when we left the country in three weeks time, so saved a lot of things to see and do until then, a time when we could enjoy them without getting soaking wet. However, one thing you can't miss in the city, or the country as a whole, is *Shwedagon Paya*, the Golden Pagoda that dominates the city skyline from afar.

The day after the water festival finished we decided to visit Shwedagon Pagoda. The staff at the hotel told us it would be a great day to visit as families would be celebrating New Year by visiting so we'd see it at a really good time. And it was great, but great also means busy. And busy in Myanmar as a tourist means an endless stream of "Selfie one?" and "Please selfie?" as you walk anywhere.

This is something new from my last visit. I remember seeing a man sat relaxing on a chair, head resting in his hands clasped on the back of his neck at a table on the pavement. On the table were two corded telephones, their wires reaching upwards and tapping into the phone line above his head. Nowadays everyone has a smartphone of some kind.

Another thing that has changed is the dawn of the ATM, something that I've taken for granted as long as I've had a bank card. Myanmar is an example of why you shouldn't stop your children from eating sweets from time to time. If you stop your child having sweets, then they're only going to OD on sugar the first time they're at a friend's sleepover. You restrict modern trappings from a country and you'll have a whole line up of ATMs at Shwedagon Paya as soon as they are introduced. Which is true by the way, there is a row of at least four ATMs on the Pagoda itself.

I'm not one to deny change to places. I think that's an egotistical idea embedded in a selfish desire to be the best or have places to go on holiday for the 'Gram that make you look like you've gone back in time. It's unhealthy and unhelpful.

Change happens, no place should be denied that. But visiting Myanmar seven years apart felt like seeing an old friend for the first time in as long. They've got a new haircut, a new job, a new partner, but underneath it all you can see the person you once knew is still very much there, even if it might not be obvious to those meeting your friend for the first time.

One thing that hasn't changed is how friendly the people are. I know, I know, it's a cliché to say "The people are so nice!" but it's another level in Myanmar. People have had very limited contact with foreigners until relatively recently so are curious. They want to talk, to practice their English, to take selfies with you.

On our way to the Pagoda, passing street vendors selling live fish and birds along the straight road towards the Pagoda, we were offered bowls of food and cups of brightly coloured drink multiple times. This was a feature of the end of Thingyan. It was all free and, even if the drinks were incredibly sweetened, it was very much appreciated due to the heat. The food in particular was great.

We were ushered to two tiny plastic chairs on the kerbside that anywhere else in the world would be called footstools, and told to sit. A minute later, two metal bowls of noodle soup and vegetables arrived. The woman smiled as she handed the bowls over and I thanked her with a 'chay zu bay'.

"You like food?" a man sat next to us asked.

"Mmmm! Saq deh! Kaun deh, naw?" *It's spicy, It's good, isn't it?* I replied through the hot water of the soup tingling my lips with its spice.

We chatted for a few minutes while we ate our noodles, safe in the knowledge that we definitely were immune in our food zone from the last few pickup trucks chucking water.

When you visit Pagodas and religious sites in Myanmar, like in many other parts of the world, you have to remove your shoes. This wasn't a problem for me as I was travelling with a pair of easy slip-on sandals that I'd wear on days like this. But for Ashley, who's not exactly a flip flop kinda guy, it became quite the ordeal to take shoes off at each site. So I'm glad we visited Myanmar first before the irritation got too much that we stopped visiting religious sites unless they were unique. In Myanmar, it feels like everything is unique.

Shoes off and tucked away downstairs, we headed up the steps through the crowds to the top of the Pagoda. The white tile floor was scolding on bare feet, especially when you couldn't tiptoe across it a little faster to catch some shade because there were so many people. After walking around what felt like Oxford Street on Christmas Eve twice to get our money's worth, we decided to head back down and across to a park we'd spotted on the map and heard music coming from on our way in.

There were stalls selling fried food, canoes laiden with yellow blossom flowers we'd seen everywhere over Thingyan (known as Padauk which is the national flower of Myanmar) and, most remarkably, a foam party happening at the top of the park. We walked down in the other direction to the foam party and came across a stand where I got to use lots of Burmese!

Underneath a gazebo, a single table stood manned by around six young Burmese. There wasn't much on the table, just a wooden circular block with something pale and yellow on top of it. I recognised it instantly as *thanaka*, the natural paste that many Burmese wear on their faces as makeup, reputedly known for its sunscreen and anti-aging properties. In a country not really internationally recognised for the typical things a country is noted for such as food, thanaka is something quite distinctly Burmese. (While we're on the subject of food, Burmese food is comforting, tasty, and often spicy. If you can find some, try some!)

"Come!" one of the young women underneath the gazebo invited me over after seeing me looking curiously. I obeyed.

Moments later, hands were all over my face delicately applying the thanaka for the first time in my life.

"Hla deh naw? Hla deh?!" *It's pretty, right?!* I asked.

Eyes widened and heads nodded in response. Then they turned to my left. It was Ashley's turn to get some thanaka applied. We'd never felt more welcomed into a foreign celebration.

***

The next evening we took the bus to Bagan. Bagan is another "must-see" in the country. Plains of dusty land spiked at irregular and frequent intervals with (mostly) rusty red brick temples and pagodas. It would take weeks to see and appreciate all of Bagan's temples individually, especially allowing time for the inevitable conversations with each sand painting vendor. Everyone's an artist in Bagan. And that's no bad thing. The small cluster of towns has been a hotbed of tourism for many years in a country with large areas travellers are often warned not to visit on and off, doing wonders for local business here in Bagan.

Last time I visited Bagan, despite how much of my time there I didn't enjoy, I had two of the best days of my entire time in Myanmar as I'd met some friendly travellers my age on the bus - two American girls from Wisconsin and a British guy. We clubbed our money together to take horse carts around Bagan on our first day there, which was magical.

"So when we get to Bagan, there's a few options." I told Ashley as we settled in to our surprisingly comfy (but still not quite topping the one we took from Encarnación to Asunción) bus.

"Right…"

"It's quite big. So we definitely don't want to go on foot. We could hire bikes, or we could hire a horse cart, which is good because you get a guide."

"Can we do bikes both days?" Ashley had two things he wasn't interested in doing on our trip that he'd made clear from the start: horses and white water rapids.

"I thought you might say that! We wouldn't be *riding* the horses, we just get to sit in the back of the cart, relaxing, looking at the view." I knew my efforts to convince him out of riding a bike for two days in a row would be fruitless but I gave it a go nonetheless.

"I just don't like horses. If we can bike, then I'd definitely prefer to bike both days."

"I thought you might say that." I replied again, smiling knowingly.

Remarkably refreshed after a surprisingly pleasant bus ride from Yangon to Bagan, we arrived still in darkness around 4.30am at Bagan Bus Station. As we stepped off the bus, we were met with a barrage of drivers each offering us a ride to our hotel for 5000 Kyat more than it should have been. I guess that's what happens when you arrive in darkness.

One guy, however, offered to take us both for half the price of the other, more persistent drivers. The difference? This guy would take us by horse cart, not taxi.

"It's only 8,000 compared to 15,000 they want for a taxi. It's a good deal, right?" I said to Ashley.

"Yeah, let's do that. That way at least we've ridden a horse cart in Bagan and we don't have to do it again in the daytime!"

"Exactly!"

As we rode in from the out of town bus station to our hotel, we watched the sun rise gently over the first peaks of temples we began to see. We stopped at the patrol office to pay our $20 each to enter the Bagan Archaeological Zone, quite the increase from the $10 I paid seven years ago, and not much further down the road, we arrived at our hotel.

Our place in Yangon didn't look much from the outside, and it was nice on the inside, with very friendly and helpful staff above all else, but there were some signs that it was a cheaper hotel - crumbling paint, small simple breakfast, and a cosy narrow hallway. Bagan however, sparked the first of a long thread of fancy Burmese hotels for ridiculously low prices. It was time to live it up.

Despite arriving just as dawn broke, we were very soon allowed into our room, offered an extra breakfast for that day, and even had someone carry our luggage up the staircase to our room. Two double beds, a large bathroom, a mini fridge, and a large array of toiletries awaited us.

Breakfast was served on the rooftop, and it was buffet style, as we'd soon grow accustomed to in the country, with an array of noodles, rice, eggs, toast, and more. Oh, and the views were pretty special. From the rooftop, we carried on our sunrise tour of Bagan we'd experienced in the horsecart with the mist clearing slowly over the tips of temples across the plains to reveal rusty red brick and shimmering white peaks gently scattered seemingly at random across the landscape in every direction you looked.

Despite all its amazing features, our hotel didn't have any bicycles left for rent that day so we started walking towards the town to find a bike rental, which we did pretty quickly.

"Hello? Ming guh lah bah?" I said, gingerly stepping into the dusty bike garage messy with screws and nails and tools scattered in piles across what looked like every surface. The air was thick with dust and the light was dark.

A woman emerged from the back room, "Ming guh lah bah! Bike?" she said, smiling upon seeing us there.

"Yes please...err...hniq?" I replied with my index and middle finger showing her a peace sign to confirm my potential mistranslation of the number two.

"H'ouq keh." she picked two bikes for us, "H'ouq keh? Good?"

"Mmmm, h'ouq keh. Err...bah de lau leh?" *How much?*

I couldn't quite believe the price she quoted me. Just £2 each for a bike for the whole day. And in such an incredibly touristy spot. Despite their high contact with international tourists compared to other parts of the country, many in Bagan have remained good honest people rather than falling into overcharging or scamming richer foreign tourists, which would be an easy thing to fall into. We agreed to return the bikes by 8pm and set off on our way, our first challenge of the day being crossing the road right in front of us.

"There's lots of artists in this town, Ash" I told him, warned him almost, as we rode along, "Everyone is an artist. Either that or they'll be children trying to sell you a copy of Burmese Days by George Orwell."

The Burmese Days books seem to have faded out of fashion, but everyone is still indeed an artist, as they were on my first visit. Entering our very first temple of the day, we were met by a kind man who explained the history of that temple, how his family have been left in charge of it (supposedly) and it costs a lot of money to maintain, so he paints. After an exchange and settling on a fair price for both him and Ashley, Ashley bought a sand painting for his classroom.

"And now you have one, it'll be easy to not buy another one because you can show them - "Look! I already have one!"" I said as we headed back towards our bikes to go to the next temple.

We had a great day exploring Bagan, meandering from one temple site to the next, some large with coaches parked out front, others tiny and all to ourselves, not even with a sandpainter in sight.

"It looks like it's getting ready to rain, should we find somewhere for a drink?" I called forward to Ashley as we struggled to stay cycling in a straight line with the sudden wind that had picked up.

"Good idea!"

It was around 4pm and after breakfast, we'd only eaten a handful of snacks we'd brought with us for the ride. I ordered one carrot juice. Then another fruit juice because the first was so refreshing and it was so cheap.

After the wind had calmed down, we set off on the journey back to the bike shop. Twenty minutes in, my stomach suddenly didn't feel right.

"Ash, can we go right back to the hotel? I don't feel too good…" I shouted back to Ashley.

We rode straight to the hotel and I went upstairs to lie down while Ashley rode his bike back to the bike shop, then ran back to pick mine up and rode that one to the shop and ran back again. I'd barely moved in that time.

"I don't know if I can go out for dinner." Another thing we'd grown accustomed to in Myanmar opposed to the eating in we'd done more in Latin America, "Maybe we can eat here at the hotel restaurant? I think I can manage that."

I couldn't. After a couple of forced spoonfuls of my fried rice, I had to ask if I could take my plate down to my room because I couldn't finish it.

Later that night, my suspicions were confirmed when I was sick. The following morning I didn't fare much better. Was it the breakfast? The fruit juices? Or something else? Likely the ice in the fruit juices. Although I was annoyed I'd miss the second day cycling Bagan, I wasn't particularly surprised I'd taken ill. My previous trip here had been tainted with up and down illness resulting in a stay in a Bangkok hospital on my return to Thailand. I was not going to let that happen again. I decided to rest it out now while I had the chance and set Ashley the mission of finding the best view across Bagan and photographing it.

***

After Bagan, our next stop was Mandalay, which had me singing The Road to Mandalay by Robbie Williams more times than I care to count. We caught a minibus this time, organised by our hotel. "OK Travel" they were called, which we would soon discover wasn't the only thing in Myanmar to be "OK".

After a few hotel pickups around town, we stopped at the OK Travel depot, where we picked up a crate of water bottles for us passengers, all labelled with "OK Water".

On our drive to Mandalay, we began to notice other businesses randomly en route, also defining themselves as just "OK": "OK Restaurant", "OK Internet".

A quick Google search while writing this has just taught me that "OK Cashews" exists in Myanmar, as done "OK Dollar", a new taxi app, and the granddaddy of them all, "OK Myanmar Co Ltd". I'm not even sure what the last one does, but I'm glad to know their services are simply "OK". Not excellent, not great, not even good, just OK.

Maybe we can learn from this. Maybe all businesses should promote their products and services as "OK", maybe even "distinctly average", "mediocre", or "just alright, really." That way, no one is ever disappointed, only ever happy with the bog standard service they expected, or ecstatic with the excellent service provided by "OK." That said, the service was above average on our minibus. They should rebrand as "More than OK". I think that would work wonders for them.

Our hotel in Mandalay was another elaborate place that would cost at least four times what it cost us were it in most other places outside of Myanmar. It was a mostly-finished building with a rooftop terrace, large breakfast room, and an elevator - possibly the first I'd ever been in in Myanmar. Our room wasn't quite as big as you'd expect from a place that gave us a tray of welcome papaya and drinks on arrival in reception, yet it was better than most hotels we'd stayed in, so we were happy. We weren't happy however, with Mandalay.

Mandalay is a busy, polluted city with endless rows of traffic, rarely stopping for the few pedestrian traffic lights that exist in the town. It's not exactly what you'd call a walker's city. Most streets didn't have pavements, and those that did, namely around the square Mandalay Palace moat, were still covered in semi-deconstructed stages and bleachers from the water festival, now a week ago. When we did see workers there to complete the job, they were mostly sat in the shade underneath trees sharing their lunch tiffins (layered lunchboxes, the ultimate picnic). So most of our time getting around Mandalay was spent hopping from kerbside balances to avoid open drains to jumping into the road to avoid the lack of kerbside and drain cover. Fun times.

A small break from the madness came the day we walked up Mandalay Hill. The views from the top when you eventually get there overlook the entire city, including the elaborate golf club that very few locals would get a glimpse of any other way. The hill is easy to identify from the south entrance (which is north of the city) due to the two large white lion statues guarding the steps at the entrance. Remarkably, it's free to climb and visit, although you'll likely end up spending something either on food and drinks or souvenirs as you climb the longer than expected staircases taking you from one temple to another until you reach the big one at the very top. I purchased three pieces of art by a man who was using just ink and a razor to create lovely black and white vistas of typical Burmese sights - Bagan, Pagodas, U Bein teak bridge (the world's longest teak bridge, don't you know) and Inle Lake. I told him they were "hla deh" - *pretty* - and he smiled and offered me three for a good price.

***

After navigating traffic and coping with various power cuts in the hotel (something that happened in almost every hotel and shopping centre we went in in the country at some point) the next most difficult thing about Mandalay was leaving the place. We'd decided that instead of Inle Lake (Ashley had decided that he doesn't like bodies of water and it's where I got sick last time and had to be escorted to the doctor's hut on a push bike sidecar in a flood) we would visit Nay Pyi Taw, the mysterious capital city built in secret and declared as the capital in just 2005, making it one of the newest capital cities in the world. It was one of the most fascinating places I've ever visited.

The story goes that upon being told by a clairvoyant that bad times were ahead because Yangon was too close to the sea for attack, the then guy in charge decided to build a new capital city (one that hadn't been influenced over the years by the country's colonial past).

The spot they picked lies halfway between Mandalay and Yangon, right in the middle of the country. The only problem being that the small villages that occupied the land at the time were surrounded by marshy lands - not ideal building ground.

Nevertheless, construction went ahead, without much information being shared with the outside world until announcing Nay Pyi Taw as the new capital of Myanmar in 2005. Needless to say, the majority of embassies and international organisations didn't exactly recognise this new capital. And the embassies in particular showed this with action by choosing to remain in Yangon, a crumbling city for the most part but a city with healthcare and education nonetheless.

The problem with Nay Pyi Taw is they planned ahead a little too much. Nay Pyi Taw is geographically four and a half times the size of London with just an eighth of the population. London has eight million. Nay Pyi Taw has one million, spread out over an area ten times the size of Singapore. You can't knock their ambition. But Nay Pyi Taw does leave you wondering if it will ever attract enough population and tourists to fill the twenty-lane highways and countless oversized hotels.

We arrived late at night by train from Mandalay at the one train station in this vast city, a mere 7km from our hotel.

The other thing about a city so big with such a small population is that public transport isn't exactly cost effective to run, meaning that as a tourist the only ways to get around are by taxi (much more expensive than anywhere else in the country) or moped (you don't have to ask too many people before you find one up for rent). We took a taxi from the station to our hotel, awestruck even in the darkness by the size and superficial grandeur of the hotels we passed along the way, wondering what on earth ours would look like. Until we turned in. We didn't have to wonder anymore. It was huge. A wide road led past the pool reflecting the little light there was, tennis courts just visible in the distance. A tall building towered over the tiny taxi.

We thanked the taxi driver who carried our bags to the door before they were instantly picked up by a man with a youthful face wearing the classic Burmese male combo of a beautifully fine-chequered longhi with a tucked white shirt, who walked us into the oversized (and empty) reception area.

I can't quite believe I've got this far into writing the Myanmar chapter and haven't yet talked about the longhi! The longhi is what you might call from an outsider's perspective a "male skirt". But actually, that's doing it a disservice. It's not like a kilt, the Scottish "male skirt" that no one really dusts off until a wedding or Rabbie Burns Night. It's what the large majority of Burmese men wear everyday, even as modern fashion trends seep into the country. Loose white long-sleeved shirts are tucked comfortably into a wrap of dark fabric often with a fine-chequered pattern, which is then tied into a big knot below the belly button, and mostly worn over flip flops. It's not uncommon to see men adjust themselves in public.

Although surprisingly, I've never been flashed at. The 'Longhi Adjust' is quite a skill.

The young-faced man showed us to our room, which was in a different building out the back. We passed the swimming pool, water just glistening in the moonlight, and the tennis courts, crisp and clean, probably out of lack of regular use. Our room was large, spacious, with all the extras we'd grown used to in Myanmar - a mini fridge, a TV, a desk, piles of free toiletries.

"Oh my God! You're not going to believe this!" I called to Ashley from the bathroom, where I'd gone to inspect the free toiletries situation.

"What?" he replied as he walked to the bathroom, "Oh, no way!"

"A bath! An actual bath! I never want to leave! Can we just spend our last three months in Nay Pyi Taw?!"

We hadn't had a bath for the whole trip so far, nine months. The closest we'd come was the Tabacón hot springs in Costa Rica but that doesn't really count - that's a different kind of treat.

But more was to come.

The following morning we headed for breakfast in a room just adjacent to the reception lobby, but not after paying a visit to the gym. Yes! This hotel had a gym! And no one had used it in a while, apparent by the fact that the woman on reception who unlocked it for us also had to switch the machines on at the sockets.

There was only a small handful of tables with guests at breakfast, I'd say five at most, and there were as many staff members, all stood attentively by the end of the buffet table, keen to top up tea and coffee.

We enquired at reception about the shuttle bus service into the "centre" (there's no real centre of Nay Pyi Taw), which actually was going to cost the price of a taxi. So we asked if they had any mopeds to hire. This turned out cheaper and within minutes, the receptionist's boyfriend arrived (who was also the guy who'd carried our bags the night before) and lent us his moped for the day for a fraction of the price of a taxi or shuttle.

Now, I have to be clear here. I'm what some people might call boring when it comes to travel. I prefer the term 'sensible' myself. I have a little rule I always keep in the back of my mind: "Would I do this at home?" If the answer is no, then I don't do it. If the answer is yes, then I do it. Simple.

Would I rent a moped at home? No. Never. Not in a million years. I'd be terrified to even start the engine. So I'm definitely not one for the whole "Yeah! Southeast Asia! Rent a moped! #YOLO!". Nope.

Ashley however, *did* used to ride a moped at home. The fact that it was close to fifteen years ago didn't matter. It was our best choice to actually see Nay Pyi Taw given its vast size. On top of that, Nay Pyi Taw is not Ho Chi Minh City. The size and lack of population made it a good place to rent a moped, especially if your moped driver hasn't ridden in fifteen years. There's not much that can go wrong. Plus - twenty lane highway? Yes please.

We started by riding out to the Nay Pyi Taw Water Fountain Garden, a large, slightly surreal (I mean, this is Nay Pyi Taw) park with various fountains and water features spread across the site navigated by paved paths, even the woodland path up to the observation tower is paved. That said, as it was daytime, most of the fountains weren't on, and on top of that, some of the features were beginning to look a little tatty around the edges.

Next up, now Ashley was feeling a little more comfortable with the moped, we headed across towards the parliament buildings, which is where the roads begin to expand in front of you. If Nay Pyi Taw is known for anything at this stage in its short history, it's the twenty-lane motorways, but actually, that's a bit of a myth. Most roads are only ten lanes wide. Only! However, as you get closer and closer to the government buildings, the roads gradually expand first to twelve, then fourteen, then sixteen, eighteen, and finally twenty lanes. Ten lanes per direction of traffic. It is the ultimate in forward planning.

Although with vehicles the way they are, I'm not sure how safe twenty lanes of Burmese traffic would be. Back when the British were still here, cars drove on the left-hand side of the road, meaning that all cars were right-hand drive, just like my own car at home in the UK.

But, as is the way when your colonial rulers depart, the Burmese rulers at the time (well, twenty two years later) decided to mix things up and switch sides to drive on the right. Why? One theory is that the guy in charge spoke to an astrologer, much like the rumoured birth of Nay Pyi Taw.

Nowadays however, Myanmar mostly imports its cars from Japan, a country that drives on the left, meaning that the cars are mostly *still* right-hand drive. So they drive on the right, with right-hand drive cars. Overtaking and turning is lots of fun. Thankfully we didn't have to worry too much about all of this on our little moped.

As we rode down the vast twenty-lane motorway, we saw just two other vehicles, both mopeds. We turned back, looping around the roundabout just before reaching the parliament building itself and headed down towards the "centre" of the city, by which I mean the shopping centre.

In every place we'd visited so far in Myanmar (with the exception of tiny Bagan town) there was an 'Ocean Supercenter'. In Yangon there were multiple malls, none of which existed on my first visit. But it was Ocean Supercenter that stood out as the dominant chain nationwide. In Nay Pyi Taw too, this was the main mall and just as we parked up the moped and placed our helmets on the seat, rain started to fall. Slowly at first, in large, bulky spacious drops, but then within minutes it was falling hard and heavy. So much so that it caused a power cut in the whole mall. In the semi-darkness, we headed downstairs to the cafes and restaurants and managed to order (between my minimal Burmese and the waiters basic English) two vegetarian plates of Shan noodles. Moments later, a large metal teapot with a sturdy handle was placed on our table alongside two tiny teacups. The noodles arrived soon after and we ate in the dark watching the rain fall heavy outside.

We visited the supermarket upstairs and filled my backpack with groceries to make ourselves a little dinner in the room that evening. Even if we wanted to eat out, there was nowhere within a 10km radius of the hotel, and we'd have no moped by that time of night. By this point in our trip we'd got pretty efficient at preparing meals with a kettle only.

Noodles, chopped fresh veg, and a little curry paste makes for an easy kettle-only meal.

Whilst we were in the supermarket, the power came back on, and as we left, the heat outside had already dried the rain on the moped seat, even though it was still quite cloudy. We rode back to the train station, all twenty two kilometers of it without stopping, our longest non-stop trip that day, and booked our ticket out for a day later than we'd originally planned, giving us a little extra time to enjoy the luxuriously weird and empty hotel.

The sun came out on our journey back to the hotel, which meant there was still time to make use of the pool. There were seven people already in the pool - four young people drinking bottles of beer and smoking oversized cigars in a small circular offshoot from the main pool, and a father with his two young children. I'm pretty sure that collectively we were the entirety of guests that day.

I don't think I've ever been anywhere as bewildering and intriguing as Nay Pyi Taw. It doesn't answer any questions, just opens up more for deliberation: will there ever be enough people in Nay Pyi Taw to warrant its size? Will those twenty-lane motorways ever experience bottleneck traffic jams? What do the locals think? How many locals that aren't in government living here lived here before it was built? Will the embassies ever move here?

At the time of writing, as I mentioned, very few countries have agreed to move their embassies to Nay Pyi Taw. The British Embassy in Yangon still cites itself as the "British Embassy in Rangoon" on their sign, Rangoon being the name given to the city by the British. Change is happening in

Myanmar, but it'll be a long time before Nay Pyi Taw fills those roads, if ever.

***

Our train out of Nay Pyi Taw took us to the small town of Bago, where we spent one night on the way to Mawlamyine, the town at the end of the so-called Death Railway. Bago is a busy town for its small size, yet hidden away are various religious sites worth checking out if you're passing through. Upon arrival, we tried to book our next transport to take us to Mawlamyine.

"After Bago, we want to go to Mawlamyine. Is there a train? Bus? Which is best?"

"Err..." the young woman nervously reached for the phone and started dialing. She didn't speak English, at least not confidently enough to speak with a native. Moments later, after presumably briefing the person on the other end, she handed me the receiver.

"Hello? Ming guh lah bah?"

"Hello, you want to go Mawlamyine, yes?"

"Yes, tomorrow?"

"Ok, bus is good because train time is not good. The bus is 1 o'clock afternoon. Is ok?"

"Yes, I think so," I mouthed '1 o'clock?' to Ashley who nodded in response.

"Ok, I get you ticket. You pay now and bus leave tomorrow 1 o'clock afternoon."

"Thank you! Chay zu bey! Where? Do we have to go to the bus station?"

"Err...no. Is ok. Bus go past hotel road."

"At 1 o'clock?"

"Yes yes. Ok! Thank you! See you tomorrow!"

"Ok, bye!"

It was a brief conversation. We went back to the room and something didn't feel right. I have a good "gut" instinct and I trust it.

"Is it weird we had to pay but didn't get any confirmation? Not even a receipt?" I whispered to Ash.

"Hmm. Maybe. I think it's ok though, they seem friendly."

"But what if they're too friendly? What if it's all an act to try and make us feel comfortable but really they're gonna nick all our stuff as soon as we leave the room? I dunno...I'm gonna ask if we should get a ticket."

I headed back out to reception.

"Ticket? Do we get a ticket?" I asked.

"No, no, you get ticket on bus sometimes but it's ok, it's all ready. 1 o'clock yes? Tomorrow?"

The man who answered us had arrived on his moped in the time since we'd gone back to our room. He was talking/flirting with the receptionist when I arrived. He spoke good English. But how did he know about our bus ticket?

I went back to the room and filled Ashley in. Still a little nervous, we headed out to see a little of Bago before leaving tomorrow...hopefully.

By this time the sun was setting over the town, just as we stumbled across a peaceful pagoda tucked away at the end of a dirt track. Past the chickens panickedly crossing as we walked, past the children playing football in the dust, we discovered a silent haven with the sun slowly setting casting bright amber tones across the glowing golden stupa and Buddha statues of the temple. It was beautiful. Then it happened.

I don't remember the exact words and sounds but I do remember a loud prayer noise suddenly cracking loudly from the tiny lone speaker atop the stupa.

Then things silenced. But not for long.

The prayer sounded again.

"I think we've come at prayer time. There's no one around though..." Ash said checking for a flow of people heading towards the temple, but no, there was no one. We weaved our way through some dirt tracks as the sun continued setting before heading back to the hotel for the night.

The following morning, after confirming the bus would arrive again but still not getting a ticket, we set off early to explore the Reclining Buddha of Bago. It was nothing compared to what we'd see during our time at Mawlamyine but it was good to see.

Buddha comes in various forms. Reclining, walking, begging, multiple sitting poses. But the reclining ones are my favourite. With their head resting on one hand and a loose knowing smile on their faces, the reclining buddhas look like they know a secret about you.

Before long, it was time to get ready for our supposed bus. We headed to reception at 12.40, just to be sure. Soon, the man I'd seen on the moped when I went back to ask about the ticket arrived.

"Ready?" he said.

He parked his moped and walked with us to the end of the road, "We need cross road for Mawlamyine," he said, barely finishing his sentence before he started walking forwards into the road awash with traffic.

We waited on the other side for a few minutes, my suspicions lowered slightly, but not fully. This wasn't the man we booked our tickets with - and speaking of tickets we *still* didn't have one, or a receipt to prove we'd already paid for one!

Later than felt comfortable, around ten past one, a bus pulled up and a man got off to put our luggage underneath the bus. We said goodbye to moped man and got on. The bus was packed. People were already sitting in the aisle.

The man who'd helped with our luggage followed us on and pointed to two seats where two passengers were already sat. I'm not sure what he said exactly but they got up and made way for us to sit in their seats. I've never felt more colonial. And I didn't like it. On my last trip, I took a bus one day in Yangon and an elderly woman stood up, tapped me on the shoulder and ushered me into the seat she'd just stood from. She wouldn't take no for an answer and although I appreciated her kindness, I felt incredibly awkward.

It soon transpired however, that this bus just casually picks up anyone and everyone. If you do book, you get a guaranteed seat, so I felt a little better after figuring that out when the man came down with a clipboard and our names written very clearly in shaky English letters next to our seat numbers on his paper. Minutes later, we were off, headed down the narrow eastern coast towards Mawlamyine. But not before the guy we'd spoken to originally about the tickets poked his head on the bus to check we'd got on alright. As it turned out, we had nothing to worry about at all and buying on trust and getting no ticket is just the way it's done here. What was my gut thinking?!

***

The reason we visited Mawlamyine was because we'd both let out an audible "Oooo I want to go there!" when we saw a photo in our travel guide of a row of stone monks surrounded by greenery. The monk photo had the words "Win Sein Taw Ya" written underneath, along with the photographers name. Further research taught us that Win Sein Taw Ya was the site of the World's Largest Reclining Buddha and that it was nearby the town of Mawlamyine. Mawlamyine was also near the end of the Death Railway, which is the railway built by slave labour under Japanese command that includes the famous Bridge over the River Kwai, which is on the Thai side.

Our hotel in Mawlamyine was great because it was right next to the bus station, meaning that our evening arrival didn't include drifting around an unknown town in the darkness. Not only that, it was like a motel, consisting of blocks of two large rooms with enough space for two cars between that and the next block of two rooms. Tables and two chairs were outside each room as well for breakfast, which, as we discovered the following morning, was delicious. Our hotel in Bago was the only place that didn't provide breakfast, so we were glad to get back to having breakfast included, especially as it was so tasty in Mawlamyine.

We spent a day exploring the town itself, which included lots of up and down hills to religious sites, rows of shops, and parks with painted rocks. Well, just one park with painted rocks. By far the most impressive site was the Kyeik Than Lan pagoda, a huge pagoda that sits high above the city, with spectacular views all around. Many pagodas in Myanmar are free, but you do pay for the larger, more impressive ones. At this stage in our trip, after seeing quite a few pagodas, and burning our bare feet on the tiles in the crowds at Shwedagon Pagoda, we had already decided not to pay for any more.

I put my head around the door and didn't see a sign about payment, but there was a lady sitting at a small desk, who smiled when she saw me and ushered me in. I asked her in Burmese if it was free. She didn't directly respond "yes" but instead continued to usher us both in and told us to leave our shoes by her before heading up in the lift. Yes, a lift. Remember how Shwedagon had ATMs? Religion here has all the modernities you could wish for.

The lift brought us out on the tiled floor heading towards the grand golden stupa in front of us, shining even brighter in the hot midday sun. We dutifully circled the stupa, taking in the sights and the views along the way, including three tiny scruffy kittens falling off a ledge and hiding behind a signboard. Halfway around, ice cream began to become a prominent sight in people's hands, and we soon saw why - free ice cream cones were being given out, which also explained the abundance of food we'd seen ahead being handed out for free on the street level.

As we approached the lift again, people stopped still in front of us to give way...to ice. A group of around five men were working together to transport enormous blocks of ice from below, up in the lift, and over to the ice cream stand to help keep things cool. I'm glad we didn't get an ice cream. The chunks of ice were being taken from inside the lift and dragged across the hot, dirty floor where hundreds of bare feet had already walked that day and picking up allsorts of dirt and grit in the process. Of course, the ice cream would be in containers and relatively safe from contamination, but this wasn't the first unexpected ice transportation we'd seen during our time there.

On our journey from Bagan to Mandalay, our (OK) minibus stopped for a quick break at a restaurant by the side of the road. None of the foreign tourists were hungry. Either that or we didn't fancy the open bowls of questionable meat on offer. So instead, we stood stretching our legs in the sun close by the minibus. A young lad no older than ten heaved a huge chunk of ice to the basin of the tap in front of us. He started chinking away at the ice with his axe, breaking it into smaller more carriable pieces. The whole block of ice was covered in sawdust from the truck it had been unloaded from. The boy's rusty axe cut through, flinging some sawdust off, but by no means all of it, before he'd carry each smaller chunk through into the restaurant. I followed, pretending to be curious as to the food on offer, but really curious to where the ice went. It went into the Coca-Cola branded drinks cooler. Again, just like the ice cream, the drinks are in containers, so it's not a huge health issue, but at the same time, it's not something I could see passing health inspectors back home.

We finally entered the lift to head back down and get our shoes, our feet unavoidably getting wet in the lift from the melting ice block that had been there just moments earlier. I thanked the lady at the desk for letting us in and keeping watch of our shoes and that's when we got our tickets given to us. She touched my arm slightly and pointed, indicating to the ticket book in her other hand.

"Ba de lau leh?" I asked her how much it was. She responded 2000 Kyat which is fair, so we paid up and she handed me a postcard out of nowhere alongside our tickets, accompanied by her beaming red betel-stained smile. The postcard had a badly printed image of the pagoda we'd just seen on the front, with the saturation well and truly turned up to eleven. Still, it made for a quirky souvenir from our unexpected ice pagoda. Having seen the ice being dragged across the tiles, we avoided the street food being given out for free outside the pagoda. Besides, there were likely locals who needed it more than us. As we walked away from the pagoda, hunched people smiled up at us from their bowls of food, their mouths stained red - not from the food, but from betel.

Let's talk about betel. Whereas people in the west are battling tobacco addiction, mostly replacing it nowadays with vaping, in Myanmar, the equivalent is possibly betel nut chewing. Some do smoke long cigarette style 'cheroots', a primarily handmade traditional Burmese cigarette wrapped in a leaf and smoked. However, betel chewing appears more prominently, not least for the red spit scattered across pavements and red-stained teeth accompanying local smiles.

Betel nut is a nut found in countries across South Asia and chewed by locals in Myanmar, wrapped in a leaf with a varying mixture of other things depending on which streetside stand you buy from. Some add lime, others chili. There's a slight variety wrapped in the leaves from different stands, but I couldn't tell you much more than that as I've never had one myself.

The Government is gradually adding new laws and campaigns to tackle betel nut chewing as it's a major cause of oral cancer within the country, and responsible for many deaths each year (and...that would be why I didn't try it.)

***

The following day in Mawlamyine, we asked our hosts at breakfast how to get to Win Sein Taw Ya, the place where we'd seen the photo of the stone monks in a line. They sorted us out and even waited beside the road with us for the right pick-up for us. Which was handy seeing as none of the pickups had signs or any indication of their destination. We passed our money forward to the driver and squeezed in on opposite sides of the back of the pickup truck, realising why there were so many available for Thingyan a few weeks ago in Yangon - they were everywhere. I kept an eye on my map app, while locals kept an eye on me, curious why these two foreigners were on their pickup.

Arriving at Win Sein Taw Ya, you wouldn't know at first you were in the right place to see the World's Largest Reclining Buddha. Surprisingly, it's not really visible from the road in the direction we'd come. We started walking down the road as indicated correct by the pickup driver and soon spotted the start of our line of stone monks.

"Here they are! We've made it!" I exclaimed, feeling like I'd just met a celebrity I'd only ever seen in photos.

We decided to visit the World's Largest Reclining Buddha first and follow the stone monk line later. The closer you get, the more you see the whole thing, and the bigger you realise the Buddha is. I know that just sounds like I don't understand perception but it's true. This Buddha has 3 floors inside, each displaying a range of concrete models depicting stories from the religion. The first few rooms begin well. The concrete animals, backgrounds and people are huge, well-shaped, and nicely painted, albeit covered in dust. The deeper you go into the labyrinth of rooms however, the less impressive the displays get. First the paint is lacking, then the models become less chiseled, until finally, empty concrete rooms lay ahead inside what must be the legs to the toes of the Buddha.

We live at home on a new-build estate. I say build, with a d, because at the time of writing it's not finished - it's not yet new-*built*, with a t. So I get that perhaps to make things profitable you have to open them before they're finished, but this place was something else. Mainly because despite the World's Largest Reclining Buddha's interior displays not being finished, construction had begun on a new equally large reclining Buddha facing this one. Finish one job before starting another, perhaps? In fact, I do find myself saying that about our estate builders a lot too.

Before heading back, we made sure to follow the trail of stone monks as far as we could before the greenery by their platforms (and by our feet) got too spiky to walk through. So I'm still not sure exactly how far they went on for. Who knows, if we'd kept going we might still be there now.

It was a peaceful and remarkable sight to see such unity and continuation in one long snaking train of near identical statues. Most stood upon a blue platform with their only other colour being their painted maroon robes. Some replacement monks had brighter paints, even white or pink paint on their stone skin. And some older monks had missing parts - an ear, a nose, a hand, a head. Yet they were still the sight we'd expected. And the stone monk path was much less of a bizarre circus than the World's Largest Reclining Buddha.

Across the road was a golden stupa on a hugh hill, plus my map said "cave" so we decided to take a look before heading back to Mawlamyine. Of course, shoes off at the bottom, and up we went, walking on mostly untitled stone stairs curving around the hill weaving us to the tiny peak which housed the golden stupa...and some spectacular views.

We were still quite near the coast and so the views consisted of vast flat landscapes with the occasional hill similar to the one we were stood on jutting from the flat, breaking the green of a field to showcase its height. Some gold stupas and pagodas glistened in the hills, many of which we'd seen from the pickup truck on the way here. I wondered who visited and maintained such remote religious sites, and how often.

***

The following day we asked for transport help again from our helpful hosts at the hotel who got us on a different pickup truck to take us to the small town of Thanbyuzayat, the town at the Burmese end of the Death Railway, the train line built with slave labour ordered by the Japanese in 1943 to connect Thailand to then Burma. The most known spot along the former line nowadays is the Bridge over the River Kwai, in Thailand. At the time, we were planning to visit Thailand so though it would be interesting to pay a visit to both sides in both countries. At the Burmese end, there's a Death Railway Museum, which we didn't visit, and a well-maintained Cemetery which we did visit. Two bizarre things happened in that Cemetery.

For one, I saw my name on a grave...then it happened *again*, the second time with my middle initial as well. It's pretty creepy to see a grave with your own name on it. Even weirder to see it twice in the same graveyard.

Second, a local asked me for a selfie. This was the one place I refused out of all the requests we'd had across the country. I just held my arms out, looking around me hoping that would be enough to get the message across that this was not the time nor the place. Moved after paying our respects, we headed back for our last night in Mawlamyine, a town we'd grown to like over our few days there.

"How about we eat here tonight? Saves us heading out looking for something." Almost on cue as I said that to Ashley closing the door, the rain started. And it didn't stop. They were thick, heavy, frequent raindrops. Within minutes, there was a layer of water covering all the path and driveway outside.

"Yeah, I think so!" Ashley replied.

We ordered a feast of dishes we'd been wanting to try since we arrived - tea leaf salad, Shan noodles, and more vegetables and rice. It was delicious.

The next day was our last in Maulemine. We had the majority of a day to kill in the town before our night bus to Yangon, and meandered around the town before grabbing lunch at the Ocean Supercenter and even seeing a film (yes, we had *hours*!). We saw Avengers Infinity War. Not my choice of film, but there wasn't exactly much choice of film with just that and a film with a Burmese title on the list of showings. We headed in, complete with popcorn and drinks, taking advantage of the low prices at cinemas before we got back to the UK, and were surprised after the adverts to see a 90s style GIF of the Myanmar flag fill the screen with the words "Please stand for the National Anthem" written in both English and Burmese. We looked around and, sure enough, slowly people were getting to their feet. We followed suit as the music (presumably the national anthem) began playing. It ended without fanfare and everyone casually sat back down as if it were the most normal thing in the world, which I guess it is if you go to the cinema in Myanmar.

The film was in the original English version, and didn't have subtitles. I couldn't help but wonder how many people in the room understood enough English to understand everything going on in the film, to get the little nuances of language, the puns, the subtley, the hilarious "I don't feel so good, Mr Stark" before Spiderman slowly disintegrates into dust. If I were watching that scene and I didn't understand the language, I'd be totally lost, and that's if I'd made it this far into the film without leaving the cinema out of confusion. It will never cease to amaze me how internationally accepted English has become and I wonder if some other language will ever hold that position in the world in my lifetime.

That evening, we caught our bus back to Yangon and Ashley was not well. (Still try Burmese food!...Just maybe not when it's raining and from a small kitchen.)

He arrived in Yangon the next morning in one piece, but as soon as we arrived at the hotel, he was straight to bed, exhausted. I headed out to Junction City, the most impressive new shopping mall to grace the streets of the city centre since my last visit. As I walked straight down the road to the mall from our hotel, I felt a wave of comfort pass over me. I observed residents pulling their mail up on a string, attached to a bulldog clip to which the postman had clipped their post. I smiled at children playing as they hid behind trees and mothers, their shyness still visible through the thanaka on their faces. I effortlessly dodged holes in the pavement, navigating the streets beneath my feet like a dancer.

Remarkably, despite the illnesses we'd both fallen victim to, despite the pavements being beyond unfriendly to pedestrians, despite everything that could niggle and annoy someone not from this land, as I walked down that street, unaware of the next time I'd visit the country, I felt comfortable in Myanmar. I felt like I could live in Yangon for a year or so quite happily, and see it grow and change at the pace it is. I felt, on some deep level, a lasting connection with this country. I felt at peace.

Yet there's one big "despite" that can't be ignored. In 2011, Myanmar was a controversial place to visit. Many would argue it still is. It was inevitable that even if you tried really hard to avoid supporting the government with your tourist dollars, if you visited big sites like Bagan, you would be giving something to a government guilty of humanitarian crimes, a military junta that controlled the country under the thinly veiled guise of a 'government'.

Since then, fair(er) elections have taken place and Aung San Suu Kyi, beloved by her people and under house arrest for decades of her life, is now the de facto leader of the country. Yet things are still changing fast. In the time between my first draft and second edit of this chapter, Aung San Suu Kyi has been accused of doing too little and stripped of her status as Ambassador of Conscience by Amnesty International.

And yes, things are changing for the progress of Myanmar - international brands are moving in, ATMs are sprouting across the country like weeds, new shopping malls are making a name for themselves.

But progress doesn't just consist of commercial gains. At the time of writing (and at the time we visited) Myanmar is being condemned widely by the international community for its treatment of the Rohingya in the Western State of Rakhine. The predominantly Buddhist country has actively and undeniably treated the Muslim Rohingya atrociously. Rape, forced removal, abuse, killing. Journalists reporting the truth on the ongoing situation have been arrested, putting freedom of press at risk, something many hoped was a thing of the past.

There's no obvious answer as to why. It's just hate. It's a feeling of superiority - that "they" don't belong because "we" do, and "they" are different from "us".

Part of the current problem could be blamed on the very progress that promises to bring the country forwards and "in line" with the rest of the world after so long dragging behind under the military junta.

"Selfie one" may be just a new thing heard by us as we travelled the country, but when the selfies are taken, Facebook is opened - an app offered free of data usage for many - ready to upload those photos. And Facebook hasn't yet (at the time of writing) fully got to grips with Burmese script, never mind Burmese translations. For far too long, the options to report Facebook posts were written in English, not Burmese. And despite what you may be led to believe from the English plastering the walls and windows of the modern shopping malls, the majority of the Burmese population don't speak English, never mind read it.

This slow response from Facebook, to my mind, allowed hateful content to spread quickly and easily across the country's new favourite place to hang out - the mobile phone screen.

Of course, I'm not blaming Facebook for a genocide. But before we shake our heads and tut, reading this and observing from afar, we need to look at ourselves too. Similar things have happened across the world - hateful content spreading like wildfire and helping to cause damaging consequences. Maybe there is no "them" and "us" after all.

Vietnam

We always knew we'd have to have a more solid idea of how much time we wanted to spend in each country when we headed to Asia. After all, we'd be there for a lot less time than we were in Latin America. Vietnam, along with Myanmar, was a place we wanted to be for a bit longer, so we settled for three weeks in both countries, leaving less time for the others.

Vietnam intrigued us both. We were excited to explore the long and thin country straddling the eastern coastline of Southeast Asia. Plus we already had interviews lined up for Language Stories episode about Vietnamese, the first of which we'd recorded back in Peru.

Gaston Dorren, the author of one of my favourite books about language, Lingo, was learning Vietnamese for his upcoming book, Babel, exploring twenty of the world's most widely spoken languages. Unfortunately, our time in Vietnam didn't quite line up and Gaston visited the country while we were wrapping up our time in Latin America. So although we didn't get to meet in person for the second interview, we did speak on Skype during our first week in Vietnam, in Ho Chi Minh City.

Another possible lead for an interview was from Central Deaf Services, a school for Deaf children in the town of Da Nang, midway up the country on the coast. I emailed the first day we were in Ho Chi Minh City to confirm and we set up a time and date to meet, securing Da Nang as our next stop along our way up Vietnam.

But we still had a week to explore Ho Chi Minh City and catch up on work after three weeks of less working hours in Myanmar. And opportunities to meet people and do stuff were filling up our time there fast.

One of my students on my biggest program for online teachers, the Online Teaching Starter Kit, Jessica, lives in Ho Chi Minh City, so I spent an afternoon with her, which was great.

Not only that but Tri, from Language Accepted, messaged me on Instagram asking if I'd like to meet and he could teach me a few basic words to get by. I asked him if he'd like to do it on camera for Language Stories. He said yes. Things were coming together quickly in Vietnam!

We headed to one of the many drinks shops in our neighbourhood to meet Tri, who arrived on the back of a Grab moped. Grab is the Southeast Asian equivalent of Uber. Except it's better. Like, way better. You can choose to save money with a shared ride, you can order a Grab bike and get there faster and cheaper, or you can pick a regular car. Not only that but you get Grabpoints too, which you can spend on different stuff depending on which country you're in.

Oh, and there was another reason we lingered so long in Ho Chi Minh City: the Color Me Run. We'd done our first colour run in Mérida. It was messy, but it was a lot of fun. And Ashley won. Although there's no prizes for coming first in a colour run as most people are just in it for the 'Gram. So when we were looking for running races for Ashley to do in Asia, this seemed like a good one as it fitted in with our dates and plans quite well.

There's one big difference about these runs across the world compared to the UK. At home, you don't always get a t-shirt, and if you do, you get it at the end of the race or you pay for it. At all the races we did abroad, however, we had to go and pick up the race pack (including t-shirt!) at least a day before, most often from a shopping centre.

In Ho Chi Minh City, this meant getting a Grab six kilometres out of the city to a large mall two days in a row, as the race would be starting from the same place the following day. It also meant getting this Grab from outside a big cafe near our apartment that had wifi we could join from the street, because where we were staying the streets were too tiny for cars!

The shopping mall and surrounding area were a spacious relief from the tight busy streets of the majority of the city. Yet for all it's obvious causes of stress, the city has a friendliness to its bustle. Everyone is going somewhere or doing something and working hard.

The following day we repeated the same routine: walk to the cafe on the corner with wifi, book a Grab to take us to the race start line, and we were on our way, slowly lifted out of the city and to the suburbs. It was clear from the start this was a very casual event. There were food tents with free samples - and I'm not talking protein bars and energy gels typical of many races, more so free doughnuts.

We took a few photos with our coloured powder before the colours would mix into a muddy dark green as the race went on and more colours and sweat and water were added to the mix, and hung around the field by the start line waiting to be called over to the start.

"It's supposed to start in five minutes. Surely, we should have all been called over by now?"

People were still being entertained by the DJ at the stage at the other end of the field. No one seems worried about starting the race.

The race start time came and went, and about thirty minutes after we were due to start running, we were all called to the start line. I've never known a race start late, even with the stereotypical casual lateness of Latin American culture, every race Ashley had done there had been on time.

Eventually we set off, and it wasn't long before we reached the first colour station...well, I reached, Ashley was long gone by that point. It was blue. Powder and foam. And clean still. Somehow I was one of the first runners to reach the station - and I'm a slow and steady runner!

I kept going, passing various colour stations and each time getting a new dusting of a different colour to mix with my current palette. I heard a little voice from below tell me I'd run four kilometres. My Strava man from the running app on my phone.

I was nearly done! Hooray! It was a hot day after all, and sweat wouldn't mix well with this coloured powder. I approached the end of the road I was running on and turned left, joining the mass of people running.

Where had these guys all come from? Had I missed a corner somewhere? Oh well, I was near the end. Nearly done. Wait a minute...I've seen that weird abandoned farm machinery thing before. And that building. Is the route a loop?

"Distance: Five kilometres. Time:...." My Strava man started talking again, and I was not near the promised finish line. I realised what had happened as I saw a blue foam color station ahead of me. I was running the route again. I'd be running almost ten kilometres! For the first time in months! In this heat! On my own!

The blue colour station was a lot messier by the second time I reached it. The foam had formed a blue puddle of soggy ground beneath the inflatable arch that was spraying the foam.

The other color stations weren't much better. Most of the volunteers, who'd been so cheerful on my first loop, had now run out of coloured powder and enthusiasm, and were handing out water without cheering instead. Although most "runners" didn't need it as they were sat chilling by the side of the road, scraping powder from the road with their fingers and smearing it over their faces, hair, and clothes before taking a dozen or so selfies for social media.

That's when I realised why the event had such a casual start time. No-one was here to run! People just wanted photos, to up the saturation on that filter and make it look like they were living the dream when in actual fact they were sweating on a kerb with street dust in their eyes.

I ran when I could on my accidental second lap, but the sheer mass of walkers prevented me a lot of the way, and besides, no one else was running at this stage in the crowd. I looked like the odd one out when I did run, despite this, you know, being advertised as a Color *Run*. Fuming, I reached the finish line, where Ashley was waiting for me.

"How was that? I was getting worried about you," he said as I came back onto the field through the barrier, similar to that of a music festival.

"Well, I ran nine kilometres! I say ran, I mean I ran about five then had to walk and *try* to run. There was no one to tell you when to turn, no sign, and there was just a mass of people so I figured they must be going the right way and I'd gone the wrong way because hardly anyone was behind me, so I turned left instead of right and ended up running it all again! How did you do?"

"I came first."

No surprises. I was getting quite used to Ashley winning these smaller running events after winning twice in Mexico and coming third in the trail run in Paraguay while Michael the Millipede quietly slept in our room.

"But it was weird. Like they weren't ready here for anyone to finish at that time. And people were still starting, just walking with phones and stuff, it was odd." he continued.

"Yes! The selfies! Oh my God! I think 90% of people didn't run any of this at all!"

I feel like I should clear something up here. I'm all for people getting involved with events and activities at any fitness level. I think that's great. But I saw so many people that looked genuinely disinterested until they picked up their phone and struck a pose, and I don't understand why you would do such a messy event with 'run' in the title and not want to get messy or run. Maybe this is what Instagram has done to society. We'd already seen it so many times on our trip - from young women posing in the Cuban ocean while their friends took multiple shots from various angles to this. If you don't have photographic evidence, did it really happen?

After our free bubble tea purchased with vouchers from our race pack, we bought a pack of wet wipes from the supermarket downstairs in the mall and proceeded to stand outside what's probably the swankiest mall in Ho Chi Minh City and wipe ourselves clean. Well, as clean as possible. Then came the tricky bit: getting home.

I hailed a Grab using the wifi from the mall, and when it arrived, he refused us entry to his car by shaking his head and driving off with no further explanation, at least not one in a language we both understood.

"But we can't get any cleaner without a shower!" I said to Ashley as he drove off.

Thankfully, there was a kind, regular taxi driver waiting who agreed to take us after he took off his cotton seat covers. The ride cost twice what a Grab would have cost.

Still colorful, but by now mostly with patchy smears of green and blue on our legs, we walked back from the main road down through the narrow alleys to our apartment. Showering took around three or four times longer than usual but sure enough, we were eventually clean again, and ready for our night train to Da Nang the following day.

We didn't know what to expect after our "first class" train in Myanmar bringing a mouse along for the ride in the seat in front of us. I doubt he paid. Thankfully, the Vietnamese trains turned out to be a little better. For starters, we got a bed! We'd booked the top bunks in a six bed room, the cheapest of the three tiers, based on our experience of night trains in China a few years before.

We settled in and watched a Derren Brown Netflix special we'd downloaded for the journey, with the space between us and individual headphones calling for multiple wide-mouthed looks at each other to communicate throughout the show. Soon after, we settled down to sleep and when we awoke, we were just a couple of hours outside of Da Nang.

***

Da Nang isn't necessarily on the tourist route for most visitors to the country. Many use the towns of Hoi An or Hue to break up the journey between Ho Chi Minh City and Hanoi. Yes, everywhere in Vietnam begins with a 'H' apparently. Except Da Nang. Da Nang is an exception to the H rule, and sits comfortably between Hoi An and Hue, seemingly happy to let the bulk of tourists visit those two towns instead to keep Da Nang a liveable place. It was definitely the most liveable place we visited in all of Vietnam.

We were here to meet Nancy and Jeff, the founders of Central Deaf Services. I didn't know much about Vietnamese Sign Language, but I did know after meeting Tio Antonio and speaking with James Kegl about Nicaraguan Sign Language, that I was keen to cover more Sign Languages in future episodes of Language Stories. We weren't visiting the school until our second day in the city, so had most of the first day in Da Nang to ourselves to walk around and explore.

The beach is long, with various watersports happening along the shore. Da Nang may not yet be as popular as the neighbouring towns of Hue and Hoi An, but judging by the number of half-built hotels springing up facing the beach, it soon will be. Currently, it seems it's a hotspot for Chinese and Korean tourists, who visit so frequently that restaurant signage and menus is often translated into Chinese and/or Korean before English. There's also a simmering undercurrent of "digital nomads", evident from the long-haired white men who sit topless outside of cafes with English-only menus where most locals couldn't afford to eat.

The next day, we booked a Grab to take us to the school around 8.30am.

"Hey! So where are you going today?" our hotel owner asked as we waited.

My answer of "We're going to a Deaf School to make a documentary about language" was met with a blank stare and slow nod from our overly nosy hotel owner.

"Will you go to Hoi An? I have a great tour available and there's already a group of people going so it'll definitely be departing today..."

"No, sorry. We won't have time today."

Clearly we weren't hitting the expected regular tourist sights.

We arrived at the school, which, being a school for Deaf children, was much quieter than most schools at the start of the day. It was lovely.

Nancy and Jeff showed us around the classrooms and explained how the school operates.

We sat down to film with them both and Ashley filmed bits as we walked around the school that morning. Nancy and Jeff told us about the situation of sign language in Vietnam, where three sign languages are recognised: Hanoi, Haiphong, and Ho Chi Minh City. As well as teaching the children who attend the school each day, the teachers (who are all Vietnamese and Deaf themselves) teach at three of the four schools with Deaf children in the city. On certain days each week after school, parents and family members are also invited to come and learn sign language so they can communicate with their Deaf children. There's a lot of wonderful work going on there.

We left, thinking that would be it, until we got an email from Nancy that lunchtime asking if we'd like to come back and interview one of the teachers who had just agreed to be interviewed.

We had plans that afternoon, so we headed back the following morning and interviewed one of the teachers for our only non-English interview of the entire second season of Language Stories! I asked questions in English, which were then translated probably via Vietnamese by the

Vietnamese translator who signed my questions to the teacher. The teacher then responded in Vietnamese Sign Language and the translator repeated out loud what she said not in Vietnamese, but in English, not her first language. Jeff also stood by, on hand for any tricker translations from English to help me simplify any questions so they could be easily translated from Vietnamese into Vietnamese Sign Language. I know! Impressive stuff!

Phương, the teacher we interviewed was about my age with her hair tied back, glasses and a broad smile. She told us about what it was like for her growing up and attending school as a Deaf child and how things are different for Deaf children nowadays. When she was first at school, she didn't understand anything and would play with her friend instead of paying attention to the teacher. Gradually, throughout her education, new schools and opportunities opened up and after some years of successful Deaf education, Phương was invited to teach at Central Deaf Services in Da Nang.

After the interview, Jeff mentioned a cafe in the town where all staff are Deaf or hard of hearing. He then offered to take us there, and left after introducing us to the owner and a Deaf waiter who was happy to be interviewed by us turning up completely out of the blue. We sat with Binh and an interpreter for around 20 minutes. Much like Phương's school experience, things weren't always easy for Binh growing up. He's grateful to now be working in the cafe and told us how he enjoys meeting Western visitors. Towards the end of our interview, we asked the interpreter how she learnt sign language.

"I don't know why but I love it. I think God put the Deaf people in my head and in my heart."

It was an inspiring morning, and we were quite sad to have to be leaving Da Nang that afternoon, but I was very excited about our next destination: Phong Nha.

***

In 2011, on my first trip to Asia, I visited Gunung Mulu National Park in Malaysia, on Borneo. Mulu is an incredible caving destination and at the time boasted the biggest cave in the world. I didn't really know much about caves at the time. I'd been to a few show caves, I'd oohed and ahhed at luminously lit stalagmites and stalactites with the best of them. But I'd never travelled that far for a cave. Mulu isn't easy to get to. First, you have to get to Malaysian Borneo, most likely by plane to Kuching, Kota Kinabalu or Miri. Then you have to catch a small propeller plane from Miri to Mulu. Mulu is unreachable by road (although there are some propositions to build a road from Miri to Mulu) so at present it really is very remote. And you have to stay at the accommodation within the National Park - the cheapest of which being a large shared dorm building. I don't know what drew me to Mulu. I think it was simply the fact that it was "the biggest cave in the world".

"Well, if it's the biggest, it'll be worth visiting." I thought.

It was. Mulu was phenomenal and really got me into caves. And yes, I realise "it really got me into caves" sounds like an incredibly geeky sentence. But I don't care. Caves are cool. Everywhere now - the beach, the forest, the hills - you are connected in some way to the world. There's people or cars nearby, there's noise coming from somewhere, there's 4G - you're not alone. In a cave, it's the ultimate silence. You're truly "at one with nature" because you are quite literally *inside* nature. You're inside the earth. Yes, you can climb to the top of a mountain, you can dive deep down in the ocean, but nothing compares to actually being inside the earth in a cave. I love caves. I wish it was still socially acceptable for people to live in them. I'd be first in line.

Anyway, Phong Nha. Everything I'd read about Phong Nha was claiming that they had the "world's biggest cave", just as Mulu had claimed. So I did some more research. It turns out that Son Doong was discovered fully (well, perhaps not, I guess it could still be bigger) around 2009 and overtook Deer Cave at Mulu as the world's largest cave! Fuzzy memories started coming back to me of our guide in Mulu showing us the cave map before we went in and saying something like "This is the biggest cave in the world." and then mumbling, "But they've just discovered one in Vietnam that might be bigger but there's still exploring to be done there." before finishing with, "So anyway, we're about to go in the biggest cave in the world."

The thing is Son Doong is being incredibly well-preserved since its discovery and well under 1000 visitors are allowed per year, and they pay $3000 per person for the four day adventure. It's on my lifetime to do list. But not happening this time round at such short notice. That wasn't a problem however as there are so many other great caves to explore at Phong Nha.

As soon as we arrived in the town late at night, our hotel owners came to meet us at the bus station and walked us back to the hotel. Plastic folders were pretty much thrust into our hands with various tour options each with its own piece of A4 paper to promote it. Normally this would annoy me at 10 o'clock at night but if caves are involved, let me see. I don't want to waste a day.

We picked two day tours. One for the following day involved a well-lit showcave with a boardwalk followed by ziplining to another and wading through that cave to a mud bath after lunch. The day after was the one we were most excited about - kayaking into a cave and bouldering for another kilometre before settling down to lunch deep inside the cave and then going on a little further to a swimming pool inside the cave. Yes please.

As imagined, the first day was much more open to tourists. It surprised me no end to learn that most people who come to Phong Nha come only for one day's worth of cave exploring before heading off again. One day?! And I was worried our three days wouldn't be enough!

The day started well and the showcave was impressive, and a little less busy than what was to come. We headed to the next cave where we sat having lunch underneath the top of the zipline and overlooking the end of the zipline. Perfect to observe what was to come next..over and over again.

The zipline was constantly in use. No sooner had someone been unclipped at the bottom was someone else let loose from the platform above the restaurant. It was fun, but I was really here for the cave.

Bobbing in the water, life jackets pushing our heads up, we all waited for the last few in our group to zipline into the water before heading into the cave. This cave was much more adventurous than the morning show-cave, and started off quite enjoyable as we waded through muddy passages following our guide.

Gradually though, as we got closer to the mud pool, the noise got louder, echoes filled the cave, and we had to stop more frequently to let other people pass back out of the cave. This was a busy cave. This was everything I hated about tourist caves. This was not the ultimate silence deep inside the earth.

We reached the pool, where we'd been told firmly by our guide (and overheard from many other guides too) not to throw the mud. And of course, there's always one...or seven. A group of obnoxious young folk flirted as if for the first time, throwing mud at each others manbuns and bikini-clad bodies. Yay, cave silence. It didn't fully ruin the day, and our first day tour was still a memorable and worthwhile experience, but it was nothing compared to what was to come tomorrow.

The next day, we awoke, had breakfast nice and early again, and waited downstairs for our minibus. There were only four others in our group this time, an older couple from Quebec and two Korean guys. From the get go, you could sense this would be a much calmer day.

We stopped off at a hotel to pick up our gear - lifejackets, shoes, helmets, etc, and then headed across to the cave. On a bank by the river leading into the cave, our minibus stopped and we all clambered out, making our way down to the small dock, where four inflatable kayaks sat waiting, including one for our guide. I was told to sit in the front and Ashley behind me, and within minutes, we were out in the middle of the water on our own in a kayak for the first time.

"Why are we going around in a circle?!" I called back to Ashley.

"I don't know! Maybe, because I can see you, I'll call a side, you paddle then we're both going the same way?"

"Ok!" I called back, oar resting horizontal across the kayak, awaiting my next instruction.

"Ok, left!" Ashley said, as I dutifully put the left paddle of my oar into the water and pushed back. We moved a bit.

"Ok, now right…"Ashley said, I did the same on my right side.

"Are we going forward?" I called.

"I think so...Let's do it again and see if we can get to the entrance of the cave"

Slowly, we got the hang of it. Or rather, I invented my own unique method of kayaking which involved pushing the oar forwards instead of backwards from time to time to straighten up. Not pro, but it did the job.

We all kayaked into the cave, headlamps clicking on in unison as we passed the bit where the outdoor light was enough, and it wasn't long before we were told to pull up to the right side on a sand bank.

"How do we start kayaking again? I don't know if I can get the thing moving again!" I whispered to Ashley as we stepped out of our kayak.

Stopping proved worth it. We'd stopped to see some ancient cave writing on a spot tucked away within the cave, written by the Cham people who lived in the region many years ago. Nowadays there are still small numbers of Cham people in modern-day Cambodia, but none in this part of Vietnam. The writing was cool - I mean, language in a cave? That's like my dream day! But there were bits of it that looked like modern graffiti and it made me question how much of what we were seeing was actual original Cham writing and how much was just someone declaring their love 4 u 4eva.

Moving on from the Cham writing, we had a longer distance to kayak before our next stop, which was our last on this leg of the journey. As we all fumbled around getting the things we wanted to take with us out of bags and into pockets, our porter went on ahead, carrying lunch. We followed in his direction, climbing over rocks and boulders, truly on our own in the cave now, away from the first kilometre or so where boats full of other tourists circled in and out.

Eventually, we made it to a plateau, a long flat plain, where our porter was waiting. He'd put electric lanterns down on the rock, and was laying the last few trays of food onto a picnic blanket. We ate lunch right there, deep in this cave. We were the only people to do that on that day. That's pretty magical.

Lunch was a delicious combination of Vietnamese make-it-yourself fresh spring rolls and banh mi baguettes, which was, oddly enough for communist not-so-friendly-with-the-USA Vietnam, washed down with a red can of Coca-Cola each.

When we'd finished, our guide turned off all the lights and for those few moments, we were in the darkest of darknesses, alone inside a cave with just a handful of other people. I realise that for many people reading this, that may sound terrifying, but please do try caving if you get a chance. There's something quite comforting and relaxing about finding yourself in complete and utter silence and darkness, something so difficult to achieve in modern life.

After lunch, we only had a little further to go into the cave before heading back, but this was the really special bit: the swimming pool. We clambered and climbed, not always gracefully over more rocks to reach the pool. It was big. Bigger than you could imagine a pool inside the earth to be.

"Ok, so now you all have to jump off from here, one by one." our guide said, with a dry wit.

Everybody laughed it off, as we all stripped down to our swimwear (and lifejackets) and made our way to the lower level rocks where we could gently dip our toes before submerging our bodies at a comfortable pace.

Except for Ashley. Ashley was up for it. He was ready to jump. And he did.

I stood at the edge from where he'd just jumped and looked down. It was a long drop. You might remember from the cenotes in Mexico that I'm not a huge fan of jumping into water at the best of times.

"You can do it! Come on! It's not so bad!" Ashley shouted back up to me.

"It's very deep here so no problem hitting rocks, and you keep lifejacket on, you will be ok." the guide was next to me, feeding me equal encouragement.

I hesitated. Then I opted out and went down to the low rocks where everyone else had by now tentatively made their way in. I did the same and swam around to Ashley.

"I couldn't do it. I just don't like jumping into water" I said.

"That's ok!" Ashley replied.

There was quite literally no pressure from anyone to jump. Ashley was fine, the guide was fine, no one else had jumped. So I don't know quite what it was that compelled me to get out of the water and back up to the high ledge.

I stood for longer than before, counting to three and pulling myself back multiple times. I walked away from the edge. Then suddenly I turned back around, and I did it.

I landed. Everyone cheered. I was still alive.

After an incredible day, doing so many things for the first time, I think it was knowing I'd likely never be back here again that encouraged me just enough to complete the day and jump in the pool.

Dry clothes becoming damp against our wet swimwear, we began to head back out of the cave. This is the easy bit, right?

More or less. Until one of the Korean guys in front of me dropped his bag between two large rocks as he climbed across them. I was stood behind him at the time, my reactions too slow to reach out and grab the bag for fear of falling myself as both hands were being used to keep balance.

In what felt like slow motion, we both watched the bag fall until moments after we could see it no more, we heard a distant thud of it landing somewhere. We looked up at each other. Everyone else had heard too.

"Is everything ok? What happened?" said our guide as he made his way back to us.

"I drop my bag" the Korean guy replied. Remarkably calm, he turned to walk onwards, seemingly already believing that he'd never see it again.

"Oh…" our guide stepped between us and looked down, shining his torchlight, "Down here, yeah? One moment."

He shouted something to the porter ahead of us in Vietnamese and the porter soon returned into view, before the two of them disappeared down between the rocks.

The six of us left at the top found passable places to sit while we waited. A silent feeling of 'well, it's clearly gone forever but it's nice they're trying' swept over the group. Remarkably, minutes later, the guide emerged.

"Is this it?" he shouted up.

"Yes!" the Korean guy replied.

We looked around at each other in awe, jaws wide, and soon we were back on our way as if nothing had ever happened.

We kayaked our way to the entrance of the cave (this time basically like pros...ok, well not quite, but better than before) and then we waited.

"It's raining so we can't kayak out to the dock yet. We need to wait for the rain to stop." our guide informed us.

"Wait, so...we can clamber over all those wet rocks, and it's totally fine to swim in that pool with the current pulling you to your potential death, and there's no problem whatsoever with jumping into the pool...but we can't kayak outside because it's *raining*?" I asked Ashley, somewhat sarcastically. He smiled back.

Rain isn't quite like drizzle at home in the UK in places like Vietnam. More often than not, big tropical raindrops are followed by thunder and lightning. The possibility of our kayak getting hit by lightning was something that our guide wouldn't risk. I know, I feel like there were bigger risks inside the cave too. But, regardless, we waited until the rain cleared.

When we got back to our hotel that evening I told Ashley that it had been one of my favourite days of the whole trip. Then I thought again. I think it was one of the best days of my life. Definitely top ten.

***

From Phong Nha, we took a night bus to Hanoi which connected us with a second bus to Sapa, where I'd been planning on making an episode of Language Stories about Hmong.

However, every company I could find online that arranges tours and homestays with Hmong locals, had replied to my email asking if they know someone who'd be happy to be interviewed, with a generic "please let us know which package you want and we can book it for you" email.

So, we were arriving with nothing booked. We had one night arranged in a cheap hotel in the town of Sapa itself, and were relying on various accounts I'd read online of locals gathering around you as you got off the buses, keen to take you on a trek to their village for the night.

We got lucky.

"Trekking? Trekking? You want come trekking?" one woman asked with a beaming smile.

"Yes, but not today. Tomorrow maybe?"

"Yes tomorrow, tomorrow. One night? Two night? We trek, sleep in my home in village and I show you many things."

"Ok, and how much?"

"$30 one person."

"$30 for everything?" This was not what I was expecting. The cheapest thing I'd found online was $60.

"Yes! Trekking, sleeping, eating, and trekking back next day."

I turned to Ashley who was being equally bombarded. I thought against interrupting and turned back around to the ladies in front of me.

"And you speak Hmong?"

"Yes! Yes!" the ladies faces lit up, "We are Hmong people, we speak Hmong yes!"

"Ok, good! We are making videos about languages, and we want to speak with you about Hmong. Is this ok? To speak on camera about Hmong language, and culture…"

They spoke amongst themselves, probably in Hmong, and another younger woman was presented to me.

"You want to know about Hmong? You want to interview me?" she said, smiling. Her English was better than the woman I'd been speaking with.

"Yes please! If that's ok?"

"Yes, yes, and trekking tomorrow yes? Not today?"

"Yes, tomorrow please! One night. $30 yes?"

She nodded, confirming the price. I chatted with Ashley briefly before agreeing with her that we'd meet at 8am the following morning on this corner. A bracelet was placed on my arm and she put out her little finger.

"Tomorrow, 8am, right here. We come for you. You be here, yes? Pinky promise?" she said.

"Pinky promise!" I replied, locking my little finger in with hers.

The following morning, we dutifully headed down to where we'd agreed to meet and after a nervous fifteen minute wait, one of the ladies from the day before appeared around the corner. She wasn't the one I'd pinky promised but was definitely with her yesterday.

"Sorry!" she said as she approached us, "I was eat breakfast! You are ready?"

"Yes," we nodded in response.

"Ok, let's go."

We started by walking past the cafes with numerous men sat outside smoking from long bamboo pipes that look suspiciously like oversized versions of bongs you'd find on that shady stall at the marketplace back home. When I say a long pipe, I don't just mean pointing outwards from the mouth. These pipes are long to the floor. Clips on the internet show tourists trying to "be a local" and collapsing after taking one puff on the thing.

We made our way towards the market. After a few minutes at the market, we began to leave the town taking stairs and hilly cobbled trails up and out past houses through the trees. It wasn't long before we caught up with another group of trekkers. Our guide started talking to their guide. After about another five minutes, she turned to us and said, "I go now because I walk yesterday so very tired. She is my sister. She go with you now."

"Ok, and we sleep at your house? Will she take us to your house?"

"Yes, all ok!" she replied, practically already halfway back down the hill.

Ashley and I looked at each other and shrugged our shoulders. We kept walking.

We had been on our own with the first guide, but now there was around eight of us, including us two new additions to the group.

After a long walk, frequently bumping into other groups of trekkers and local guides, and a lunch stop midway, we made it to the house where we'd be staying at mid-afternoon. The views across the rice paddy fields and hills were amazing. And there was wi-fi! We'd weaved our way to the top of these hills and there was wi-fi?!

"So, when do you think we should ask about filming for Language Stories?" Ashley asked me quietly as we sat on the porch.

"I'm not sure, I'm thinking tomorrow morning but we'll see how it goes. I haven't seen the girl that I pinky promised yet…"

That night we ate well. Plates upon plates of food were brought out to the hall in the building with the bedrooms, where we all sat around low tables and tucked in. It was then I recognised, Chua, the woman I'd pinky promised. She saw me and got up to come and talk.

"Hello! You want to talk about Hmong, yes?"

"Mmm! Yes, please! Do you want to talk now or are you here tomorrow?"

"Tomorrow is good. Now I've drank some happy water already so not good for camera!" she laughed infectiously.

At various points on the trek that day we'd come across fields of cannabis growing, which the guide referred to as what they use for "happy tea". "Happy water" on the other hand is (by all accounts) an alcoholic spirit they make with rice, although some online accounts do state other ingredients such as opium.

We agreed to meet early tomorrow morning and she would come with clothes to talk about on camera. It sounded great and she sounded keen.

The following morning, after breakfast, Chua arrived and we were ready to film.

"Here, wear this so you can look Hmong!" she said with a smile, holding out a pile of dark indigo clothes with bright well-stitched patterns peeking through the folds of fabric.

We started with the legs and Chua tied the black indigo panels to my calves before handing me a pair of short trousers to pull up over my own. Next came the jacket, a heavy, stiff and shimmery indigo jacket with rows of beautifully cross-stitched coloured pattern around the waist.

Dressed, we were ready to film. Chua was very sweet and honest in her interview and I got the impression she was genuinely happy to be asked about her culture. She explained how the Hmong language isn't written down because when her ancestors came from Mongolia they lost their books in the river.

"Oh! Hmong, Mongolia...is that where the name comes from?!" I asked, making etymological connections between the two words.

"Yes! Our ancestors are from Mongolia."

When it came time to researching for this episode back home, it soon became apparent that many academics have disproven the 'Hmong from Mongolia' theory. I felt somewhat sad for Chua. She has this story of her heritage that she's proud of, that may actually be untrue. Everyone wants to know where they come from, and I suppose we're keen to retell the bits of the story that we like and want to keep, especially if we've never been told it's untrue.

An hour or so later we headed out together for our trek. Just Ashley, me, and Chua. Everyone else was going together with the guide from yesterday but I think she wanted more time with us to talk about Hmong language and culture, which I was grateful for.

We walked all around the village and right up to the highest point at the top of a waterfall overlooking the whole valley. The views across countless rice paddies are spectacular.

As we talked and walked, I learnt that Chua had never been anywhere beyond Sapa. I asked if she'd like to go to Hanoi one time and she said she wasn't too fussed.

When we returned home, someone said to me how travel is great because "it's all about becoming a better version of you when you get home". I disagree. Travel is about becoming a better version of you, yes, but when you think less selfishly than that, it becomes about much more. One of those things is about sharing what you know with others as much as they share it with you. Chua doesn't want to travel further than the village a thirty minutes drive away (or an eight hour trek away!) but that doesn't mean she'll never "become a better version of herself". She meets people from across the world each and every day and learns from them. Even if she didn't meet those people, that doesn't mean she's never got the option to "become a better version of herself". Travel isn't just about what you take home to improve your life, travel is also about what you leave behind to help improve the lives of *others*; be it thoughts, things, knowledge, or friendship for a day.

Chua and I have led very different lives, yet somehow, through simply being the same age and gender and talking with her, I felt that if I lived there or she lived here, we'd be friends. She's smart and funny, and she has a good heart. I'd love the chance to meet her again someday. But also, I'm not naive. I know she meets hundreds of travellers passing through each year just like me and Ashley. Would she remember me if we met again? Either way, I remember her, and still have the friendship bracelet she tied around my wrist.

***

After Sapa, we had just one more stop in Vietnam: Hanoi. We also had one potential interview lined up for Hanoi, and after a final confirmation message, we set and date and time to meet.

I'd found Vietnam Teaching Group online, and reached out to their Facebook page to see if they'd like to discuss the Vietnamese language with us for Language Stories. What we didn't know is that we'd be coming full circle.

We approached the cafe entrance tucked into the corner of the narrow street and were met with a wave and an "Are you Lindsay?" from a young woman already sat waiting for us. Ashley headed in to get drinks and I stayed with who I soon discovered was Sapphire to explain a little more about Language Stories.

"So, it's a series, we've just finished publishing the first series in Latin America, and now we're filming the second one in Southeast Asia. It's all about different languages and speaking to people like you, teachers, and learners, as well as other people doing interesting things with the languages for each episode too. So one episode will be about Vietnamese. We've spoken already with Gaston Dorren, who wrote the book..."

"Gaston Dorren?! I know him! I taught him Vietnamese! He writes books about language?!" she exclaimed.

"Yes! Wait...you taught him?! You actually taught Gaston when he was here in Vietnam?!" I couldn't believe our luck.

"Yes I did!"

"That's so funny!"

Sapphire had invited a friend and fellow teacher Shinegi and we interviewed them both together, very happy and still amazed that our first episode for season two had come together so well!
In fact, we had three ready from Vietnam: Vietnamese, Vietnamese Sign Language and Hmong.

Vietnam had been well worth the extra time we spent there. The question now was, would we be spending too little time in Laos and Cambodia as a result?

Laos

Season 2, Episode 3: Teaching English in Laos

Laos was the first country I missed as a result of going to hospital in Bangkok on my last trip to Asia. The place I'd wanted to go to most that time round. Luang Prabang, the Plain of Jars, Si Phan Don, caves...there was a lot I wanted to see. But after three weeks of moving pretty fast around Vietnam, we opted to keep things simple and spent one week in Luang Prabang and one week in Vientiane.

I thought I knew what to expect from Luang Prabang - a backpacker town with topless white guys "finding themselves" in every direction. Actually, it was much nicer than that. The town-wide curfew on alcohol and noise to allow the monks to get some sleep before their early rise probably helps. It's a small town, perhaps even too small for the swell of tourists it receives being the biggest tourist draw to the country. Yet they cope.

It was nothing short of a treat to be able to walk down the street in Luang Prabang and not feel that you were risking your life crossing the road after our time in the Vietnamese cities. And besides, we had work to do, we needed to be here for a while.

I'd discovered the website Lao Learns English when searching for language things going on in Laos and knew I had to get in touch. I got a reply from Evan, who lives in the US, and who told me that Jer, the teacher in the town, would be happy to meet with us. But we had some time before then.

So we took our first day in the country to explore the town. The main drag is a mixture of cafes and restaurants, and shops and tour agencies. Not that we'd need a tour agency with the amount of times we were offered a trip to the waterfall by the *jạmbǫh* ('jumbo' - like a tuk-tuk truck) drivers on our walk into town.

With no plans or direction, we reached the end of the town, as clarified to us by the river now in front of us creating the edge of the town. We turned left and weaved our way back, taking a slight detour up a hill, which turned out to be one of the most popular attractions in the town, Mount Phousi. The hill is adorned with a collection of small shrines and Buddha statues, mostly golden in the sun, that you stumble across as you climb the stairs to the top.

We climbed up and made our way to the top. As we walked around the monument at the top, I noticed an eldery Lao woman weaving a leaf of some kind into a small basket, presumably to be filled with little colourful flowers like the other baskets on the table in front of her. Also on the table in front of her was a plastic woven basket with a similar but differently coloured lid placed on top. Inside were lots of small birds, chirping.

I got my phrasebook out to tell the woman that the baskets she was making are pretty. Ashley started to film me flicking through the pages, but all she saw was a camera pointed in her direction. She said something that sounded aggressive and hostile in Lao and covered the bird basket, a sure sign she knew that what she was doing is frowned upon and unacceptable in other parts of the world, possible even in Laos too (we never did find out). We left.

***

One of the often cited highlights of Luang Prabang is the night market. It is quite a sight. The sleepy calm main street transforms at night into an unrecognizable marketplace. Sellers lay out their wares on tarpaulins illuminated with big, bright, white bulbs. Down a narrow side street is the food. We headed there for our first evening in Luang Prabang and were pleased to find a big banner "Vegetarian Buffet Lao Food" hung above rows of bowls of different curries, vegetables, rice, noodles...yes please. We both don't eat meat and had struggled with street food so far in Asia as a result, often ending up with self-mixed instant noodles and tofu and fresh vegetables in the room in Myanmar, and did the same but with noodles replaced by baguettes in Vietnam. So it was a real treat to see a place like this.

The next day, we'd arranged to do a Hmong batik class which we'd found online at Backstreet Academy. After meeting and speaking with Chua in Sapa (and trying on her indigo clothes!), we were interested to learn more about the traditions of textiles and clothing of the different groups of Hmong people, and we thought it would be interesting footage for the Hmong episode of Language Stories.

"Hello? Sabaidee?" I said as I gently walked into the shop attached to the workshop.

A thin man in a loose white vest top appeared from the door at the back of the shop.

"Ahh, hello! Batik?"

"Yes. I'm Lindsay, this is Ashley." I replied.

"Hello, hello! Please come, sit."

We were ushered into the workshop nextdoor where two low stools were waiting for us next to a pile of wooden blocks with metal details attached to the bottom: the stamps. Across the workshop was a small fire on the ground with a metal pot on top. We could hear the wax gently bubbling inside.

"Ok, so here is your fabric," the man said as he came back into the room, presenting us each with a teatowel-sized rectangle of hemp cloth, "And wax is here. So you go…" he reached across to the stamps, "stamp, and in wax, then press on fabric. But first this is only test fabric."

We spent a few minutes experimenting with the amount of wax we needed on each stamp before being presented with our actual pieces of fabric, the ones we'd be taking home. At first, I don't think either of us knew what we wanted to create so we just started by picking the stamp patterns we liked until Ashley decided what to do.

"I know what I can do!" he said.

"What's that?"

"Well, I've got this pattern thing going on," he was referring to the small stamps of curls he'd started at the top of his piece, "That could be steam from a coffee cup! With everything I've learnt about coffee, that seems pretty appropriate."

"Ohh, I like it! That's fun!" I looked back down at mine, the patterns around the edges complete, and if I say so myself, looking pretty good, "I wonder if I write coffee in different languages? Then they're a matching pair but mine is language-related so it's obviously mine."

I checked my phrasebook for coffee in the languages I didn't know how to spell - Khmer, Lao, Thai, Vietnamese and carefully wrote them out with the wax pen that had also been in the pile of stamps. I say pen, it's not like a biro. It's a wooden handle with a metal curved tip leading to a point, which writes like a pen with the wax. Slowly but surely our pieces came together, and before long we were done.

"Good! Good! So now, we soak in indigo dye and tomorrow you come back to get them."

We put our pieces in the barrel of indigo dye by the door and said our goodbyes. It would soon be time to meet Jer. We walked back to our hotel, swapped day bags for camera bags, and headed to where we'd agreed to meet him.

Sure enough, a younger than expected man soon approached us and introduced himself as Jer. We made our way to a cafe down by the riverside and started filming. It turned out that Jer is actually Hmong, a different Hmong group to Chua who we'd met in Sapa, so we asked him about that too.

After the interview, Jer offered us the chance to visit his class that evening but we didn't want to surprise the class by showing up with a camera out of the blue, so we agreed to visit the following day, allowing him a chance to tell the class we'd be coming. Before Jer left us, he agreed a good price with a taxi driver to pick us up and bring us back to Luang Prabang the following day as Jer's house, also where his classroom is, is in a small village outside of the town.

Jer built his classroom from scratch with the help of his friends and family in his family's yard. He teaches English every evening Monday to Friday, and takes his students to the night market in Luang Prabang on Thursday evening to practice what they've learnt that week with foreign tourists. When we showed up to class the following evening, this is what we got to practice:

Hello, where are you from? Please may I practice my English with you? I live in Luang Prabang. Do you like Luang Prabang? How long have you been here? Where have you been? Did you visit the waterfall? What did you think?

Jer had done a good job creating a useful resource full of relevant language for his students.

There were two different classes the evening we attended, divided by age and ability. Both Ashley and I got the chance to stand up and teach parts of the lessons. Ashley is a primary school teacher at home, and although we met working in a school together as Learning Support Assistants, I'd never seen him actually teach a class. It was a joy to see. Especially knowing how much he was missing work by this point.

When we're at home and he comes home and tells me of his assessments where his teaching has been awarded an 'outstanding' rating, it's obviously amazing but it didn't mean as much until I saw it with my own eyes. And this was a lesson he wasn't expecting to teach! Thrown in at the deep end, so to speak! By this point in the trip, we knew he'd be going back to work at the same school he'd taught at before we left and a part of me yearned for us to get on a plane the following day so he could have the chance to dive right back into the job he loved.

There was a part of me that felt selfish for wanting this trip, for almost holding Ashley back from his career progression by effectively taking a year and Tippexing it out on his CV. But since we've returned, he's taught a whole topic on Japan (Japan chapter coming up in this book soon), the Mayans, and has a wealth of knowledge about Latin America, Incas, and Asia to share with his classes of the future. He even had children come in after a couple of lessons about Japan and say "ohayo gozaimasu", something they'd gone off and learnt it themselves, inspired by his teaching. That makes me happy, and proud. And not just because it's language-related. Because it's proof that the year was worth it. We both know we did the right thing.

Jer never needed to call for the taxi driver to pick us up again. Instead two of the older students who rode in on mopeds offered to take us into town on the back of their bikes. We arrived right in the middle of the Night Market, the town looking busier than it ever had. Inspired, we headed home.

***

We had one more thing lined up for our time in Luang Prabang, a Hmong cooking class. We were picked up by tuk-tuk with our guide who took us out to a local village high up a dirt road. The tuk-tuk couldn't drive all the way up, so we had to walk the rest of the way to the house where we'd be doing the class. It was just us - perfect.

The house was a wooden one, with a straw roof reaching out over the side to shelter the mud earth yard around one side of the house, which was separated from the road by a handbuilt mud wall. A lady with a bright smile opened the gate and let us in. There was a mass of bright vegetables on the table - platefuls of vibrant, green, leafy herbs and vegetables; a bowl of thin, long aubergines; another bowl with two strange-looking bulbous burgundy things; two long sticks, and a Lao-English picture dictionary.

The two strange-looking bulbous burgundy things turned out to be banana flowers. Yes, as in the flower from a banana tree! And the two long sticks were rattan. Yes, as in that thing that baskets and woven chairs are made of!

We started with the rattan, which we threw straight onto the fire as they were. The thick woody outer layer means that this is the easiest way to cook them and eventually get to the flesh inside.

Next up was preparing the vegetables, which each required washing five different times. It's hard to know if this was just how they did things up here (the leafy green stuff had been picked from the forests that morning) or if they'd been told to wash things this many times to avoid tourists like us getting sick and leaving bad reviews. Either way, with no running water or sink on hand, there was a lot of refilling the bowls from the water barrel of fresh water by the tap around the front of the house. We weren't allowed to wash the vegetables there as this was also where the family washed themselves. Eventually, the vegetables were all clean and cut, and placed into various pans spread over two or three small fires started by the father of the family hosting us.

Soon it was time to get mashing! Dips are apparently quite a feature of Laotian cuisine, a fact I learnt when looking for an experience like this one. We were making dips. We mixed the ingredients into their various combinations and mashed them together, the mother of the family adding copious amounts of salt to each dip after every taste test. For the amount of food and time it took to prepare, I have to be honest and say it didn't make an impressive amount of dip, but as the dips were quite bitter (and salty) that wasn't a problem. We said our goodbyes and headed back into Luang Prabang with our guide.

The last couple of days were spent relaxing in this ridiculously chilled-out town. We rented bikes and rode out to the next town; we paid a visit to the fancy-looking, pricey coffee shop for a drink and cake (to honour our new coffee-inspired indigo artworks, you understand); and we enjoyed an abundance of mangosteen that I purchased from a lady by the roadside one afternoon.

If you've never had mangosteen, I can't recommend them enough. They really are my favourite fruit. I just wish they were more widely available in the UK. They come in a hard purple shell, with an almost comical green-leaved plume on top. Once you break through the shell (dying your fingers bright pink in the process) or you cut through the shell at the centre and twist open, you're met with a white, semi-translucent segmented ball of deliciousness. I can't describe the flavour with words that would do it justice but they are a true joy.

***

Vientiane is a place many travellers in the region skip or pass through quickly on their way between countries. We'd be here for a week. We had two interviews lined up, and the last of season one of Language Stories to release. It'd be a busy week.

The city often gets the label of the most chilled-out capital in the world, and rightfully so. There is traffic, but a lot less than its neighbouring country cities. There are malls, but a lot smaller and less manic than its neighbouring countries. Basically, Vientiane is a place that has everything you'd expect from a big capital city, but just with the volume turned down a notch or two.

We were staying in a new "loft" apartment, a term I'd only just learnt from booking the place. It describes an Ikea-worthy designed place with a ladder leading to a mezzanine where the bed is, and, in this loft apartment, a small sofa area too. Downstairs was a compact kitchen area, a breakfast bar for eating (and working, in our case), a desk, a sofa, and a newly finished bathroom...with a bath. Southeast Asia was bringing out all the luxury with these baths now - first in Myanmar and now Laos. We were spoilt for choice after having gone so long without a bath. This was definitely one of the nicest places we'd stayed all year. We were glad we'd be here for so long.

Our first interview was with ARDA languages school, a school that teaches both English to Laotians and Lao to foreigners. We spoke with Rachel about the Lao language, herself being a Brit who has learnt the language after living in the country for years.

The second was arranged through Martin from Momobooks who I'd contacted initially about the episode and who recommended I contact these people on the ground in Laos. It turned out that
these people work for the Education for Development Fund in Laos. Distributing Momobooks to schools in the country is only part of what they do. Their work focuses on reaching remote schools in Laos and providing them with the means to teach English and other subjects, be those means technology, technology training, or Momobooks. It's valuable and inspiring work.

But that was only a fraction of our time, the rest of the week was spent between work, the malls, running along the riverfront, and a visit to COPE, a centre that provides prosthetic limbs to Laotians who have physical disabilities, often due to the war.

Much like a room at the War Museum we'd visited in Vietnam, it was fascinating to see how Laos handles disability, especially when the country is the most bombed in history as a result of fallout from the Americans bombing Vietnam during the Vietnam War.

As tragic an event as it was, I do wonder if the high number of people left with missing limbs and physical disabilities altered the perception of disability in the country. At least in the centre, the reaction appeared positive - an attitude to help and assist people, and to treat them normally came through. It is an interesting place worth a visit if you're in Vientiane, even for a short while.

I can see why people skip Vientiane, or pass through briefly, but I'm glad we had longer in this chilled capital city. It didn't take long for the place to become one of my favourite places in Asia.

Cambodia

Cambodia. Known to most as a place of gap year travellers, Angelina Jolie adopting children, Angkor Wat and a history of genocide, if known at all. I'd struggled to find interviewees for a Language Stories episode, so we wouldn't get to know it much more ourselves, but were keen to make our eight days there count to learn as much as we could about the place.

We arrived in the tourist hotspot of the country, Siem Reap, the town that serves as the jumping off point for visitors to Angkor Wat. Angkor Wat is a remarkable sight. It's a temple complex that serves as the biggest tourist draw to the country. For many years, history covered the site until it was rediscovered by the French in the mid-19th century. Bit by bit, they uncovered temple after temple to unearth one of the architectural wonders of the world.

By all accounts, it was quite a big area, and impossible to cover in a day by foot, so we opted for a bike tour after stumbling upon Grasshopper Tours online and visiting their office to find out more the following day.

After booking, we found a lovely cafe where we stopped for a drink, and discovered they offer a vegetarian Cambodian cooking class. We booked that too for the day after and our time in Siem Reap was mostly set!

We arrived bright and early the following morning at the Grasshopper office and got measured up for our bikes. Before long we began the worst bit of the whole bike ride - through the streets of Siem Reap on our way out of the town. Crossing the road was bad enough but biking as part of the traffic was pretty terrifying and I discovered I had a tendency to end up right at the back, separated from the group, Ashley unable to turn around in the traffic to come and meet me. Regardless, I kept on trucking and we soon found ourselves at the Angkor Wat ticket office, where we'd visited the day before.

"If we'd known we were coming here again we needn't have bothered coming all the way out here to get tickets yesterday!" we said to each other as we waited for the final few in our group to get their tickets. It had been a long walk out from the centre of the town to the ticket office the previous afternoon. And not an overly enjoyable one in part thanks to the Cambodian tuk-tuk driver who insisted on cruising beside us, sure we'd give up and need his services eventually. If only he'd conversed with the Salvadoran guide on that volcano, he'd have known not to underestimate me. His persistence only made us more determined to get there by walking alone. Yes, I may have a stubborn streak.

Still a good three kilometres from the site entrance, we took the scenic route, which was a lot longer - and definitely more exciting than the long straight tarmacked road we could have taken. We veered off the main road and onto a muddy track littered with stones and rocks poking their way through the mud desperate to expose one of their sides to a mud-free world….and to our tyres. We bounced and bopped our way through the really rocky bits, carefully negotiated the narrow bits, and smiled and said hello to the children in the village bits. The children (and even adults in some cases) were clearly used to the group daily cycling past their homes and ran out to greet us, stopping what they were doing to practice their hellos and smiles on us tourists. The villages were a far cry from the modern paved streets of Siem Reap, with wells and water pumps a common sight along the route. It was strange to think we'd only rode a few kilometres out of town. This is probably how a large number of Cambodians live, hidden from view of tourist glimpses into the tapestry of the country.

Soon we were met with a tarmacked road, and turned up towards Angkor Wat. We reached the ticket checkpoint. I always wonder with places like this if the guides become slightly blasé to the whole thing. Somewhere that for many is a once in a lifetime experience, for the guides is simply their daily life.

"What do you do?"

"I work at Machu Picchu."

"I'm a gardener at Tikal."

"I take tours around Angkor Wat."

Would places like that become boring if they're simply a place of work, I wonder?

I remember when I visited Gunung Mulu National Park (the place that had the biggest cave until Vietnam's Soong Dong took the crown) the guide I had on most of my tours was incredible. Everything she pointed out, she did so with a sense of genuine wonder and amazement. You could tell that she loved where she grew up, where she lived, and now where she worked. She was the living and breathing example of "at one with nature".

We headed in past the ticket checkpoint and soon stopped at our first temple - Angkor Wat - but not what it looked like in the photos. We were at the back of the site, the quieter entrance. As would become clear throughout the day, these temples were also the epitome of "at one with nature", with vines and tree roots hugging the stone structures and curving them out of shape in places as they found a path between two large stones. This "nature taking over" element to the place is one of the reasons it became a filming spot of the Tomb Raider film with Angelina Jolie, who went on to adopt her first child Maddox Chivan from the country a few years later. Jolie is still quite a celebrated person in the country, especially since the release of her directorial debut First They Killed My Father, a heartbreaking film about a little girl's life under the Khmer Rouge. Respectfully, the film is presented in Khmer, with a Cambodian cast.

Next we visited Ta Prohm, the temple where scenes from Tomb Raider were filmed. It was definitely one of the busier ones, but with good reason. At one point as you walk around, there's a tree propped up with metal bars to stop it from falling upon any unsuspecting tourist because it's unclear which is stronger: the tree or the stone wall it's grown itself against. After lunch at a busy restaurant outside the front of one temple site, we saw a few more temples, before rounding off the day with a pause at the front of Angkor Wat, the most famous vista from the whole complex.

Next came the tricky bit again - riding back into the town. Once again, I was firmly at the back of the pack as we made our way through the streets. At one point, I got held up by a traffic light and lost the group completely for a few moments before I eventually reached the other side of the crossroads. By the time we reached the office, I was grateful to get off the bike.

We'd agreed that if we biked around Angkor Wat, we'd get a massage after. We made our way around the back of our hotel to a street lined with tourist restaurants and massage parlours and picked one based on a combination of price and which looked less likely to offer 'extras'. On that front we picked well, but perhaps we should have added more criteria.

We lay on thin mattresses on the floor, nakedness covered by a small towel, next to each other while a masseuse each pounded our flesh and muscles. My masseuse's phone rang. I thought she'd ignore it or put it on silent, but no, she answered. As I flipped onto my back exposing bits thanks to the smaller than average towel I discovered she hadn't only answered the phone, she was on FaceTime. And my naked body was the background. It wasn't what you'd describe as a relaxing massage. Experience, yes. Relaxing massage, no.

The next day, it was cooking time. We arrived at the cafe at our appointed time of 11am, ready to cook in time for lunch. We were making amok, a traditional Cambodian curry often served in a banana leaf; vegetable spring rolls, which we learnt to wrap correctly at last; and papaya salad.

We'd taken quite a few cooking classes by this point on the trip - from our Mexican market trip and local cooking day, to pupusas in our El Salvadorian hostel, and our Hmong cooking class in Laos. This one in Cambodia was by far the most efficient. It was like they wanted us in and out in record time. They'd clearly done this a lot before. All the food was laid out ready, some bits even pre-cut, in the order we'd need. The camping stove stood next to the food on the table, with the pan ready to go on the rings.

We started with the spring rolls, which we left to sit while we then made the papaya salad and finally the amok. Once we were done, we headed downstairs and found ourselves a table as instructed as our freshly made food was brought down to us, served with a big bowl of rice. It was really good. We left stuffed.

***

After Siem Reap, our final stop in Cambodia was Phnom Penh, the capital. We'd found a running event there, which we'd booked online back in Paraguay, and so arrived in the city a few days before.

Although we didn't have time to visit the Killing Fields, we did visit S21 or Tuol Sleng, a school that the Khmer Rouge converted to an interrogation centre, essentially a prison. It was a moving experience, especially because Ashley teaches and spends most of his working day in a similar building. Chalkboards still graced the walls of some of the classrooms on the top floor, making for an eerie contrast to the smaller rooms downstairs, in which the chalkboard on the wall was replaced with a photograph of the room as it was found, sometimes including a prisoner on the bed. In some of the photos the prisoners were dead.

It's horrific to imagine what the Khmer Rouge did during the short period they ruled the country, and it's so recent that it smarts. At the end of the visit, sits one of the last survivors of S21 who has written a book, and is happy to sign them and chat if you purchase a copy. He lived in this place against his will during what was likely the darkest period of his life, and yet here he still is, returning every day to sit at a table in the same place and share his story with visitors in the flesh. Suddenly, everything we'd just read on the walls of S21 felt more real. The unbelievable became believable.

I saw a short BBC video about this man after we returned home. His name is Chum Mey and he is one of only seven survivors. In the video he describes what his life was like during the few months he spent in Tuol Sleng. He describes how he was locked in a small cell with only two spoonfuls of porridge water a day. He describes how he would eat cockroaches, lizards, rats, anything he saw crawling around on the floor near him in his cell. The video ends with him explaining that he has to be there everyday and smile to stop the tourists crying at what they are seeing. Because if they cry, he'll cry too.

***

After a couple of days catching up with work, it was time for the International Phnom Penh Half Marathon for Ashley (and the 10k for me!). I'd signed up to a lot of the same races as Ashley in Asia, as running had proven to be something I didn't really enjoy in the moped-ridden streets of most of the places we'd been. I figured organised events would be a chance to do a little exercise. Oh, how wrong I was with Phnom Penh.

Typically for a running event that follows a road, some portion of said road will be blocked off for exclusive use by the runners, because, you know, it's a paid for event. People are paying for safety and the chance to run in places you don't always get the chance. This was not the case in Phnom Penh, a race described as "International", meaning you would expect some sort of international standard of safety. Oh no.

There were in places some haphazardly placed traffic cones and policemen, but very little telling off for the numerous mopeds, bikes and even cars that crossed the path of the runners. I started by trying to count them. This did not last long before I lost count. Around the seventh kilometre, the space for runners appeared to become less and less and I'd finally had enough. I just wanted to finish and curl up in a safe corner where I wouldn't be at risk of death-by-moped. But I wasn't giving up without a fight.

"Hey, this is for runners! You need to wait!" I started shouting to every bike that pulled out into the flow of runners, mostly expecting they wouldn't be able to understand my English or hear me through their helmets but hoping that my body language and tone would get the message across.

One bike pulled right out into the runners path without even looking and proceeded to drive alongside us. I said my line to the bike. The female passenger turned to me and mumbled something through her helmet along the lines of "this bit is for you", pointing to the white line narrowly marking the edge of the road. It was infuriating. I've never ran such a chaotic event, even the color run in Ho Chi Minh City doesn't hold a candle to that Phnom Penh race. It was hellish.

Thankfully at the finish line, Ashley confirmed I wasn't imagining things and that he'd had an equally frustrating time risking his life with every step.

With that being our most recent memory, we were somewhat excited to leave Cambodia, not least because our next destination was an unexpected one, and one of our favourite places: Japan.

Japan

Back in Vientiane, we needed to decide how to spend the
ten days we had between leaving Cambodia and arriving in
Penang, Malaysia. The obvious answer was Thailand. But
neither of us was overly excited about Thailand. So instead,
we started searching on Skyscanner for all possible options
leaving Phnom Penh on the date we'd be leaving Cambodia.

"We could fly to Japan!" I said, somewhat half jokingly.

Somehow it became reality. I think the 'how' can be placed
on the fact that we'd been to Japan together for the first time
back when we visited Asia in 2012. And we'd loved it.

The flight we found was in and out of Osaka, meaning we'd
be well-located to visit Kyoto, or maybe even Nara, Kobe,
and even Hiroshima if we got a train pass! We calmed
ourselves down and decided to keep things simple, with a
couple of nights in Osaka sandwiching four nights in Kyoto.

We left our hotel in Phnom Penh via Grab taxi early in the
morning and made our way to the airport. We did all the
airport things - check in, security, going to the toilet about

seventeen times to keep busy. And soon enough, we were sat on our flight to Osaka. It was a big plane, with three lines of three seats in each row. We were in the middle, sat next to what turned out to be a Malaysian man.

"Did you hear about the earthquake? We just found out." he told us after a little small talk.

"Earthquake? What? Now? In Japan?" Ashley responded.

"Yes, in Osaka today. My wife just read on the news on her phone but they have said nothing here on the plane, so I hope it's ok."

"Wow, yeah, I hope it's ok too." Ashley muttered in response turning to look at me, "Did you hear that? There's been an earthquake in Osaka today."

"What? Well, they're still flying us there right so it must be ok...I guess..right?"

"I dunno! How do we keep chasing natural disasters?!"

After the hurricane in Cuba, and earthquakes changing our plans in Mexico, we'd just discovered a week or so ago in Vientiane that the volcano forming the backdrop of Ashley's Guatemalan run had erupted, causing devastation in Antigua. If we weren't chasing disasters, they were slowly following us.

The plane took off with no mention of the earthquake. It was so casual and calm in fact, that even when we landed we were beginning to doubt the Malaysian man's report of a 6.1 earthquake that very morning. We got off the plane, through security, got our luggage, and headed out to wait for the bus.

By now it was 10pm and everyone was going about their business - staff collecting luggage trolleys, drivers smoking outside of their buses, passengers waiting for taxis and buses...had there really been an earthquake? I called the hotel and confirmed where we needed to wait for the shuttle bus.

We arrived at the hotel, checked in, went up to our room, and still would have been none the wiser to the earthquake had the Malaysian man on the plane not told us. Yet, sure enough, we checked the internet and there had been an earthquake in Osaka around 8am that morning. Japan being Japan, they'd carried on their day regardless and, at least by 10pm when we arrived, everything was moving normally again.

We saw no damage, heard of no injuries, and had no delays because of it. It really goes to show the difference between somewhere like Japan suffering an earthquake versus somewhere like Indonesia, which was hit by a similar earthquake weeks later to devastating consequences. Having the money to be put into infrastructure means Japan can beat Britain at their own game in the keeping calm and carrying on stakes.

As we'd arrived quite late and Kansai airport is quite a way from Osaka itself, we spent the night at a hotel near the airport and made our way into Osaka the following morning.

I'd picked our Osaka hotel primarily because of the photo of the robot in reception, Pepper. Pepper did not disappoint. As soon as I could, I pushed a few buttons and got her dancing along to Gangnam Style and Madonna. Pepper is my hero.

Our room itself was small and "Japanese style" according to the booking we'd made. This meant tatami mats and a mattress and bedding to be folding out into the space for sleep.

Tatami mats are those beautifully-scented woven straw floor tiles that you've probably seen in photos of traditional Japanese tea ceremonies. Shoes had to be removed and if we spilled food or drink on them in our hotel room, we would have had to pay a hefty fine for a new floor.

There were male and female toilets on each floor and then showers for females on the all-female floor and a proper spa for males on the ground floor. This was something that had always amused us from our first visit to Japan.

We stayed in a capsule hotel in Tokyo for a week and one night went for a bath in the separate gendered bathrooms. I had a spa bathtub (the water changed color each day from a range of luminous and dubious hues) and lots of fancy toiletries for free use at the mirrors and dressing tables. That was all. But it seemed like a lot. I was back in our capsule first to soon be joined by a very pink Ashley.

"Are you alright? You're very pink in the face..."

"Yeah! I've been in the sauna!"

"Wait, what sauna?!"

"Yeah. We've got a spa jacuzzi, well, two actually, a sauna, a massage chair, a..."

"I'm sorry, what?! I have fluorescent bathwater, that's it!"

It turns out this is quite typical practice in Japanese hotels with men getting better bathroom facilities than women, something we were reminded of by Ashley in Osaka having a door leading to what I can only imagine to be a spa-shaped wonderland to get him clean. Japanese male bathrooms are an inaccessible Narnia for females.

Osaka felt like a calmer, quieter Tokyo. It was lovely. We walked our way from the hotel down through the streets past vending machines galore, and delicious looking restaurants tucked away until all of a sudden a giant pufferfish loomed above us at a pedestrian crossroads. This is Japan. This is the Japan that you see from the outside. This is the Japan you expect.

After marvelling at the pufferfish and overwhelming amount of Japanese text now adorning shopfronts and restaurant menus in the streets, backed by an array of bold colours, we headed ever closer to the centre of the city. This took us along the main drag of Denden Town, Osaka's answer to Tokyo's Akihabara, or Electric Town, another side of Japan we see superficially from the outside - of "otaku" or "geek" culture.

Denden Town was a lot simpler in comparison to Akihabara but the gaming shops, cheap fast food spots, and unashamed sex shops could clearly be seen. This led us closer to the river, the home of one of Osaka's most famous sights, the Glico Man Sign in Dotonbori-dori, the shopping heart of the city. Ashley posed for a photo, imitating the Glico Man's celebratory finish line arms in the air, and we spent the rest of the day meandering around Osaka and enjoying taking in the new city.

The following day, we decided to venture out of Osaka, and with good reason: we were going to the Cup Noodle Museum. It's probably common knowledge that the Cup Noodle was invented in Japan, but the museum proved to be so much more interesting than that. For example, did you know that the Cup Noodle was invented as a partial solution to hunger? Or that they were important in the development of space food? I didn't either. The more you know.

The best part of the museum, however, had to be the 'Make Your Own Cup Noodle' activity. For 300 Yen, you can decorate your own Cup Noodle Pot and pick your own fillings (including cranking the handle to tip in your noodles!) and leave satisfied with an air-filled plastic pouch full of your very own Cup Noodle. It was fun. The town home to the Cup Noodle Museum is a small one, and made for an interesting contrast to the size of Osaka.

***

A quintessential part of any trip to Japan surely has to be riding the bullet train. Seeing images of these things for decades and being told of their efficiency and speed is enough to make even the hardiest of London commuters a little jealous as they wait for their three-times delayed train home. With our bags in tow, we made our way to the station to head to Kyoto in just fifteen minutes - a journey that takes around forty-five minutes on the regular train.

The bullet train didn't disappoint...except perhaps in one area. I have to be honest and say I was sort of hoping that I'd be pushed back into my chair, G-forces playing games with my mouth, exposing my teeth as my hair blew backward and my eyes widened enough to rival Alex in A Clockwork Orange when he's pinned down being rehabilitated. That didn't happen. That's probably a good thing. In fact, it felt slower than I was expecting. It clearly wasn't though, as we made it to Kyoto in less than fifteen minutes, as promised, and then proceeded to take at least four times that amount of time to get to grips with the bus ticket system and arrive at our accommodation for the next four nights.

The noise from the traffic quietened. The streets became narrower. And then we spotted it. Hidden amongst a residential neighbourhood was a small, quaint accommodation. Not quite a hotel, not quite a hostel, not quite a B and B.

It was a strange place. There were a handful of rooms upstairs and around two downstairs, one of which was ours, with a communal living and dining space and a kitchen off to one side. Outside was a small patio, where guests gathered, mostly to smoke it seemed if the smell seeping into our room was anything to go by. Our room was downstairs at the back, the sliding door leading straight to the communal living space, and the floor-length window out to the patio. Privacy was minimal, but it was large and clean so no real complaints. Until 4am.

We'd tried to get to sleep around 11pm, despite the loud voice of an obnoxious Frenchman on the patio droning on into the night. Somehow we managed and slept lightly for a bit. What felt like moments later, I awoke, still to the sound of the obnoxious Frenchman's voice, clear as anything. And loud. So loud.

I heard Ashley shuffle, and sensed he was awake, "What time is it?" I asked, expecting him to say ten past eleven.

"3.30am," he replied in a whisper checking his phone to respond.

We tried to lull ourselves back to sleep but it was a wasted effort. Whoever the guy was talking to wasn't getting much chance to speak, but that didn't seem to bother the French guy. He just kept talking. After thirty minutes of failed attempts to sleep, I'd had enough. If I can hear them, they can hear me.

I sat up.

"It's 4am and you're talking very loudly."

Silence. I lay back down. Sniggers.

"Err...can you...err...translate...?" the Frenchman responded, as if he hadn't been speaking in English all night.

I sat up again. Fuming.

"Il est quatre heures du matin! Vous parlez trop fort!"

Silence. Only this time, not followed by sniggers.

So next time someone tries to tell you that language learning is a waste of time, remind them that you never know when there'll be a native speaker chatting away outside your window until 4am that needs a telling off.

Aside from that (he left the following day and we never saw him again) Kyoto was a delight. It's a much calmer city than Osaka with an abundance of sights. There's quite a few temples (I'm being modest there) and plenty of things to break it up with (I'm talking tea ceremonies and animal cafes among other things). That said, coming towards the end of a temple-filled trip in Asia, we decided to hit the key temples we wanted to see in just one day.

The accommodation rented bikes on a trust system - pop some money in the box, write down your name and the number of the bike and off you go. So we did. I planned a rough route that would visit a small handful of the most impressive temples, the highly-Instagrammable bamboo forest, and end in an onsen. Because all good days should end in an onsen. The roads were clear, the shops were just beginning to open up their shutters, and the city was waking up. We were leaving early.

Our first stop was Kinkaku-ji, the Golden Temple. That's the one you've probably seen in photos if you Google Image search Kyoto. It's golden (as the name might suggest) and it glimmered beautifully in the sun on the day of our visit. What the photos don't show you however is the mass of people to the left and right of the camera. Maybe 360° cameras have a purpose: to show the *real* view of tourist sights. Despite arriving before it opened, there was still a queue that Alton Towers would've been proud of and the crowds didn't seem to disperse upon entering.

Towards the end of our visit I did get interviewed by some Japanese schoolgirls for an English project. After all the interviews we'd done so far on this trip, it was fun to be on the receiving end. They asked me what I like about Japan, where I'm from, where I'm visiting in Japan, my favourite Japanese food etc. At the end, they asked to take my photo to prove that they spoke with a real person and didn't just make the answers up, which means I'm probably on a classroom display in a Japanese school somewhere now. I think I'm fine with this.

After Kinkaku-ji, we cycled to Ryōan-ji, as did some others who'd begun at Kinkaku-ji it seemed. But definitely not everyone, Ryōan-ji was much quieter, which was fitting as it's known for its Zen Garden. I didn't realise I'd not seen a Zen Garden in real life until then. Well, except for a desk-sized version. Combined with the perfectly sized tatami woven mats fitting elegantly into the floorspace in the hall behind us, the Zen Garden was actually having the desired effect of being very calming. I found myself preferring it to Kinkaku-ji, which was a surprise.

Next up was our lunch spot before Arashiyama, a bamboo forest. We'd packed plenty of food for lunch, stocked up from a trip to Lawson 100 the night before. Lawson is a chain of convenience stores in Japan, or *konbini* as they're known. Lawson 100 is an offshoot of that where everything is priced at 100 Yen, roughly £1. And they sell good food too! Over our time in Japan, popping into Lawson 100 on the way home from an evening became a habit that no doubt saved us a small fortune in eating out.

Of all the stops we had planned for the day, the bamboo forest was the one I was most excited for. Well, after the onsen that is. But, to be honest, it was the most disappointing. After struggling to find somewhere to park our bikes on the main street below the forest park, we made our way up with the crowds towards what we hoped was the bamboo forest itself. After a short walk through what I'll call here 'regular' forest, a sign points you in the direction of what you came for.

Sure, the bamboo is tall. Sure, it's very green and relatively pretty. But what Instagram doesn't show is the etchings of initials, dates, and hearts carelessly carved into the bamboo by tourists; the short path through the bamboo forest than ends before it feels like it's really begun; the small, strong Japanese men pulling carts with tourist couples through the path forcing you to stand aside and constantly be on the lookout for the next one behind you.

It was awful. I kind of hate it when people say tourism has ruined a place because it feels like there's an element of snobbery to that statement. Phrases like "Get there before the tourists ruin it!" or "Visit this amazing place off the tourist trail!" lure you in, making you feel like you're "better" than the average tourist, even though if you go anywhere that's not home to see and do stuff, then you're a tourist too. Tourism can be a game-changer for so many places around the world, for good and bad. Yet here, it was a reflection of the bad. Very few of the carvings in the bamboo stalks were etched in Japanese. We didn't stay as long as we'd initially intended and soon found ourselves back on our bikes, keen to escape the hot and sweaty crowds. Our next stop was the onsen.

Regardless of how many countries you visit, I think there are many tiny traits that reveal yourself to be from one place or another. Mine that reveals me as a Brit? My dislike of public nudity. We'd already "been there, done that" on the public pool nudity front in Iceland at various thermal springs on route during a trip there a couple of years before. There at least, it was just the changing rooms with everything hanging out. The springs we visited had a rule about bathing suits in the water, which I was grateful for. Don't get me wrong, I'm very comfortable with my body. And I have no objection to anyone else being comfortable with theirs. I just...I don't know...I'm British.

We'd read up on onsens and were aware of the nudity and seperate gender baths in many of them, so thankfully it didn't come as a shock, and I did keep a towel with me, although I couldn't quite perfect the towel delicately balanced on top of the head whilst relaxing in the water pose. Onsen yoga.

There were showers all around the back of the room, many with people sat on small stools spraying their wet bodies with the hoses. Steam rose high to the roof, met only with the decibels of voices chattering, gossiping, and telling children to stand still so as not to get soap in their eyes. A selection of pools lay before all of that, looking out through the glass to even more pools outside, each with a temperature sign on the wall above. Emerging from the changing rooms I was like a kid in a candy shop. I do love a good spa.

After sampling each pool for an appropriate amount of time to judge if it was my favourite one or not, I conducted a second tour, with my eye on the clock between each dip to ensure I wouldn't leave Ashley waiting. He's not as much of a fan of spas as I am.

Oddly enough, it was him that left me waiting. But not for long, and we were soon by our bikes again ready to head back towards the city of Kyoto to our accommodation. Ashley opened his map app as we unlocked our bikes.

"I've checked the map. We can go straight along this road, but it might get busy with traffic and it's gonna get dark slowly. I'm not sure these little reflectors hold up to much. Or…"

It was a big 'or'. The kind when the person speaking definitely prefers the second idea.

"...we can ride back on this trail. It might take a bit longer, but it's the same route we just rode here on from the bamboo forest. So it should be clear. What do you think?"

I don't know what came over me. I guess I must have been feeling incredibly relaxed after my onsen, despite the British trauma of the public nudity.

"Let's take that longer trail one! It looks like it'll be a lovely evening!" I replied, shocking myself slightly at the words pouring out of my mouth uncontrollably.

"Oh! Ok! Are you sure?" Ashley was equally as surprised.

"Yep! Let's go!" I replied, almost half way down the road on my bike already.

And it was a beautiful evening. Dusk lingered long over the Kyoto skies as we wove the twenty-something kilometres back to our accommodation. We stopped at a konbini in the city and grabbed some dinner, which we took down to eat by the river. We finally arrived back at around 10pm. And if ever there were a perfect day, this was probably it.

Temples, zen gardens, bamboo forests, onsen, dusk riverside cycling...oh, and we watched England beat Panama 6-0 in the World Cup that evening too.

But of course, all good things must come to an end, and after our few days in Kyoto, it was time to head back to Osaka.

The "slow" train pulled into Osaka station just as efficiently and effectively as the bullet train that had taken us in the other direction and we made our way back to our hotel and my kindred spirit Pepper the robot.

Soon enough, after a couple more days enjoying Osaka, our ten day gap was finally up and we had to get to our penultimate country of the trip: Malaysia.

Malaysia

Season 2, Episode 5: Make Hokkien Cool Again

Season 2, Episode 7: Kristang: A Tale of Two Cities

After our lack of filming in Cambodia and Japan, filming for season two of Language Stories quickly picked up again when we reached Malaysia, but not right away. We were visiting Penang and Melaka before our final country of the whole trip, Singapore.

In Penang, I wanted to make an episode about Penang Hokkien, and Hokkien in general really. However, everyone I'd found online was spread around the world and there was no one in Penang to film. One person I was emailing about the episode even told me that "we only really care about the language when we leave."

Regardless, we paid a visit to Penang, photographing and filming signs exampling Hokkien alongside Mandarin, Cantonese, Malay and English, in varying orders and ranges on different signs. Also, Ashley had found a half marathon in Penang!

We arrived at our hotel, a grotty little room on the edge of Little India opposite a huge Chinese temple. Eager not to catch something from the walls, we headed out quickly and strolled around the centre, following street art down alleyways when we saw it.

Georgetown, the main town on Penang, is quite well-known for its street art scene. After emerging from one alleyway with a Pikachu and other characters painted on the wall, we stumbled upon a few street vendors selling books including one guy with an old copy of "Colloquial Malay" casually sitting there waiting for me to pick it up. I did. I paid for it. Now it lives with me.

Soon enough, we inevitably found ourselves at the out of town mall, where we saw (what I thought was) the Britishest of all restaurants: a cheeky Nando's.

Now, a few things to clear up. Firstly, we're actually not big Nando's fans (I know, British blasphemy). Secondly, I did some very quick googling after our Nando's trip in Penang and discovered Nando's is South African! How it has become such a British "thing" in the form of a cheeky Nando's, I'll never understand.

By the end of our time in Penang, it was time for Ashley's half marathon. And by time, I mean it was 4am. The heat was expected to become unbearable early on, clearly. That's not exactly what happened. After Ashley had left, the 10k runners were still waiting to start when the rain started. And we're talking tropical rain - big thick raindrops that fall on you, each one wetting you like a bucket tipping onto your shoulders. I found shelter with the other spectators and the 10k runners waiting to start underneath a porchway roof by an entrance to a building.

"10k! All 10k runners to the start!" Barely anyone moved. Barely anyone began the 10k race because the rain was that bad. So collectively, we lingered as the bucket raindrops continued to fall on the runners already out there.

After around an hour and a half, I started to look out for Ashley. I put my umbrella up and headed to the finish line. He arrived, drenched, glasses covered in drops of water. Most of the times when he finishes a race and I'm watching, I feel a pang of guilt that I should be exercising or should have joined the event. Not that day. I was quite happy under the porchway roof, thank you very much.

From Penang, we caught the bus to Melaka, a port city further down the coast with a colonial past, where we'd be back on the Language Stories trail.

***

I'd never been to Melaka before, but Ashley had. It was the reverse of Penang - where I'd been before but Ashley hadn't.

He'd always told me that he thought I'd like Melaka, and I did. There's a lot to like if you're curious about languages and culture. The architecture casually flows from European red brick churches into Chinese and Indian temples. The food is a reflection of the cultural influences on the place too. With a slight European edge to the Chinese and Indian influenced Malaysian cuisine you can get across the country. But it wasn't until we went to the Portuguese Settlement that I really fell head over heels for the place. We'd arranged to interview Sara, a local who'd been recommended to me by another interviewee that didn't work out. Sara, I'd been told, "teaches Kristang classes in Melaka". This was the only lead I had.

We had another interview lined up with Kevin Martens Wong of Kodrah Kristang in Singapore, but even though there are roughly ten times as many speakers of the language in Melaka, Sara was the only person I'd found online to interview in Melaka.

Kristang, in case you're wondering at this point, is a creole language derived from the local languages Malay, Chinese and others too, but heavily relying on Portuguese, the language of colonisers many years ago. Despite various language policies that excluded Kristang over the years, around a thousand speakers remained who use the language in their everyday life here in the Portuguese Settlement in Melaka.

We headed out to the Portuguese Settlement one evening before dusk hit, and I was instantly struck by how different it was to the rest of the city. As we reached the end of the street where we'd walked down into the Portuguese Settlement, we were met by quite a sight. In front of us, before the harbour where a small handful of fishermen were wrapping up for the day, there was a Christ the Redeemer statue, standing proud casting a shadow onto the car park behind him as he gazed out over the houses making up part of the Portuguese Settlement. Across the carpark, restaurants with words like "Lisbon" and "Porto" on their signboards stood. I walked over to check the menus. They turned out to be graced with Portuguese treats such as bacalao cod and custard tarts. This wasn't the Melaka we'd grown to know over the past few days.

Soon it was time to head down to Sara's house. I'd messaged to confirm it was still ok for us to come earlier that day and she'd replied with "I'll be teaching the children singing tonight. It might be interesting for you to see!".

I was left unsure from her message if we'd still get the chance for an interview. I didn't want to interrupt family time, but regardless, this was our only lead in Melaka. Some footage was better than no footage.

"Hello?" we tentatively rang the bell at the gate.

"Ahh hello hello! Come in!" a woman I assumed must be Sara appeared from the house and opened the gate for us. We followed her lead and removed our shoes before entering. The front door led straight to the living room, where at least seven children sat around talking amongst themselves and giggling and whispering as we entered.

"You've arrived at a good time! We are about to start singing! So they have to practice for a performance this weekend at the festival here in the Portuguese Settlement. I think I mentioned the dancing happening to you on WhatsApp?"

I nodded. Sure enough Sara had mentioned the dancing going on that coming weekend for a local festival that she said would be a good place to see Kristang culture in real life. But unfortunately, we'd be in Singapore, and being so close to the end of the trip, we couldn't change our plans.

"Ok, everybody ready? Let's go!" Sara started singing, pointing word by word as she sang to the lyrics written clearly on large pieces of coloured paper and displayed in front of the group, leaning against the wall.

I was impressed that I could make out a few words from my knowledge of Portuguese and Spanish! It didn't take long for Kristang to draw me in.

Thankfully, we weren't interrupting family time. The children weren't all Sara's. They were children from the neighbourhood who came to her house every weekday evening to learn a little Kristang.

After a few rounds of singing, the children were sent home and Sara sat down on the sofa next to us to be interviewed. I explained a little more about the series and asked if she was ready to go.

"Yes. Oh, before we start, I want to show you some things!" Sara got up and went over to a corner of the room, shortly returning with a box and some books.

"This is a game made by a guy in Singapore. So he starts to teach the language there, and last year he hosted the first Kristang Festival so I went and spoke with him and I got this game."

"Is that Kevin, by any chance? We're meeting him in a few days in Singapore!" I replied.

"Ahh, yes. Kevin made this." Sara smiled, knowingly. "Also, this is a book that I helped to write that teaches Kristang."

Sara passed me the book. My eyes lit up.

"Is there anywhere I can get this in Melaka?" I said.

"Yes, I can take you to the author's house after we're done and he should have a spare copy. Maybe he can speak to you too."

We did the interview. It was interesting to learn that Sara invites the children we'd seen into her home every evening to sing and learn some Kristang. And she does it completely for free. She simply wants the language to live and be passed on to the next generation.

After, Sara's husband drove us all round to the author's house. It was dark now and we were simply expecting to pop in, buy the book, and head back to our accommodation again.

Instead, after Sara introduced us to Philomena, who also worked on the book, we were invited in and learnt about her efforts to help keep the language alive and relevant for younger generations too. Every day she posted a video on Facebook sharing one new Kristang word and giving examples of its use.

Her brother, Michael soon emerged from his nap, complete with the book, which I would later learn was signed by him. We explained what Language Stories is about and thanked him for letting us into his house so late in the evening with a video camera, and casually asked if there was anything he'd like to say about the language for the episode. They both agreed. And for the next two and a half hours, we sat mesmerised as we learnt more about Kristang during our longest interview throughout our whole trip.

Michael and Philomena were so generous with their time and I was grateful I could buy the book to repay their kindness even a little. Around 10pm, we called a Grab and said our thank yous and goodbyes, my heart full of joy at the people we'd met that evening.

It was incredibly inspiring to meet so many people passionate to promote and keep their language in use. It was clear however from our time interviewing for the episode in Melaka that there was some disagreement on the best way to revive/keep using a language between the Melaka speakers of Kristang and the Singaporeans.

In Melaka, where the language originally flourished, they seem to very much take the view of language evolving naturally, and absorbing words from other languages as that happens - computer, Tweet, etc - the usual suspects. However, in Singapore, it seems they take a different approach and create new Kristang words when they encounter vocabulary. For example, "panda" would be influenced by the languages of the users in Singapore, such as Hokkien and Malay, to be structured similarly in Kristang.

As Michael summed up quite nicely, in Melaka, they favour "Evolution not revolution" when it comes to the Kristang language. Now we just had to hear the Singapore side of the story.

But first, we had one day left in Melaka, and we'd found just the place to spend it. Once we knew we were going to Japan and planned to make the mini series there, we also knew we had to stay at the "Fantasy Hotel" in Melaka, in particular in the Hello Kitty room for final filming for the Japan series. It was creepy, I'm not gonna lie.

The hotel has themed rooms, each with a character or general theme dominating all aspects of the place from wallpaper to bed sheets to decor. We even had a Hello Kitty toilet seat and soap dispenser. I'll say it one more time: it was creepy. We left our lovely hotel on the other side of town at check out time to head across to the Fantasy Hotel in the hope we'd be able to leave our bags until check in time there.

"Hello, we have a reservation, Williams, Hello Kitty room, one night." Words I never thought I'd say falling out of my mouth there.

"Ok, Williams.yes, Booking.com, one night. I cannot confirm the room choice as it's first come first served and you have to reserve the room in advance."

What? Was she telling us we'd just left a lovely, quiet B and B with a pool and a French family in the next room to practice my French with to be put in a totally random creepy room that was in no way related to Japan? Not having that.

"But we did reserve. I sent a message when I reserved the room requesting the Hello Kitty room." As I started to speak, I realised how weird it sounded to be a grown couple acting very adamant that they get the Hello Kitty room.

"Yes but it is first come first served."

"But I am first come, I should be first served! I have confirmation…" I reached into my bag looking for my phone to bring up the message from the hotel confirming our (bizarre) choice of the Hello Kitty room.

"Ok, ok, I can see. I can confirm you have Hello Kitty room." she replied, looking again at her computer screen as I fumbled for my phone.

Thank goodness I didn't have to get too defensive of the strange room that we'd soon find ourselves in. We left our bags and headed into the city for a couple of hours, where we shared a cendol. Desserts in this part of the world can be an acquired taste to the unacquainted. Many consist of huge piles of shaved ice, covered with lashings of what others might consider savory snacks - beans, sweetcorn - and, weirdly not as sweet as they look, brightly colours jelly balls and strands, all topped off with rich caramel syrup and/or coconut milk. Cendol is one of those desserts. Oddly, it kinda works. The ice makes for a refreshing break from the sometimes stifling heat outside, and the flavours somehow work too, even the things that you'd typically consider savory.

That afternoon, we headed back to the hotel and thankfully got the Hello Kitty room, which meant no excessive "Give me the Hello Kitty room now!"s needed. Phew.

The room was ridiculous. The walls were covered in bright pink Hello Kitty wallpaper, the beds had big Hello Kitty face pillows on top of the Hello Kitty sheets, the dressing table, the mirror. Everywhere you looked, Hello Kitty looked back at you. It was terrifying. We filmed the cutaways for the Japan series and headed back out for dinner as soon as we could for a break from the garish room.

I don't know if it was the excessive Hello Kitty or something I ate but the following morning I was sick. I woke up suddenly and ran to the bathroom instantly being sick into the toilet. We had to take the bus to Singapore today.

After breakfast, I felt a little better but took a pill just in case, and we caught our taxi to the bus station. I still felt fine. Then out of the blue, walking around one half of the bus station looking for the ticket booth selling tickets to Singapore, I asked Ashley to stop. I took my bags off, suddenly weak, and stood a little dazed and confused by a pillar.

"Ok. I think I'm ok now. Sorry, I don't know what came over me."

I put my bags back on and we walked another few feet before I called forward to Ashley again.

"Ash! I need to sit…" I collapsed into a massage chair to my right, dropping my bags down by the side of the chair.

"I don't know what's wrong. I don't feel well. It's not…I'm not…sick…I just…." my thoughts and words tailed off as a feeling not dissimilar to the altitude sickness I'd experienced in Peru washed over me.

The room became distant and my ears played a sound creating a depth between me and the room. I couldn't hear.

"Toilet" I managed to muster, wondering if I was still feeling sick after all and if being sick would make me feel better.

Ashley passed me some change to pay for the toilet and I got myself up out of the chair.

I remember walking a few steps.

Then I remember a Malaysian woman saying "Be ok, be ok" and Ashley asking if I was alright.

I collapsed in the bus station. And just then as I was coming round, I remember a man coming over to us saying "You can't lie here", as if I'd chosen to collapse right in the middle of a public bus station. A casual lie down.

With Ashley's help, I made my way back to the massage chair and lay myself on the floor in front of it. It felt good to lie down, sitting wasn't comfortable. But of course, soon it was time to get on the bus.

Ashley carried everything, which by this point included an extra suitcase of stuff we got in Japan, and I slowly walked towards the door, sitting myself on the ledge just past the door on the outside. A few minutes later we were on the bus, and for the first time in my life, I was that annoying person on the bus who puts their seat right back. I did look back to apologise and say I was ill, but I didn't look back long enough to give them time to respond. I was too ill for that. And besides lying felt ok, sitting wasn't nice. This was going to be a long journey.

Singapore

Season 2, Episode 2: Singapore Takes The Floor
Season 2, Episode 7: Kristang: A Tale of Two Cities

A few tired, weak and uncomfortable hours later we arrived at the Singaporean border and had to get off the bus with all our luggage for the border controls. By now I was feeling much better than the morning, but still a little delicate. The Malaysian side went smoothly, but as we arrived at the Singaporean side, Ashley picked the right lane at immigration and whizzed through ahead of me.

I, on the other hand, definitely picked the wrong lane. The girl that served me was young, and likely new at the job seeing as she was the only person during our recent trips to Singapore to ring someone about the fact that I ticked the box honestly for entering Singapore with a different name before - my maiden name. Even the first time we entered after arriving from Paraguay when we had the yellow fever box ticked as well, no one asked to see our yellow fever certificates. Why was she stalling me on today of all days?

She put the phone down and looked back to me, "Just one moment please. Because you say different name, he will check with you in the office."

"Ok…" I said, instantly feeling guilty despite having done nothing wrong. It's like when you hear a police siren, there's a sudden urge to hide.

Shortly, another Singaporean border officer arrived and took me and my luggage to a side room where I had to wait like a criminal, unsure if my bus had already left without me but sure than Ashley didn't know where I was and that I had no way to tell him. After what felt like an eternity, I got called forward to the desk by the man that had my passport in his hand.

"So you enter Singapore with a different name, yes?"

"Yes, my maiden name. I think...yes, three times in 2011 and 2012."

"Ok, and now you're married, so different name?"

"Yes."

"Ok, follow me."

I followed him into a room and had my face scanned by a machine before being instructed to sit back down in the waiting area in the main office. A while later, I was given my passport back and free to go. Just as I turned, Ashley was being shown into the room by another officer.

"Hello! They pulled me over because I'd been to Singapore with a different name!" I said as he approached, looking confused and worried.

"Oh, ok! I didn't know where you'd gone. I lost you!"

"I know, I was behind and then ahhh, I don't know! Where's the bus? I was worried it would have gone!"

"It's still here. There's someone else stuck I think."

Bizarrely, despite my long escapade in the immigration office, we weren't the last people on the bus. Eventually, we set off from the border and arrived at our final destination, a fifteen minute walk from the place we were staying, and because of the location of the MRT stations, an even longer ride on the underground. We went overground. Ashley carried most of the luggage and I carried the two smaller bags, feeling a little stronger now than before and we made our way to our hotel. It was worse than our place in Penang, but it was a place to rest, which I embraced. Within minutes of arriving around 6pm, I fell asleep on the bed and didn't wake up until morning.

The following day we didn't have any interviews until the afternoon, so I gave myself the morning to recover in the room until we left at lunch to head to our first Singapore interview. This one was a language meetup in a food court.

We spoke with many of the language learners there and interviewed some of the volunteers who help to run certain sessions too. It was really interesting to hear about language learning from a different perspective. At home, many people learn French, Spanish, German etc and then Japanese,

Korean, Chinese are the more "exotic" languages to learn, but of course in Singapore, things are the other way around.

And of course, they have food courts to do these things in rather than pubs and bars. Although the food courts can be as noisy as a British pub in the evening, they do give you the option to buy a wider range of drinks to enjoy as you chat. I don't drink alcohol so always look like a right nerd at pub language meetups because all I really want to drink at that time of night is a hot chocolate or chamomile tea. So to be honest, I don't go much because it's loud and I'm going to have to buy a drink I don't really want (I typically get orange juice, which looks less weird than a mug with a hot drink). Whereas in Singapore, I could totally see myself enjoying a couple of hours in a food court each weekend chatting and practising languages.

***

Our next interview was with Kevin Martens Wong, founder of Kodrah Kristang in Singapore. After so many people had recommended I speak with Kevin for the series and I'd heard the Melaka side of the Kristang story, I was keen to hear what he had to say. And of course, we met in a food court before his class one evening.

Kevin was clearly in demand as two other young women sat patiently waiting to interview Kevin whilst I asked my questions. Kevin discovered the language aged twenty-two whilst writing an article for a linguistics magazine. It didn't take long for him to learn that this was incidentally a language that his ancestors spoke. After a year or so of learning the language, he started to teach Kristang classes to the relatively small Eurasian population (and other locals) in Singapore. With the support and involvement of elder speakers of the language, he has compiled a revitalisation plan for the language as far forward as 2035. It's fascinating stuff.

Next up we went to meet Lilian Lee, founder of Say What With Friends, a Singaporean company through and through that ozzed Singaporean nostalgia and multilingualism through the fun stuff she creates including came games to learn Singlish, Hokkien, Malay, Cantonese, Japanese and Mandarin. And yet again, we met in a food court. I like Singapore for that.

Lilian showed us up the escalator to the food court. Small units, each with a brightly-lit signboard above and a different speciality on offer, hugged the walls of the space. All around, circular tables and seats attached to the floor helped to form groups of people all eating, drinking, and chatting. We found some food and Lilian reserved a table with a packet of tissues, a very Singaporean thing to do.

Lilian handed me a couple of packs of her cards to keep - Singlish and Hokkien - before going on to explain how the game works. She then told us how because of the many dialects of Chinese (or different Chinese languages altogether) spoken in Singapore, it's interesting to see Chinese Singaporeans speak to each other in English from time to time. One reason for this is that, as Lilian went on to explain, in the 60s and 70s the Singaporean government tried to ban dialects and Chinese languages other than Mandarin.

Our final interview was with Zinkie, founder of Singlish Mama Shop. After a morning enjoying the National Gallery, Ash and I headed to the cafe where we were meeting Zinkie.

"These are for you!" Zinkie said, presenting stickers and a huge A3 prototype of her project 'What The Singlish?' on the table in front of us. I was glad we'd picked up an extra suitcase in Japan to carry all these new gifts home!

Zinkie went on to talk me through some of the Singlish expressions on her stickers and explain her reasons behind the project. She's a full-time photographer, but wanted to bring Singlish and Singaporean identity into this particular project. The book is a collection of fun photographs taken by Zinkie around Singapore. At the back of the book, there's a few pages of stickers for the reader to add their own take on each scene using Singlish words and phrases. It's a fun take on a 'visual dictionary', the subtitle of the book.

***

Once all our interviews were done, we left our dive of a hotel in Chinatown and took ourselves and our luggage for a well-deserved final night in Singapore and of our trip at Marina Bay Sands.

This city is so important to me. It's the place I first travelled to on my own when I arrived in Asia back in 2011. I loved it from the word go so it's the place Ashley decided to buy my engagement ring years later on a visit without me. It's the place I first saw four languages side by side, increasing my curiosity that led to Language Stories. And most importantly, it's the place where we were ending our incredible year-long trip across continents making Language Stories.

We still had some cash in our wedding gift list account so splashed out on a night in the Club Suite at Marina Bay Sands, which included all food. We vowed to not leave the hotel from check in to check out to really make the most of it. It seemed a fitting end to our trip.

We arrived for check in a few hours early, and went straight up to our room. As we opened the door and placed the keycard in the slot, the lights lit themselves and the curtains drew themselves back to reveal Gardens By The Bay. We dumped our bags and proceeded to "ooo" and "ahh" our way around the room admiring the little touches and features until it was time for lunch. After a delicious buffet lunch, we took to the infinity pool. The infinity pool is right on top of the three towers that make up Marina Bay Sands and overlooks the city, with smaller jacuzzis on the side looking out to Gardens By The Bay.

We hung out in the pool for a couple of hours before heading back down to get changed for dinner. There was a knock on the door.

"Hello?" I said, opening the door partly.

"Hello, Mrs Williams?"

I nodded in confirmation.

"I hope everything is satisfactory with your stay. Please enjoy these complimentary macarons.."

The man handed me a tray with a bowl of macarons and a card that said "With compliments, Marina Bay Sands"

"Oh, thank you!" I said. He bowed slightly and smiled as I closed the door.

"Complimentary macarons?! Complimentary macarons?!" I excitedly took the tray round to Ashley, "This is my life now. I don't want to stay anywhere unless there's complimentary macarons. This is the new bar that's been set for my hotel experiences - complimentary macarons!"

"Was that even on the list of stuff we get?"

"No! I think we definitely would have remembered 'complimentary macarons'! This is it. A new standard has been set for all hotels from here on in."

We were very excited about the complimentary macarons, as you might be able to tell. And even more so when we discovered the 'With compliments' card was actually edible rice paper on a chocolate plaque. Once the macaron tray was empty, and lunch was over, we headed back upstairs to the infinity pool to see the sun set over the city before dinner.

Dinner was a lot busier than lunch, but equally delicious. After, we had time for one more stop at the infinity pool to catch the light show over the bay from a different angle to what we'd got used to from seeing it previously on the ground outside the shopping centre in front of the hotel.

All in all, Marina Bay Sands was rather expensive, but definitely worth it as a grand finale to our trip. Although, that's not strictly true, as our flight actually left early in the morning, meaning we had one more night in Singapore that we'd decided to spend at the airport instead of Marina Bay Sands so we didn't have to check out insanely early from our very expensive room and miss breakfast. So we'd reserved our night there on our *penultimate* night in the city.

But if there's an airport in the world you're going to spend a night in, Singapore is a good bet as Changi Airport is consistently voted the world's best airport. Although not much is going on at night, it is a lot more comfortable than most, especially Lima where we'd spent two nights either end of our time in Cusco.

Plus, England were doing incredibly well in the World Cup and had reached the semi-finals, where they'd meet Croatia. It was a beautiful story. It had been twenty years since they'd got this far (although from the faith in the team each World Cup, you wouldn't think it had been that long); Gareth Southgate was the player to miss the penalty that lost them that match twenty years ago and he was now the manager; everyone seemed to have rallied behind them at home with Marks and Spencers selling out of the "It's Coming Home" waistcoat that Gareth Southgate had been wearing from the sidelines of matches. And as for us? Well, we *were* coming home, from the Lion City (Singapore), so surely the World Cup would be coming home with the Three Lions (the England Football Team)?

We stayed up until the wee hours and managed to miss out on comfy seats in the fanzone at the airport, meaning we watched the match stood up against our luggage trolley from the back, but we were there! Everyone was cheering for England, no one was cheering Croatia (sorry, Croatia) so it was a bit of a downer when England lost. And it made us wonder if our paths would follow a similar fate given our luck with planes crossing continents so far on the trip.

Thankfully it didn't and within a good few hours, we were back on British soil and soon heading home after a trip we'd never forget.

Coming Home

What no one ever talks about when it comes to such big trips is coming home.

"Go while you're young!"

"Do it now while you can!"

"See everything! Go everywhere! Meet everyone!"

All the advice, the words of wisdom, the books - everything is focused on the joys of travel: the getting ready to go, the going, the being there. It would be very easy to fall into 'post-travel blues' and to feel a sense of loss, of regret, of sadness at no longer being away and doing all of these amazing things that had been so frequently highlighted as 'once in a lifetime' before you left. If it's 'once in a lifetime' and you've done it, now what? I have to be very honest and say that we were both glad to come home. Luckily, we didn't fall into any post-travel blues.

The trip was incredible and travelling long-term was a great experience. However, it's not all rainbows and butterflies.

Robberies from hostels in Nicaragua, flights being cancelled in Brazil, altitude sickness in Peru, getting stuck in a hurricane in Cuba, collapsing in a bus station in Malaysia. Remarkably, these are the stories that get told the most. I've told the story of our cancelled flight many more times than I have the story of meeting Galapagos tortoises. I'm sure you can guess which experience I preferred.

My point is that there's no reason to feel down when you come home. Your travels may be over (for now, at least) but it happened, and that's amazing. You'll always have the stories, good and bad.

That's what appealed to me about making Language Stories. Not only were we making our own stories that year, we were able to tell other people's stories too. Stories are one of the oldest forms of art, ideas and exchange. The more stories we get to hear, to watch, and to read telling of people, situations, and languages different to us; the more we learn about the world we all share. And the more we learn, the more we want to go and explore the rest of it.

Until next time, keep learning languages, and keep sharing stories.

Resources

Below is a list of links related to Language Stories in each country we visited for easy reference in case you're curious to learn more.

Of course, as the internet is ever in flux, these links may vary throughout the lifetime of this book. If a link no longer works, search engines should get you there too.

If you enjoyed this book, please take a minute to leave a review on Amazon to help other people find the book. Thank you.

Enjoy!

LANGUAGE STORIES

Language Stories is a podcast and video language documentary series.

You can enjoy the podcasts on your favourite podcast player or here:

https://languagestories.fireside.fm

You can enjoy the videos for each episode here:
https://www.youtube.com/playlist?list=PLByFxX2gaCXZAUP
fr1ooB9tsQUxxShETa

Be sure to subscribe where you get podcasts and on YouTube to be up to date with future episodes.

If you enjoy Language Stories, the best things you can do to support the project (now you've already got a copy of this book!) is leave a review on Apple Podcasts and tell a friend about the series. Thank you.

USA

Endangered Language Alliance:
http://elalliance.org/

Fluent in 3 Months:
https://www.fluentin3months.com/

Wikitongues:
https://wikitongues.org/

CANADA

LangFest:
https://montreal.langfest.org/

MEXICO

Radio Yúuyum:
http://www.yuuyum.org/

PatBoy:
https://facebook.com/patboy.rapmaya

Vicente Canché Móo:
http://vicentecanche.blogspot.mx/

Siskia Lagomarsino:
http://thepolyglotist.com/

BELIZE

Northern Belizean Spanish:
https://www.facebook.com/NorthernBelizeanSpanish/

Timothy McKeon:
https://medium.com/@timothymckeon

GUATEMALA

Carlos and Family:
https://www.airbnb.co.uk/rooms/21225204

Galeria Pop Wuj:
http://galeriapopwuj.wixsite.com/galeriapopwuj

NICARAGUA

Nicaraguan Sign Language Projects:
http://www.nicaraguansignlanguageprojects.org/

Café de las Sonrisas:
http://tioantonio.org/

PARAGUAY

Guaranglish:
http://www.guaranglish.com/

IDIPAR:
http://www.idipar.com.py/

Paraguay - Other Places Travel Guide:
http://discoveringparaguay.com/home/

VIETNAM

Central Deaf Services:
http://www.handsforvietnam.org

Happy Heart Cafe:
https://www.facebook.com/happyheartdanang/

Language Accepted:
https://www.instagram.com/languageaccepted/

Gaston Dorren:
https://languagewriter.com/

Vietnamese Teaching Group:
http://vietnameseteaching.net/en/

Chua's Sapa Tour and Homestay:
https://www.facebook.com/ChuaSapaTourAndHomestay/

Jasmine Tierra:
https://www.facebook.com/KuvJasmineTierra/

LAOS

Lao Learns English:
http://www.laoslearnsenglish.org/

EDF:
http://www.edflao.org/en/

ARDA:
http://www.ardalaos.com/

Momobooks:
https://www.momobooks.org/

MALAYSIA

Michael Singho:
http://www.umpress.com.my/index.php?route=product/produ
ct&product_id=644

Philomena Singho:
https://www.facebook.com/LingguaDeMai/

Sara Frederica Santa Maria:
https://www.facebook.com/Malacca-Portuguese-Cristang-
Language-Class-1932909556995794/

Penang Hokkien Podcast:
http://penanghokkien.com/

Speak Hokkien Campaign:
https://www.speakhokkien.org/

SINGAPORE

Singlish Mama Shop:
http://ishoothabits.com/

Say What?:
http://www.saywhatwithfriends.com/

Eva Comics:
http://evacomics.com/

Kodrah Kristang:
https://kodrah.kristang.com/

'Others' Is Not a Race:
https://www.booksactuallyshop.com/products/others-is-not-a-race

Acknowledgements

Naturally, Language Stories and this book was made possible by everyone who agreed to speak with us for the series. Many are linked above, but in addition, I'd like to thank Carlos Castillo, and Davie Prine. Also, thank you to Àdhamh Ó Broin, Maureen Millward and everyone else who helped us with the interviews for these first two series of Language Stories.

Thank you also to our families for looking after our home and our tortoise while we were away, and for being supportive and inspiring throughout our lives.

And, of course, thank you to Ashley. This trip and Language Stories would not have been possible with either one of us trying to do this alone. We make a good team. Where next?

About the Author

Lindsay Williams always had a curiosity for language. From spotting that most of the words on Italian road signs ended in vowels to actually *wanting* to order the baguettes on holiday in France, the warning signs were there. It wasn't until Shakira released Laundry Service and she asked for a Spanish dictionary for her birthday to translate the Spanish on the album that things got what might be described as serious. Since then, Lindsay has gone on to study more languages than her fingers can count, including a degree in Modern Language Studies along the way. After founding Lindsay Does Languages to inspire independent language learners to go further when doing it solo, she now hopes it's contagious.

More from Lindsay Williams

The best place to keep up to date with everything going on at Lindsay Does Languages is:
http://lindsaydoeslanguages.com

Be sure also to subscribe to my email list (and get free access to my Little Language Library of resources for language learners and teachers) here:
http://lindsaydoeslanguages.com/signup

I also regularly share videos for language learners on my YouTube channel here:
https://youtube.com/user/lindsaydoeslanguages

And of course, you can follow and subscribe across social media.

Facebook Page:
https://www.facebook.com/lindsaydoeslanguages/

#WeDoLanguages Facebook Group:
https://www.facebook.com/groups/wedolanguages/

Teach Languages Online Facebook Group:
https://www.facebook.com/groups/teachlanguagesonline/

Twitter:
https://twitter.com/ldlanguages

Instagram:
https://instagram.com/lindsaydoeslanguages/

Pinterest:
https://pinterest.co.uk/ldlanguages/

46133415R00201

Made in the USA
Middletown, DE
24 May 2019